CHRIST ON THE CROSS

IN DARKNESS   IN LIGHT

CHRIST ON THE CROSS

IN DARKNESS   IN LIGHT

AN EXPOSTION OF
THE TWENTY SECOND PSALM

BY JOHN STEVENSON

Scattering Seed Press
www.scatteringseed.org

CONTENTS

CHRIST ON THE CROSS
IN DARKNESS

CHRIST ON THE CROSS
IN LIGHT

PUBLISHERS' FORWARD

Upon reading the work before you, Charles Spurgeon told the students in his pastoral college the book was, "Exceedingly precious in its unfolding of the Redeemer's sorrows. We have derived personal spiritual benefit from the perusal of this gracious exposition..." He recommended it to all his students stating he was, "unable to judge it critically" because he had received such blessing from it.

Very little is known about John Stevenson. He was British and served as curate in the district of Cornwall, England. He wrote only four books in his lifetime, three of them being individual commentaries on different Psalms. The work before you is an exposition of Psalm 22, first published in 1841. Though it is an exposition, it reads like a book.

As you would expect with a book that was written one hundred seventy five years ago, some updating to the language was necessary. We have performed minimal editing, making the work readable in modern English without losing or diluting the original meaning. More details to the editorial approach we have taken can be found in the postscript.

You will find a richness of depth and understanding in these pages of the sufferings of Christ that is rarely encountered. The interaction taking place within the Godhead while Christ was on the cross is explained in heart warming detail.

Christ is set forth in all of His splendor as our Surety. It is a main theme of the book. Before God, the Surety is one who takes responsibility for the performance of righteousness demanded from the sinner, and the payment of the sinner's debts to God. These righteous demands were fulfilled by One who has a relationship to the Father as that of Son. It is a filial relationship. It is the filial relationship to the Father (Christ as Son), while substituting Himself as our surety that produced Christ's greatest trial. It was the greatest trial for the Father also. For as Christ stood in the sinners place, He did so maintaining perfect innocence throughout His entire time on the Cross. How the Father dealt with the substitute as the sin-bearer while He still remained His innocent Son is a mystery beyond full comprehension. The child of God will spend eternity exploring this mystery.

May you be richly blessed and brought to deeper admiration and awe as you read what your Savior has done for you.

In Christ,

Ryan Ellsworth
Scattering Seed Ministries

THE
TWENTY SECOND PSALM

To the chief Musician upon Aijeleth Shahar,
a Psalm of David.

[1] My God, My God, why have You forsaken Me? Why are You so far from helping Me, and from the words of My groaning?

[2] O My God, I cry in the daytime, but You do not hear; and in the night season, and am not silent.

[3] But You are holy, enthroned in the praises of Israel.

[4] Our fathers trusted in You; they trusted, and You delivered them.

[5] They cried to You, and were delivered; they trusted in You, and were not ashamed.

[6] But I am a worm, and no man; a reproach of men, and despised by the people.

[7] All those who see Me ridicule Me; they shoot out the lip, they shake the head, saying,

[8] "He trusted in the LORD, let Him rescue Him; let Him deliver Him, since He delights in Him!"

[9] But You are He who took Me out of the womb; You made Me trust while on My mother's breasts.

[10] I was cast upon You from birth. From My mother's womb You have been My God.

[11] Be not far from Me, for trouble is near; for there is none to help.

[12] Many bulls have surrounded Me; strong bulls of Bashan have encircled Me.

[13] They gape at Me with their mouths, like a raging and roaring lion.

[14] I am poured out like water, and all My bones are out of joint; My heart is like wax; it has melted within Me.

[15] My strength is dried up like a potsherd, and My tongue clings to My jaws; You have brought Me to the dust of death.

[16] For dogs have surrounded Me; the congregation of the wicked has enclosed Me. They pierced My hands and My feet;

[17] I can count all My bones. They look and stare at Me.

[18] They divide My garments among them, and for My clothing they cast lots.

[19] But You, O LORD, do not be far from Me; O My Strength, hasten to help Me!

[20] Deliver Me from the sword, My precious life from the power of the dog.

[21] Save Me from the lion's mouth and from the horns of the wild oxen!

You have answered Me.

[22] I will declare Your name to My brethren; in the midst of the assembly I will praise You.

[23] You who fear the LORD, praise Him! All you descendants of Jacob, glorify Him, and fear Him, all you offspring of Israel!

[24] For He has not despised nor abhorred the affliction of the afflicted; nor has He hidden His face from Him; but when He cried to Him, He heard.

[25] My praise shall be of You in the great assembly; I will pay My vows before those who fear Him.

[26] The poor shall eat and be satisfied; those who seek Him will praise the LORD. Let your heart live forever!

[27] All the ends of the world shall remember and turn to the LORD, and all the families of the nations shall worship before You.

[28] For the kingdom is the LORD's, and He rules over the nations.

[29] All the prosperous of the earth shall eat and worship; all those who go down to the dust shall bow before Him, even he who cannot keep himself alive.

[30] A posterity shall serve Him. It will be recounted of the Lord to the next generation,

[31] They will come and declare His righteousness to a people who will be born, that He has done this.

INTRODUCTION

CHRISTIAN READERS,

GRACE and peace be multiplied unto you, through the knowledge of God, and of Jesus our Lord! May you be "partakers of his sufferings," only in such measure as shall prepare you to bear "his exceeding weight of glory." The constant aim of the Apostle, should be ours also—to "know the fellowship of Christ's sufferings, and to be conformed to his death," (Phil. 3:10). "All Christians have been taught in one school," says an admirable author; "all have known the power of affliction in some of its varied forms, of inward conflict, or outward trouble. Before I was afflicted I went astray, 'but now,' each of them is ready to say, 'but now have I kept Your word.' I never prized it before. I could indeed scarcely be said to know it. I never understood its comfort until affliction expounded it to me. I never till now saw its suitableness in my case."[1]

Is this the reader's experience? In some measure we trust it is, for we must *all* bear the cross before we can wear the crown. The "Book of Consolations" is peculiarly fitted to the *downcast*. The Savior's gift of a "Comforter" is highly prized by the members of his Church when they are left *comfortless*. Whenever then, amid your trials, you turn to that Book, lift up your heart in secret earnest prayer for this gift. You shall thus obtain a double benefit by your affliction; the Spirit will open your understanding to understand the Scriptures, and the key of spiritual knowledge thus put into your hand will open to you the Sanctuary of Christian sympathy, where you shall find the man of sorrows, whose tears will mingle

---

[1] Bridges on Psalm 119:67.

with yours, and the sight of whose agonies will cause you to forget your own.

The twenty-second psalm sets him before us in the darkest hour of his earthly history. His loud cry of agony attracts our attention to the passage in which it was foretold, and insensibly our minds are led on to the perusal of the whole psalm. It proves to be emphatically one of those passages in which the prophets, by the Spirit of Christ within them, testified beforehand the sufferings of Christ, and the glory that should follow (1 Pet. 1:11). In this way the psalm diverts the sorrow of the Christian, by exhibiting the untold sorrows of his Lord, and elevates his mind above all earthly trials as he proceeds by making him a partaker, through hope, of the glory that is yet to be revealed. With his stripes our souls are healed (Isa. 53:5). We cannot murmur when we contemplate such an unmurmuring Master. Who will love sin any longer, after he has seen how it has pierced his Savior? How can we call our afflictions severe, when we "consider Him who endured such hostility from sinners against Himself?" (Heb. 13:3).

The Author desires to commend this psalm of the Redeemer's sorrow and joy to the frequent and attentive perusal of his fellow Christians. This humble endeavor to unfold some of its contents, he designs only for those hours of spiritual depression, or of family or personal affliction, when, criticism being disarmed, the reader looks only for a few simple words of consolation, or would seek to lose remembrance of his sorrows in contemplating those of the deeply tried fellow sufferer. He feels that much has been left unsaid. But as the volume is already larger than was anticipated, his object will be accomplished if the views here presented may, through the gracious Spirit, impart consolation even to a single individual, and by their imperfection incite others to turn aside and contemplate for themselves this great sight, which a saint of old beheld under the appropriate emblem of "a bush burning and not consumed," (Exodus 3:2).

As the psalm does not refer to the whole of the period in which our blessed Lord hung upon the cross, the reader is requested to set before his mind part of the previous history and circumstances. It is supposed that our divine Surety was crucified about, or not long after, nine o'clock in the morning. Immediately on his being nailed to the cross, we conceive that our merciful High Priest prayed for his murderers, "Father, forgive them, for they know not what they do," (Luke 23:34). After he had hung some little time on the cross, our Lord affectionately consigned his mother to the care of the beloved disciple John, saying to the one, "Behold your son," and to the other, "Behold your mother," (John 19:26, 27). Next after this, and before midday, it is probable that our Lord accepted the prayer of the penitent thief with this gracious assurance, "Assuredly, I say to you, today you will be with Me in Paradise," (Luke 23:43). At the sixth hour, that is, in our reckoning, at twelve o'clock, the supernatural darkness commenced. Instead of meridian brightness, there was a solemn gloom for about three hours. The moon being then at the full, the darkness could not possibly be caused by an eclipse, which besides, never continues for so long a period. From twelve o'clock until three our blessed Lord appears to have been silent, enduring a great inward conflict. About the ninth hour, that is, about three o'clock, he gave utterance to his feelings in the first words of this psalm, "My God! My God! Why have You forsaken me?" From this we infer that he applied the Psalm to himself. And as it was usual at that period for the Hebrews to quote the commencement of a psalm in an audible manner, in order that those around might join in its mental or vocal repetition, we have some reason to conclude that our dying Redeemer occupied his thoughts with "speaking to himself," and to God, in the words of this psalm (Eph. 5:19). The applicability of every sentence of it to his condition strengthens that opinion. This is the view attempted to be set forth in the following account. We conceive that our Lord, while under the darkness and desertion, repeated after his loud cry, the remainder of this psalm, and that in the 19th, 20th, and 21st verses, he plead so unrelentingly for the immediate return of his Father's comforting presence, that light broke forth instantly, and then he mentally exclaimed, "You have answered me!" The supernatural gloom was dispelled from the face of nature, and the light and peace of the Father's countenance were restored to the heart of Christ. In gratitude and joy our Lord continued to repeat to himself the remainder of the psalm and expressly declared that "God has not hidden His face from Him," (verse 24); and he affirmed his determination to "pay his vows." As he repeated this thought of the 25th verse, we conceive that in accordance with it, Jesus exclaimed, "I thirst," for St. John informs us that this was prompted rather by a sense of duty, than an impulse of nature. Continuing the course of the psalm, the Savior's heart was comforted with the vision of joy that was set before him (Heb. 12:2). He saw of the labor of his soul (Isa. 53:11) and was satisfied to witness the whole earth filled with the knowledge of the glory of God, and all nations rendering the homage of Christian worship (verses 27-29). He beheld his seed celebrating his righteousness through time and through eternity, and exulting in the glorious truth that he had perfectly "fulfilled it" (ver. 31). Here the psalm terminates, and we conceive that our blessed Master, as if satisfied with this sight, and conscious that all the work of suffering and of obedience in his mortal life was completed, now gave utterance to the second "loud voice," and, in accordance with this everlasting testimony of his Church, exclaimed, "It is finished!" Having said this, the Savior of the world bowed his head, and of his own accord gave up that life which no man could take from him (John 10:18) for, breathing out his soul he said, "Father, into Your hands I commit my spirit" (Luke 23:46).

This psalm depicts the Savior's condition, and unfolds his mental history, from the period of the first loud cry to that of the second. It opens with sorrow, and concludes with joy. Its time is but those few minutes which its meditative and deliberate perusal would occupy.

It commences with that most severe of all his trials, the hiding of his Father's face, and terminates with a vision of his everlasting joy in his Church. The change in the middle of the psalm is most important and comforting. It teaches that the Redeemer did not die under darkness. It assures us that his latest moments were those of peace and communion, not of trepidation and estrangement. The Christian's heart rejoices to know that his adorable and gracious Lord did not depart out of this life in bitter anguish of spirit, complaining that his Father had forsaken him, but in gratitude and exultation of soul, testifying that he had not hid his face from him, but had heard and answered his petition (verse 24).

We are now, Christian reader, about to consider the most important and mysterious part of our Lord's important and mysterious life. Yet let no Christian shrink from the contemplation of the "great mystery of godliness, God manifest in the flesh" (1 Tim. 3:16). So far as it is "revealed," it, "belongs unto us" (Deut. 29:29). Remember also, that there is nothing mysterious in itself. Knowledge, like the light, makes all things plain. Mystery is but a watchword of creature ignorance. As we advance from the lowest scale of being to the highest, we find that every rank calls that above it a mystery, and that beneath it a simplicity. God looks down from the height of being, and deems universal nature a simplicity. He only, whose name is "I am that I am," is the great mystery of eternity. "We shall understand all mysteries and all knowledge" (1 Cor. 13:2), but we shall be forever learning something further of the mystery of the Godhead, which passes knowledge. What we shall learn regarding God shall instantly cease to be mysterious, and we shall plainly and fully comprehend it. What we shall not have learned concerning the Divine Being will appear so mysterious and wonderful, that the fresh zest of inquiry shall be kept eternally alive. Thus our reverential love and adoring admiration of God shall be continually increasing, and the happiness of heaven augmenting without end. The ecstatic sensation of discovery, and the high delight of intelligent inquiry, will co-exist in our hearts, and impart to eternity the appearance and feeling neither of a past, nor of a future, but of a full and satisfactory present. If thus it shall prove in eternity, so ought it to be in time. "Grow," says the apostle, "in the knowledge of our Lord and Savior Jesus Christ" (2 Pet. 3:18). The Spirit of light is promised by him as a guide into all truth. Let us therefore, "search the Scriptures, for they testify of Jesus" (John 5:39). The reading of the Word is one of the ordinances of God's appointment for the benefit of our souls. While engaged in its perusal, and at all times, let us constantly pray that God would "illuminate our minds and understandings with the bright beams of his Holy Spirit, that we may daily grow in the saving knowledge of the heavenly mystery of our redemption, wrought by our dear Lord and Savior Jesus Christ."[2] This Psalm brings that redemption, and this Savior, vividly before our view. That its perusal may be accompanied with greater benefit, we would humbly suggest the following as topics for meditation.

Endeavor to bring fully before your mind, First, the **SUFFERER,** the Lord Jesus Christ, God over all, in your nature, dying as your Surety. Second, the **CAUSE** of suffering, sin; your sin, and the sin of the world. Third, the **AGENTS,** the Law, Satan, Man, and God. Fourth, the **REALITY** of Christ's sufferings; not a mere appearance of sorrow, but a real, acute, and exquisite sense of bodily agony, and of mental anguish. Fifth, the **PLACE,** Golgotha, the hill of skulls—Calvary, the mount outside the walls of Jerusalem, where criminals were put to death. Sixth, the **CIRCUMSTANCES** a public execution—three crosses and three crucified thereon—two for theft—one in the midst for sedition and blasphemy, even Jesus our blessed Savior, condemned alike in the spiritual and criminal courts of his native country. His back excoriated by the scourge, pressing on the wood, his hands and his

---

[2] Lord Bacon's Prayers.

feet pierced with nails, his sufferings mocked, his character vilified, his strength exhausted, his soul deserted, and his spirit assailed by the temptations of Satan.

When these have been considered, endeavor next to enter into the feelings of that Holy One, who endured them all. Consider the **UNPARALLELED POSITION** in which the blessed Jesus found himself placed when hanging on the cross. Contemplate this position, and his feelings, in reference, first, to his own Godhead and manhood. When the Second Person in the Holy Trinity took our nature upon him, he did not lay aside his Godhead; he laid aside only the exhibition of its glorious presence and power. In all his words and miracles, he spoke and acted by the power of the Father and the Holy Ghost. He glorified God by an invariable reference to him. "The words that I speak to you I do not speak on My own authority; but the Father who dwells in Me does the works" (John 14:10). Now also on the cross, when his body and soul sunk to their lowest possible condition, he would not have recourse to his own Godhead power to rescue and deliver them, but waited patiently upon his Father in the exercise of faith and prayer. He did not seek the glory of deliverance for himself. He kept the Almighty power of his Godhead in silent union with the utter weakness of his manhood, and did not allow the accuser to say that he used undue advantage in the combat.

Second, in reference to God the Father, and the Holy Spirit. These two persons in the Sacred Trinity rejoiced in God the Son's taking our nature. During his life on earth, they had uninterrupted and intimate communion with him, in his human soul; but when the sin of the world was laid upon that body and soul which Jesus offered up on the cross, they judicially withdrew their comforting presence, and refrained from communing with him in that human soul. Observe that it was only *judicially*. Christ was still dear to the heart of the Father. More so, if possible, most dear now, because most obedient. And mark this, that he took our *nature into* union with his Godhead, but only took our *sin upon* that humanity which he had appropriated to himself. Sin could not be taken *into* his holy nature, no more than darkness can be taken into light. But it was laid *upon* him by imputation, and because he had taken it upon him, he suffered all that it deserved. The desertion was a judicial act on the part of God towards sin. Christ suffered that desertion of the Father and of the Holy Spirit, because he had made himself to be sin for us (2 Cor. 5:21). The wrath of God, therefore, is by no means to be regarded as directed against the bearer, but only against the burden. Yet, because he bound it fast upon him, he did actually suffer that desertion which it merited.

Third, in reference to the angels. These ministering spirits were not allowed to draw near to the dying and deserted Jesus. Even that angel who had strengthened him in Gethsemane was compelled to close his half-spread wing, and leave him all alone. Christ, at this moment, was alone in the universe of being.

Fourth, in reference to the Law. The Son of God had made himself to be born under the law (Gal. 4:4) and now he was dying under its curse (Gal. 3:13). The shame and infamy of being hung on a tree, was the last and most severe of all the curses which the law of God and man denounced (Deut. 21:22, 23).

Fifth, in reference to man. Though bone of our bone, and flesh of our flesh, there was no man that would help him. His own disciples had fled, and a host of enemies and bitter revilers now surrounded him, and with cruel hatred nailed him to the tree.

Lastly, in reference to devils. "This was the hour and power of darkness" (Luke 22:53). If a legion of evil spirits could possess the body of one demoniac, (Mark 5:9; Matt. 12:45) who shall number the hosts which Satan brought against the Captain of our salvation? (Heb. 2:10). It was necessary that he should be tried in all points. The Adversary must not have it in his power to say that the Son of Man had not been fairly, or fully, tried: no room for his insinuation must be left, that Christ would have fallen like the fathers, if he had only been tempted and tried as they were. Therefore Christ was expressly "led up by the Spirit to be tempted by the devil" (Matt. 4:1). "Consider that immaculate Lamb tempted by Satan to distrust his Father's care, and turn the stones into bread; then to presume upon that care, and cast himself down from a pinnacle of the temple; and then to deny his Father altogether, and worship the devil in preference! How horrible must such suggestions be to his holy soul!" (Sermons of Charles Simeon). Now, while being crucified through weakness (2 Cor. 13:4) he gave himself, and was given by the Father and the Holy Spirit, into the hand of the Powers of Darkness, in order that, defeating all their attempts, he might triumph over them openly (Col. 2:15). This was the hour of which the Savior forewarned his disciples on the previous evening. "The ruler of this world is coming, and he has nothing in Me" (John 14:30). It is probable that Satan led on his grand attack, under cover of the darkness. Doubtless as an experienced general, he would seize the most favorable moment. No sooner had the comforting presence of God been withdrawn from the Redeemer, than the prince of the fallen spirits would summon them to the assault. Rulers, principalities, and powers, every fiend and evil spirit of hell, came round the holy human soul of Jesus, and did their utmost, during these three hours of darkness, to gain an entrance; but not one of them could find anything in Christ congenial to their own natures, on which to work. As roaming cavalry in the battle, by desperate charges, attempt to break the square of the enemy, so these spiritual foes, rushing at all points, and with all kinds of temptations, upon this only solid square of holiness which our world has ever seen, received that defeat themselves which they intended to give, and fell back with a recoil of everlasting dismay. It was not by an exertion of his almighty strength that the Savior prevailed, but by his invincible holiness, and trust in God. In the world of spirits, good and evil are as repugnant and hostile to each other, as fire and water are in this world of matter. The presence, therefore, of a perfectly holy being on our earth, must have proved a source of constant misery to Satan and his evil spirits. Observe how they dread his approach, cry out at the sound of his voice, and address him by that name which was most cognizable to their own apprehensions and abhorrence: "I know who You are—the Holy One of God" (Mark 1:24; Luke 4:34). It was his holiness from which they shrank; and it was by his unsullied holiness that he proved more than a conqueror over them in death.

Let then, this unparalleled situation in which your Lord and Savior was placed, while hanging on the cross, be more and more fully realized by frequent meditation. Remember, that he was tried in all points like as we are, yet without sin (Heb. 4:15). This was the last trial to which he was subjected, as the Foundation-stone of that eternal temple which God was about to lay. "I lay in Zion a stone for a foundation, a tried stone, a precious cornerstone, a sure foundation" (Isa. 28:16). The prince of this world, and all the powers of darkness tried it, AND FOUND NOTHING. Man tried it with every ordeal he could think of, AND FOUND NOTHING. The law tried it with its ten commandments, and its sharpest curse, AND FOUND NOTHING. God the Father, and God the Spirit, tried it by the severest test of their withdrawal, AND FOUND NOTHING. Consider what must have been the holy Savior's feelings while enduring this unparalleled trial!

Meditate much and often on the sufferings of your Lord: You may thus need less personal suffering to teach you to hate the sin that caused them. In all his afflictions let yourself be afflicted. Do not be estranged in sympathy from the best friend of your soul. Live only to be like him. Let the first desire of your heart be fixed on the attainment of holiness. All the bitter sorrows which your Surety endured for you, were intended to deliver you from the pollution of sin. All your own personal afflictions are designed to make you "partakers of his holiness" (Heb. 12:10). Seek then, earnestly seek, after holiness. The noblest and most exalted wish which the heart can entertain, is that it may be made pure and holy. The sullied stream hastens to sink every impurity, and to flow on in the clear transparency of its fountain-head. Look ever to the Fountain Head of your everlasting being. Think often of the unsullied purity of the Divine nature, of which even the lucid light is an inadequate representation. Then turn and meditate on what you have become by sin; defiled in mind and conscience (Tit. 1:15); in heart by evil thoughts, covetousness, deceit, an evil or envious eye, pride, foolishness, not to mention grosser offences (Mark 7:21, 22; James 3:6). Pray to the Spirit of holiness to teach you to hate this defiled condition of your nature. Pray to be enabled to "see" so much of the purity of "God," that like Job you may at last be brought to "abhor" yourself (Job 42:6). That this self-abhorrence and inward sorrow may not work death, but repentance to salvation (2 Cor. 7:10), still pray for the Spirit of holiness to enable you to look upon Him whom you have pierced. The bitterness of your mourning for him (Zech. 12:12) will, by the quickening Spirit, awaken within you a holy gratitude that he should have mourned for you. This grand proof of his love will constrain you to live no longer to yourself, but to him that died for you, and rose again (2 Cor. 5:14). The promises of his grace will incite you to "cleanse yourself from all filthiness of the flesh and spirit, perfecting holiness in the fear of God" (2 Cor. 7:1). And the words of your God and Redeemer, "Be holy, for I am holy" (1 Pet. 1:16), will obtain a universal response from every part of your nature, "Your heart and flesh will cry out for the living God" (Psa. 84:2). Look ever upward. The Savior's address to each of us is, "Look unto me, and be saved." Let us never turn away from the contemplation of the Savior's sorrow and the Saviors glory. By "looking unto Jesus," the Christian rises, like the nautilus, from his dark and native depths, to the pure atmosphere and warm sunshine of an upper world, spreads forth his tiny sails of faith, and hope, and love, and is gently wafted over the waters of life by the balmy gales of grace. Onward he glides, beautiful in movement, and joyful in his new existence, so long as the heavy waters of this world are excluded: that moment he swallows them he sinks. Do not be conformed then, dear Christian readers, to this world, but be transformed by the renewing of your mind (Rom. 12:2). Seek the things that are above, where Christ sits at the right hand of God (Col. 3:1). That the Spirit of Christ may rest upon you, that the blessing of the Father of mercies may descend on you, and that when Christ, who is our life, shall appear, you also may all appear with him in glory (Col. 3:4) is the earnest prayer of your grateful and humble servant in the gospel,

John Stevenson

THE TITLE OF THE PSALM

To the chief Musician upon Aijeleth Shahar,
(or "The Deer of the Dawn,") a Psalm of David.

VARIOUS opinions are entertained by the scholars in reference to those titles which stand prefixed to the majority of the Psalms. The safest conclusion is, that where they do not explain themselves, we must regard every other explanation as entirely conjectural. Such titles, as, for instance, among others, those of Psalms 3, 57, 60, 92, must be kept in view by every reader who would understand them fully. The circumstances in which they were written, and the object they were intended to serve, are thus communicated at a glance. But there are many titles, like that before us, to which, at this distant day, it is impossible to attach a definite and indisputable significance.

This title may be understood, as in the text, in reference to an instrument called "Aijeleth Shahar," upon which this psalm was to be played by the chief Musician. Others give an English translation to these Hebrew terms, as in the margin, and conclude that David gave this Psalm to the chief Musician, as one which he had written "concerning the deer of the morning," in allusion to the Messiah, who was cruelly hunted to death, but who escaped from the hands of the wicked in the morning of the resurrection. It appears incongruous that a feminine noun and emblem should be employed where the Messiah is intended, and therefore others give an entirely different translation to this title. In harmony with the Chaldee Paraphrast, and following Aquila and Jerome, they understand the term "Lemanetsach," "To the chief Musician," in the general sense of excelling, and not necessarily as limited to excellency in one department only, as that of music. They therefore interpret it, "To the Triumpher—To the

Victor, or Giver of Victory, and, To the Conqueror." In this latter sense, Parkhurst and Bishop Horsley receive it, and the terms "Aijeleth Shahar," they render, "Concerning the interposition of the dusk," or such darkness as prevails at dawn of day. "The scene of this Psalm is the crucifixion of Christ," says Parkhurst, "when the Divine Light appeared *almost* overwhelmed by the interposing powers of darkness, and when the *sun,* sympathizing with his great *antitype,* was darkened for three hours, and afforded to all believers a sensible and affecting image of what the *Sun of Righteousness* then endured." Compare Luke 22:53, with 23:44, 45. See also Parkhurst's Hebrew Lexicon, p. 617.

Could strict criticism maintain this interpretation, we would request the reader to receive it without hesitation. It harmonizes with the view we have taken of the Psalm, from its own internal evidence, and furnishes this idea, that the darkness at the crucifixion was not total, but such as exists at the earliest part of the morning. We are compelled, however, to conclude that though most interesting and appropriate, it is only an ingenious and beautiful conjecture.

"A Psalm of David." David, as the author of this and other Psalms, may be regarded in a fourfold view. 1. As a prophet, inspired by the Holy Ghost to utter the mind and will of God. 2. As a man, expressing the thoughts, the desires, and feelings, which existed in his heart, or were suggested by his circumstances. 3. As a type of Messiah, and, 4. As a pattern for believers. In the composition of this Psalm, we regard him in the first view. As we become partakers of Christ's sufferings, by sanctified personal experience of trial and sorrows, so believers and prophets of old were admitted to the same fellowship, in the same manner. While each inspired prophet wrote as he felt, and attached his own meaning to his own words, the Spirit of God directed these feelings and these words, according to his own high design. It therefore became a deeply interesting occupation to these prophets to inquire and search diligently what the Spirit within them signified, by that which he had inspired them to write (1

Pet. 1:10, 11). This also, is our happy work in the perusal of the Old Testament. "Search the Scriptures," says our blessed Savior, "for these are they which testify of ME" (John 5:39). It was the great object of his own ministry to expound the reference which these Scriptures bore to himself (Luke 24:25-27, 44; 4:17-21). The apostles and evangelists invariably interpreted them with the same reference (Acts 2:25; 3:18; 13:32, 33; 8:35). And the pen of inspiration has declared that "the testimony of Jesus is the spirit of prophecy" (Rev. 19:10). Adhering to this scripturally prescribed *subject* of exposition, we have not alluded to the circumstances of David as the *author* of the Psalm; nor indeed is it possible now to determine the time or circumstances in which it was composed, nor shall we trouble the reader with the various conjectures which have been formed. We have thought it more important to consider the Psalm purely in its prophetic import, and to fix the attention of the reader, without distraction, upon the SAVIOUR. For David being *a* prophet, and knowing that Christ would be raised up, and seeing these things beforehand, spoke of HIS sufferings, and foretold HIS glory (Compare Acts 2:30, 31, with 1 Pet. 1:11).

CHRIST ON THE CROSS IN DARKNESS

THE CRY

VERSE 1—*My God, My God, why have You forsaken Me? Why are You so far from helping Me, and from the words of My groaning?*

HOW solemn, how mysterious, O Christian are these affecting words! They absorb the mind; they overpower the heart! The view they present is almost too awful to be realized. It is difficult to persuade ourselves of the two facts which they imply. Can it be true, that the Father of mercies forsakes any human being on this side of the grave? Is it possible, that when deserted by the great God, man can address him in the language of trust and confidence?

Go to Golgotha, Christian. Behold the amazing reality. Learn the unsearchable mystery. God's last and severest infliction, and faith's strongest and highest act are being there displayed. Let the evangelists conduct you in thought to Mount Calvary. Imagine yourself to have been present when the great atonement was offered. That was the judgment day of the Savior of the world. At the tribunals of men he was condemned—under their sentence he was being executed: and while his body hung in torture on the cross, he was arraigned in spirit before the bar of God, under the imputation of human guilt. The court of heaven descended, as it were, to Mount Calvary, the strong voice from the cross rends the veil that hides the unseen world from our view. We behold the great God at the dreaded moment when the last sentence has been pronounced. These awful words, "Let the law take its course," have just been uttered. The eternal Judge appears with his face turned away, as if about to leave the throne of justice, unable to exercise the Divine prerogative of mercy. An agonizing cry thrills every heart, arrests every attention, "Eli, Eli, lama sabachthani—My God, my God, why have You forsaken me?"

Inquiring angels and men ask, Who is this that is condemned? And with unutterable astonishment they learn that it is Jesus Christ, the Son of God—He who had always loved and served his Father; whose loving heart had never swerved from its allegiance; whose whole life, from his cradle to this dying moment, was one uninterrupted flow of holy love and obedience. It is this Jesus, who in the beginning was with God, who is God; who is the only begotten, the beloved of the Father, that utters this astounding cry (Matt. 27:46, and Mark 15:34).

Whom does he address? His own Father, from whose bosom he had come forth; He who had sent angels to minister to him, who had never before "left him alone, being always with him" (John 16:32). He whose voice had twice been heard from heaven saying, "This is my beloved Son, in whom I am well pleased," (Matt. 3:17; 17:5), even He was now withdrawn.

How does he implore his return? First, with a *sudden, loud, and piercing cry.* Christ had been silent from the commencement of the darkness. The conflict was inward, deep, and overpowering. He was silent; he opened not his mouth. For nearly three hours he uttered not a word. At last his grief burst forth. He could be silent no longer. With a loud cry he gave vent to his sorrow. That voice was not more audible to the ears of his murderers, than it was piercing to the heart of his disciples and of his Father. Devils, too, heard his cry of unshaken faith. They perceived how he could appeal to his Father against all their insinuations. They were dismayed and seized with despair. Men were struck with wonder at his still remaining strength. Mary and her believing companions must have felt that cry thrill within their inmost hearts. And surely to his own Father in heaven it must have come with persuasive and affecting force; for it was the most mournful cry he had ever heard from a human voice.

Secondly, with the language of *adoption;* with the *confidence of faith.* "My God, my God." This is not the agonizing cry of a creature struggling with an unknown power, and amid its anxious efforts to escape, reiterating O God, O God. It is the cry of a child seeking to be rescued from the grasp of foes; looking towards a distant parent, and sending across an intervening gulf the fervent appeal of its confiding claim. It is the cry of conscious innocence, which knows not a cause for estrangement, which casts itself upon the being it loves, and does not think of a rebuff. It is the cry of one suddenly surrounded by circumstances never before experienced. The outpouring of a deep, inward, long-pent grief. The unburdening of a heart which but for words would break, which but for faith would never gain relief or cry, "My God, my God."

Thirdly, with the accent of *interrogation*. "*Why* have You forsaken me?" Which of these words bears most of the emphasis of the Savior's meaning? Does he denounce the act? Does he say, "Why have You *forsaken* me?" By no means. For if Job could say, "Though he slay me, yet will I trust him" (Job 13:15), much more may Jesus declare, "Though he forsake me, yet will I submit." Does he set forward self? "Why have You forsaken *me*?" Such language was altogether foreign to his lips. The meek intonations of the Savior's voice were never swollen with the emphasis of egotism. He who was lowly in heart never once urged a single personal consideration as an argument with God or man. Concerning what, then, does the Redeemer principally inquire? First, as to the reason, *why, for what* have You forsaken me? Brought, as he was now, before a new tribunal, and experiencing a new infliction, our Lord, by this interrogation, maintains his innocence, challenges his adversaries to the proof, and inquires of the great Judge, what, and whether any, new charge has been preferred against him. Christ had been cleared at both judgment seats, even though condemned. In the spiritual court, when the contradictory testimony of false witnesses could substantiate nothing against him, the Savior challenged the closest investigation, and called on Caiaphas to make impartial and full inquiry (John 18:21). In the criminal court, he needed not to utter a word on his own behalf, for even the judge pronounced him to be guiltless. "Pilate took water and washed his hands before the multitude, saying, I am innocent of the blood of this just person. You see to it" (Matt. 27:24). But now that the Redeemer is brought before the judgment seat of his Father, under the imputation of human guilt, and beholds the face of the Judge turned away from him, and that neither man nor angel offers a word on his behalf, he is entitled, and it fully becomes him, even more so, in justice he is bound, to declare his innocence, and to demand if any new accusation has been laid to his charge—My God, my God, for what reason have You forsaken me?

Secondly, our Lord inquires as to the person, why have YOU forsaken me? This was his burden, this his grief. God was absent from him. His own Father was withdrawn; and no cause had occurred to prevent his presence more than had previously existed.

Fully did our Savior know, and exquisitely did he feel the truth of that Scripture, "In God's favor is life" (Psa. 30:5). Under the hidings of his Father's face, the only begotten Son must have experienced what no human intellect can conceive, and which if it did, no human language could express. One point in it, however, ought particularly to be noticed as important in itself, and as throwing light on this interrogation. It is, that this was an entirely new sensation, by which our Lord was now tried. For more than thirty years of his human life, the Redeemer possessed a blessed consciousness of his Father's presence, his Father's love. No changeableness or shadow of turning had ever been exhibited towards him. Even in the garden of Gethsemane, the bitterness of the cup was mitigated, the darkness of the night was relieved, because there was one present there, to whom he could go and say, "My Father." But he had hung upon the cross for nearly six hours; and now from midday, when the sun ought to have shone most brightly, the darkness had been increasing. For almost three hours it had continued; and with the outward, the inward darkness seems to have commenced and terminated. The hiding of the sun accompanied and typified the hiding of the Father's countenance. As the one was new in the history of the world, so was the other in that of Christ. No natural eclipse—no overspreading cloud—no mere gloom of a temporary fog, occasioned that darkness. Neither was it pains of body—nor desertion of friends—nor exhaustion of spirit—nor the impatience of discontent—nor the despondency of unbelief that overspread the mind of our Immanuel with this feeling of loneliness. It was a supernatural obscuration of the solar light, that enveloped the land with greyish darkness; and it was a judicial withdrawal of the light of God's countenance, that overcame the human soul of Jesus with this strange and overpowering sensation. The pains of crucifixion, the forsaking of friends, the taunts of men, and the assaults of devils, were nothing in comparison with this. For almost six hours the powers of darkness had assailed his spirit with every variety of temptation. Men and devils availed themselves of the opportunity. His hour of weakness (2 Cor. 13:4) was their "hour of power" (Luke 22:53). Outwardly and inwardly the "fiery darts" (Eph. 6:16) were thrust at him. Neither God the Father, nor God the Spirit, appeared for his help. Instead of exercising his own Godhead power to annihilate his foes in a moment, Christ presented to them the broad shield of faith and breastplate of righteousness, and stood unmoved amid their fiercest onsets, immaculate in his own holiness. Dreadfully assaulted as we read he was by man, he was doubtless more strongly assailed by spiritual foes. But he took no advantage over them from his almighty strength. He entered the combat as the second Adam; allowed his enemies to exhaust their utmost efforts of temptation; gave himself into their hands as one whom they could cause to die, but could not cause to sin; and by exhibiting the power of a pure and holy will, rejecting all and every kind of temptation, he rose where the first Adam fell, and proved himself to be "the Holy One of God."

It is obvious that our Lord must have *felt* the trial. His human soul was incessantly called upon to reject innumerable and never-ending temptations. His body was quivering in every nerve—proud and taunting men encircled his cross—fierce and wicked spirits surrounded his human soul, which now enjoyed no sensible communion with the Father and the Holy Ghost. Darkness, spiritual and material, enveloped him—neither angels nor disciples afforded him the slightest aid in this last and awful conflict. No wonder, then, that he was speechless from the sixth hour until the ninth. His human soul was engrossed with its unprecedented situation—it was bruised under the forsaking of God—harassed with the assaults of foes, and oppressed with the agonizing's of the flesh. His heart is so painfully broken, that he cannot speak. But at last, when the fury of the enemy abates, and the first halt of their despairing efforts yields him breath, he exclaims, "My God, my God, why have You forsaken me?"

When Christ here speaks of his being "forsaken," he means that he was under a suspension of that joyful and intimate communion with the Most High, which he had always enjoyed up to this moment. God the Father, and God the Holy Spirit, had withdrawn all sensible influence from Christ's human nature. He therefore speaks according to that nature, because he felt according to it: he *felt* as a *man*. The great object of his life on earth, was not to glorify himself, but his Father. Therefore in all his miracles, we find him either calling on the Father's name, or acknowledging his power, or informing his disciples that the Father who dwelt in him did the works (John 14:10). Though possessing almighty power, it was his voluntary choice and determined purpose, not to avail himself of it on every occasion, but to live as a man acting in constant dependence upon God, and so to become a pattern or example for us to follow. Instead of opposing his omnipotence to blast all his enemies, he presented his innate holiness and simple trust in God, as that in which he could withstand all their assaults. And whether the sunshine of divine love be round him, or darkness and desertion envelop body and soul, he retains the same holy, confiding, and lovingly trusting heart that he had before. In the 42nd chapter of the prophecy of

Isaiah, the Father thus directs our attention to the Son: "Behold! My Servant whom I uphold, My Elect One in whom My soul delights! I have put My Spirit upon Him." Again, in the 5th and 6th verses, he directly addresses the Son: "I, the LORD, have called You in righteousness, and will hold Your hand; I will keep You and give You as a covenant to the people, as a light to the Gentiles." Christ in the flesh is in this way exhibited to us in two respects. First, as one whom God "upholds." And secondly, as one in whom his soul "delights." And the covenant which the Father stipulates to perform with and for the Son, is also set before us in a twofold view. First, "that he will hold his hand" and "keep" him. And secondly, that he "Will give him for a covenant to the people, for a light of the Gentiles." This passage of Scripture was doubtless well known to the Savior. It formed, with many others, his title deed and security in this great work of redemption. He not only knew it in the letter, be knew it also in the spirit. He had experienced its truth. He had tested its accuracy. He had for thirty years lived in the enjoyment of all that it promised him. Sweetly and blessedly did the human soul of Jesus of Nazareth feel itself "upheld" by God. Not a moment was he destitute of the conscious "putting" and "resting" of the Spirit upon him. Every step in life the Son took, he found himself "kept" by omnipotent power, and by omniscient wisdom. His hand was held in a Father's grasp; and scarcely a day passed in which he was not able to say to some sin-darkened soul, "I am given to be the light of the world." Endeavor to realize to your mind the heavenly sensations of such a life as this. Its fullness of blessedness is greater than can be conceived. Set vividly, however, before your mind what little you can apprehend, and then imagine it to be suddenly suspended.

The same Jesus that had enjoyed the whole of what God had promised, and of what God is, was now deprived of the comfort of these promises, and of the enjoyment of God's presence. Instead of upholding, he felt a withdrawal—instead of delightful communion, there was silence and desertion—instead of strength, weakness—instead of light, darkness—instead of the

Spirit, heaviness and oppression. Let us not imagine that the Father had ceased virtually to uphold the Son, or that his soul had now no delight in him. It could not be so. He was still surely, though not sensibly, upholding him; he still felt the same delight in him. Indeed, we may conceive that, if possible, love and approbation were increased in proportion as the obedience and dutifulness of the Son was exhibited. But God was not now holding him by the hand, and keeping him in *the same sensible manner* in which he had always done before. It *was* necessary that he who was the "child born" should also be proved to be the "mighty God." It was right, that he who had always glorified the Father's power, should now be glorified in his own. Therefore, God the Father, and God the Spirit, withdrew the manifestations of their nearness and power so that the Savior might be left to the exercise of his own resources. "Therefore His own arm brought salvation for Him; and His own righteousness, it sustained Him. For He put on righteousness as a breastplate, and a helmet of salvation on His head" (Isa. 59:16, 17). Arrayed in this armor of proof, he presented himself to the hosts of darkness. On his helmeted head, and on his plated breast, he laid the sin of the world; and though the curse of the law, and the lightning of God's wrath, and the terrors of the judgment that condemned that sin, were let loose against it, yet they could not touch him, or penetrate that coat of mail. His holiness could stand. No weapon formed against him could prosper. Devils did their utmost to find the smallest opening, but his righteousness was perfect. They hated only the bearer—God hated only the burden. God's condemnation fell upon the load of imputed guilt. The strokes and shafts of the enemy were directed only against him who was taking it away. But the Savior so held fast the sin that was laid upon him, that no distinction could be made. What the Father and the law directed against the sin, must necessarily fall on him: and what devils and men aimed at the Bearer, could not make him seek a disencumbered advantage in the conflict, by letting go the burden that oppressed him, but rather hastened him forward to that tomb where he would deposit it forever, and lay it out of the way from between God and man.

It was when left alone in this terrible conflict, that our Lord cried to his Father with this loud voice. He did not grieve at the most painful of his other trials. For thousands of years he would be willing to endure them; but to be excluded from the light of his Father's countenance for a moment longer than was absolutely necessary, was what he could not and would not allow. Therefore he cries, "My God, my God, why have You forsaken me?"

Let us now consider the succeeding parts of this verse, as they stand in one connected whole, with the first. They seem to be explanatory, as well as additional exclamations and assist us in understanding the meaning of our Lord's mysterious cry. We learn by them that he does not seek to exert his own Godhead power, and secure the glory of the victory to himself—that it is no selfish cry, but one prompted by a filial desire to be helped by his Father, that the mighty Helper may have all the praise. And that it is not so much for his own satisfaction that he makes this inquiry, as for that of the members of his church, who thus learn at once two amazing facts: first, that their Lord was forsaken on the cross; and, being hereby incited to inquire the reason, learn, in the second place, that he was forsaken on their account.

"My God, my God, why have You forsaken me? Why are You so far from helping me, and from the words of my groaning?" Here there are three inquiries. First, Why have You forsaken me? second, Why are You so far from helping me? third, And from the words of my groaning? The appropriate answers to each of these furnish suitable and abundant matter for consideration.

First, Why have You forsaken me? Answer, Because you are bearing the sins of the world (John 1:29). It has been truly said, no man knows the exceeding sinfulness of sin, but he who learns it at the cross of Christ. That God should have so loved the world, as to give forth his own Son from his bosom on its behalf, teaches us how full and tender is his compassion towards fallen men. That the death of that Son should have been necessary before we could be saved, proves the inflexible justice of the righteous Judge, who will not allow his laws to be broken with impunity. But when that Son was dying on the cross, that the Father should hide his face from him, because of our iniquity, proves how revolting sin is to the holy nature of God.

It was *sin* which caused this new and strange sensation in the heart of Christ. "The Lord had now laid, or caused to meet on him, the iniquities of us all" (Isa. 53:6). The victim was placed on the altar, and our guilt transferred to his innocent head. Though Christ voluntarily placed himself in our place; though men regarded him as a sinner; yet till now he had not been so treated by his Father. It is written, "the Lord made his soul an offering for sin" (Isa. 53:10). The human soul of Jesus was offered, was given by the Persons of the Sacred Trinity on account of sin. The atonement is not only a plan of infinite wisdom, whereby the various attributes of the Godhead are brought into beautiful harmony—wherein "mercy and truth have met together; righteousness and peace have kissed each other" (Psa. 85:10)—whereby "God might be just, and the justifier of the one who has faith in Jesus" (Rom. 3:26) It is a sacrifice of something of infinite value; it is a costly gift—the gift of that pure and holy human soul, as well as of that spotless body, which God the Son had taken into union with himself. As that "prepared body" was visibly made an atoning sacrifice on the cross, as on an altar, so also was that holy soul made an offering for sin after an invisible and spiritual manner. As that body went down into the grave of the earth, and was raised again to burst apart the chains of death: so that soul was delivered for sin under the grave of the curse, that it might rise again and deliver us from the power of spiritual death. The curse was, separation from the joy and light of God's countenance. This is what we deserve. Into this we fell; but could not raise ourselves. Therefore, the Son of God took a human body and a human soul, and placed himself in this our fallen separated state—came under the curse—was excluded from God's presence—but did make for himself, and for us, a way, a glorious way, out of spiritual death into spiritual life, out of the state of banishment, into that of union, peace, and joy. The atonement, therefore, is not a mere arrangement—not a mere contrivance for the adjustment of a difficult question. It is a matter of fact—a reality—an actual substitution—a real purchase, at an immeasurable expense on the part of the Godhead. The Father and the blessed Spirit gave the Son, and the Son gave himself, for man. During all the period of his life THEY were with him, rejoicing and communing with him in his human soul. But here on the cross, they gave up that human soul—they ceased their communing with it— they made it their offering, and Jesus made it his offering, for sin. Thus sin, which is a spiritual evil, as well as temporal—the law, which has a spiritual and temporal power—and man, the sinner, who has a spiritual and material nature—were fully and individually met in each of these respects, by the spiritual offering of the soul, and the temporal, visible, and material offering of the body of the Lord Jesus Christ. And it was when this spiritual offering was being made, that our Lord experienced strange, new, and awful sensations. He had descended voluntarily into the very depths of the curse—tasted its every bitterness—and with this loud and agonizing cry, commenced his ascent upwards from a condition in which his soul could not and would not remain.

It was necessary that Christ should be acknowledged by God the Father as the sin-bearer, otherwise his surety-ship could not avail for us. And so far as we know, the only mode by which a holy Being can express his recognition of a sinner, or of a sinner's surety, is by turning from him, and causing the laws to be put in force against him. Thus did the Father act towards the Son; that so sin, even when seen on one with whom he had always been well pleased, should not be treated in the slightest degree as less odious than it really is. The turning away of God's countenance, or that Divine aversion which we so designate, though unseen by mortal eyes, was doubtless marked by those countless intelligences of other worlds who behold it in unveiled glory. Our faculties are too limited to comprehend the vast design of God in this stupendous mystery of redemption. And we are generally too selfish to allow that its lessons extend far beyond ourselves. But angels inquiring into these things would learn, and in all his vast dominions created intelligences did learn, in this desertion of the crucified Son of God, that their Creator will by no means clear the guilty (Exod. 34:7). In the death of Jesus the myriads of superior beings would be taught that same lesson which God intended we should learn by the commandment, that "sin is exceeding sinful" (Rom. 7:13). Therefore, it "pleased the Lord to bruise him." He it was who "put him to grief" (Isa. 53:10). The spirit of Christ was wrung with anguish. We know how we feel under the charge of sin from man. How much more exquisitely must Christ have felt under the imputation of sin from God!

The imputation of sin to Christ is no idle tale. It is no fond unwarranted idea in the believer's mind—a mere nominal transference, effected by the insertion of a few figures on the debit and credit side of the eternal reckoning. It was a real transaction between the Father and the Son. It was a business of life and death in which our Surety was engaged. Our case is certainly not an ideal one. Every day gives us fresh proofs by pain, sorrow, sickness, and death, that sin is something more than a mere word. We feel that we are bound under its curse. And when Christ undertook to deliver us, he was fully aware of this. He knew what he had undertaken; therefore he placed himself under the law, and under the curse of the law. He took up the burden of sin, yet he loathed it in his heart. He felt its odious weight upon his spirit, but having taken it, it was counted his. And the Father treated him accordingly. The Lord bruised him; God turned away from him; God refused for a time to speak with him. And Christ must have felt somewhat as we do when a fellow-creature lays a crime to our charge, and turns from us when we address him. In our case, the corruption of nature turns to our relief. The workings of pride and anger form a seasonable though sinful counteraction to our mortified feelings. But it could not be so with Christ. He tasted the unmitigated bitterness of the curse. His were unmixed feelings of sorrow. Sin itself grieved him. He mourned that God should have been so dishonored. He hated it not merely in its consequences, but in its essence. He knew that the great Judge, before whom he stood, did not abhor him, but the burden which he bore. His own soul detested it in an equal degree. Yet he girded it so to him that no separation could be effected. He made himself so one with our case and cause, that all that we deserved landed upon him. Let us keep this distinction clearly before our minds. Christ's person was still as holy and acceptable to the Father as before. The divine wrath could not, and did not, burn against him; but it grew hot against the sins of man. And since Christ took these sins upon his own head, he must be content to suffer all the consequences which they entailed. And he was content to suffer all, and with a ready hand he took the cup and drank it to the dregs. But when he *had* drank that cup, and when he *had* wrung out its bitterest ingredients, he was not content—we speak it deliberately and with reverence—he was not content, neither was his Father, that it should be held to his lips forever. He was now tasting a kind of spiritual death. As physical death is the separation of the body from the soul, so spiritual death is the soul's separation from God. Here is the mystery of Christ's crucifixion and loud cry; that his human soul was separated from his Father's presence; that he was made to experience exclusion and banishment from God's face. But herein lies the mystery of our redemption by that crucifixion; that Christ was not willing to remain forever separated from God; and by the energy of his own holiness did wrestle with an agonizing earnestness and importunity of entreaty until he was restored again to the enjoyment of that presence. He willingly endured that curse for us, and as willingly pressed back again into that presence from which he had allowed it to exclude him for a time. Let a mere man be once forsaken by his Creator, he never can recover himself. This is the grand prerogative of the God-man, that though submerged in the lowest depths, he can rise again by inherent power. "He has life in himself." Therefore, though the concentrated wrath of God were let loose against the sins of men, and while that wrath was not in the slightest degree diminished because these sins were taken up by One with whom the Father was well pleased, yet it did not cast the sinners that committed it into instant and eternal ruin, because one interposed himself who could bear up under it all. His power of holiness could sustain and bear away the double load of sin and of desertion, but his heart was broken under it. Do not say that, being God, he could not feel, for remember what he exclaimed when the sins of the world were laid upon his head, "My God, my God, why have You forsaken me?"

Second. "Why are You so far from helping me?" Answer. That the victory may be altogether Your own.

Of the many remarkable points in the character of Christ our Savior, his constant glorifying of God the Father is not the least worthy of observation. It is delightful to contemplate how filial reverence pervades every word and action of his life. His renunciation of self, his apparent forgetfulness that he had a separate existence to think of or to set forth—his full, cordial, and never omitted reference to his Father, as the power by whom he spoke words of life, and wrought miracles of healing; as the Being for whom alone he lived; is the most perfect picture of son-ship that the world has ever seen, or that the human mind can possibly conceive. How plainly he tells the Jews, "I can of my own self do nothing" (John 5:30). When charged with having a demon, how meekly he replies, how like a son, "I do not have a demon; but I honor My Father" (John 8:49). So entirely does he lose sight of self, so fully does he seem to recognize his own identity only in that of the Father, that he spoke to his disciples as if they should also by this time be able to do the same, "If you had known Me, you would have known My Father also; and from now on you know Him and have seen Him" (John 14:7). How amazed, how almost indignant, is he at their contented ignorance, embodied in the answer of Philip, "Lord, show us the Father, and it is sufficient for us;" for he exclaims, "Have I been with you so long, and yet you have not known Me, Philip? He who has seen Me has seen the Father; so how can you say, 'Show us the Father'? "Do you not believe that I am in the Father, and the Father in Me? The words that I speak to you I do not speak on My own authority; but the Father who dwells in Me does the works" (John 14:9-11).

This living with, and for another, is the perfection of creature existence—that other being God. We find this principle fully exhibited in Scripture. The Father speaks and acts only through the Son and through the Spirit, that all men may honor both. Christ acted for the Father—the Father glorified the Son—the Spirit glorifies both. Christ takes of the things of the Father, and gives them unto us. The Spirit takes of the things of Christ, and shows them unto us. And both the Father and the Son determine that sins against the Holy Ghost shall never be forgiven. The several Persons in the Sacred Name also bestow their threefold glory on the church, and the work of the church on earth is to glorify all the Persons of the Holy Trinity. Adam, the first member of the church, was created perfect, to live in God, and for Him alone. The perfection of Enoch, and cause of his being taken up into heaven, was that, "he walked with God." Such, also, is the intended purpose, and ought to be the high and sole business, of *our* earthly life, as members with Adam and Enoch, and all the faithful, of his universal church. Then, too, what is the summing up of eternity? Is it not the church's admission to everlasting fellowship in glory, with the Father, the Son, and the Holy Ghost? All those who acted for one another in time, acting with, and living for one another, in eternity.

To live for self, however, is the characteristic of fallen man. But when at any time he sacrifices self to another, as a servant for a master, a patriot for his country, he presents to his own mind the perfection of what he calls glorious and heroic. To give up our own interests or comfort for the happiness or preservation of another, is the noblest and highest act of generosity with which fallen humanity is acquainted. The history of the world is not lacking in instances of this magnificent disinterestedness. So far as man is concerned, it is the highest mark of esteem and honor which he can pay to a fellow creature. This it was, which Christ, as a servant and a Son, rendered every moment of his life to God. And that which it is the loftiest ambition of mortals to obtain, was continually ascending to God the Father from Jesus Christ in the human form. No mere man ever presented it before or since. And therefore, amongst the multitude of human beings from the beginning to the end of time, Christ must have stood forth isolated and alone, a peculiar object of attraction, satisfaction, and delight, to the mind of God. The only tree bearing ripe fruit in this wide moral wilderness; the single oasis in the arid desert of our nature, was that which Christ's manhood presented to the all-searching Eye. Love to God was the secret spring that set in motion all the activities of Christ's affections. Glory to God in the highest was the powerful, all-pervading principle that actuated his words, and looks, and actions. To him to live was to honor God. In death to glorify him was his all. And now, then, the moment was come, in which the Father would return this glory to his Son. The hour of Christ's desertion by the Father, was the commencement of his uninterrupted and eternal glory, as the God-man, John 13:31. True, the astonishing miracles which he wrought yielded him glory and honor, but it was not uninterrupted. Men blasphemed, and devils, though tormented, never yielded the mastery. But here on the cross, Christ, as the captain of our salvation, gained the victory over the invisible world. The Father left him alone that the spirits of darkness might feel his almighty power. It was as though he had said, "My Son has always rendered to me that honor which was due also to himself. In exerting my power, he has never magnified his own. Now let all created intelligences learn, that even while hanging on the cross in weakness, the God-Man is my almighty Son, and their almighty Lord." The moment then was come. Now was the hour and power of darkness. With combined and furious onset the spirits of evil assaulted the spirit of the Redeemer. For three hours the conflict lasted. Christ, the "Mighty God," vanquished them all, they retreated from the field of conflict in everlasting despair. From that hour to this, they remember his all-powerful energy, his invincible holiness. They tremble at his very name, and throughout eternity shall suffer the punishment of his wrath. Yet at the very moment of his victory, the Savior seeks to glorify his Father. With a loud and powerful voice he calls upon his name. That name is most appropriate. "El" signifies strength, the mighty, or powerful one. And it is as if our Lord had said, "My strength, my strength, why have You forsaken me? Why are You so far from helping me? Why am I left to fight this battle alone, and to gain a trophy of victory which I would rather lay at Your feet?" Though, then, it is not the first and principal object of this desertion, yet it is by no means an unimportant part of it, when we conclude that the reason why the Father was so far from helping Christ was, that the victory might be altogether his own.

Third. The third inquiry in this verse is, "Why are You, so far from the words of my groaning?" To which we are taught to reply, "That you may learn obedience by the things which you suffer."

Such an answer no one would venture to make, were it not dictated in the volume of inspiration. It occurs in the epistle to the Hebrews, and refers to this very period in which Christ hung upon the cross. Death was the last lesson Christ was to learn. "He became obedient unto death, even the death of the cross" (Phil. 2:8). And it is with reference to this that the apostle says, "though He was a Son, yet He learned obedience by the things which He suffered. And having been perfected, He became the author of eternal salvation to all who obey Him" (Heb. 5:8, 9). We must not understand this passage to declare, either that Christ learned obedience, as if he were ignorant of it before, or that he learned to be obedient, as if he had not been so till after suffering had taught him. It is written simply, "He learned obedience," that is, he learned what obedience is, and what all that obedience was to which he had voluntarily bound himself. Had Christ been satisfied with crucifixion unto blood; had he considered sin to be expiated when that was shed, he would have remained ignorant of the crucifixion unto death. In such a case, he must necessarily have been deficient in the grand and essential point for which he came into the world; nor could the apostle have added, that he was "made perfect." The perfection, (that is, the legal and official, not the moral perfection) of Christ, consisted in his accomplishing all that was written of him, and fulfilling all the types by which he had been foreshadowed. Death was the great event to which all Scripture testified, and which all the sacrifices under the law typified. Christ, therefore, could not be said to be "made perfect," or to have "learned obedience," till after he had tasted it. These two almost synonymous expressions involve the same difficulty, and are explained by the same interpretation. But, as being God, he was not capable of dying till he became man; so, being man, he was not qualified as a mediator, till he had passed through death.

The history of Christ may be divided into four parts: his birth, life, sufferings, and death. When it is said, that until his birth he was not acquainted experimentally with the needs and feelings of human nature, we do not, and cannot imply any ignorance in his Godhead. When it is added, that a calm quiet life could not have qualified him to be a sympathizing friend to the afflicted; and that until he had borne our grief's, and carried our sorrows, he had not learned experimentally what our trials are, we do not imply that he was previously incapable of sympathy, defective in tenderness of feeling, or ignorant of what man requires. When we say that the sufferings of life, and agonies of crucifixion, were not sufficient to qualify him to be the author of eternal salvation, until they were consummated in death, we do not imply that there were any shortcomings in these sufferings, or any deficiency in these agonies. So, when Scripture says that he learned obedience by these sufferings, and was made perfect by that death, it is not implied, either that there was any ignorance of obedience, or any imperfection of nature, in our adorable Redeemer. All these form the four parts of one great whole; and as the latter was necessarily imperfect without the former—death without sufferings—sufferings without life—life without birth; so we say, the former were imperfect without the latter—birth without life—life without sufferings—and sufferings without death.

There is also a particular emphasis to be laid on the word obedience. The original teaches us to read it with an article prefixed. "He learned *the* obedience by the things which he suffered." That is, the appointed obedience, the necessary obedience, the obedience requisite to satisfy the whole law, the obedience necessary to compensate for man's disobedience; the obedience, namely, to do and to suffer whatever God the Father pleased, to which he had bound himself.

Christ upon the cross did therefore cry, or as the original strongly expresses it, "roar," as does the wild animal under a wound; but God did not regard his words, so that he might learn and experience to the very uttermost what that obedience was which his Father required, which the law demanded, and which he himself had promised to render. As it is said of the childhood of Jesus, that "he grew in wisdom and stature, and in favor with God and man" (Luke 2:52); so may we say of his whole life from birth to death, that he was daily learning, and becoming practically and experimentally acquainted with the needs and feelings of our human nature, the sufferings of the flesh, the temptations of men and devils, and the holy determinations of God's will in reference to that atonement for sin which he was now accomplishing. Therefore the apostle declares that "we do not have a High Priest who cannot sympathize with our weaknesses, but was in all points tempted as we are, yet without sin" (Heb. 4:15).

Another, and fourth reason, may be added in answer to these several interrogations, namely, "that you may become a perfect pattern of suffering of and of patience, to all the universe, and especially to the members of your church."

Christ's afflictions were altogether of a vicarious nature. He endured trials only in the room and for the benefit of others. On the theater of this earth our Lord exhibited a lesson and a spectacle to the spirits of light and darkness which they shall never forget. To all the followers of his cross, he has left a most perfect example of the most perfect patience and submission, which they ought always to imitate. It becomes them to do so. The bringing of many sons unto glory is not accomplished until the Captain of their salvation is made perfect through sufferings (Heb. 2:10). "Therefore, let the same mind be in you which was also in Christ Jesus." "For to this you were called, because Christ also suffered for us, leaving us an example, that you should follow His steps" (1 Peter 2:21).

Reader, we have now been considering the most solemn fact, without exception, which the history of our world records. Earnestly pray that you may be suitably affected by it. Often meditate on what your Savior must have suffered at that awful moment. It is not that he was pierced with nails; it is not that he was surrounded by enemies; it is not that he was dying a most ignominious death; it is not that he was deserted by his friends; but it is that he was forsaken by his Father, on which we wish you now to fix your attention. This is the one consideration that occupied all his dying thoughts. It is a truth which not only fills, but overwhelms the mind. That the Father should leave the Son; that the God of love should forsake him who cries, "My God, my God;" and that one, who is forsaken, should yet find it in his heart to address the Being that forsakes him with the language of assurance and adoption, is a twofold mystery. Yet it is a mystery which Scripture explains. God forsook the Son, because he was bearing the sins of the world, that he might gain a complete victory over the spirits of darkness, and that he might learn all the obedience, and become a perfect example by the things which he suffered. And the Son did not forsake the Father, because his faith was perfect, his holiness unsullied, and his love stronger than death.

Here, then, in Christ your Surety, is set before you, as in a double mirror, God's method of dealing with you, and your duty in relation to God. The reasons why God forsook the Son, are the reasons, one or more of them, for which you have been, or are now, suffering, or may after this endure, the hidings of God's face. The faith, the righteousness, and the love, which Christ exhibited in this trial, are the same which you are to exercise in yours, and to seek to possess in still greater and greater degrees.

Sin is the first cause of desertion. Either some known and unrepented iniquity, or some secret and unexamined evil, is the worm that destroys the fruit of spiritual enjoyment. God has no pleasure in exclusion. He desires that your peace should flow as a river. But first he must make the fountain pure. It is not God's heart, but yours, that hinders communion; therefore, examine diligently the state of your heart. Pray for the light of God's word and Spirit, to enable you to discern and detect its every flaw, and shortcoming, and sin. Remember that it is something *in* you, not merely *upon* you that prevents the drawing near of the Lord to your soul. This is the difference between you and Christ under desertion. The sin was *upon* him, not *in* him. It was imputed, neither infused nor inborn. But in you it is both native and implanted. Seek, therefore, to have it rooted out. The light of God's countenance cannot return to you, until sin is confessed and deplored. If there is known sin, any aggravation, any iniquity regarded in your heart, it is as impossible for light and darkness to mingle, as for God and your soul to have any peaceful communion. To preach comfort to you in such a state is most dangerous. To allow you to take any of the precious promises as a pillow for your unhumbled head, would be to lull you to a fatal sleep. We trust this is not the case with you,

Christian reader. We trust that you are anxious, with a great anxiety, to be wholly free from sin, to be outwardly and inwardly holy, to possess a pure and contrite heart, that beats with love to God, and with the desire to be restored to his lost image.

Consider, then, that though there be no sin to which man can point, no sin which you do not weep over and condemn, yet there may be some secret root of bitterness springing up within you. Sin is a deceitful thing. Its first sproutings we often mistake for those of flowers. The eye alone of the husbandman instantly detects the weed. While therefore, you pray, "Keep back Your servant from presumptuous sins," do not forget also this entreaty, "Cleanse me from secret faults" (Psa. 19:12, 13). It may be that the bud of evil is already formed in your heart; and all unsuspecting and self-satisfied, you may be for going on as you are, or rather as you imagine yourself to be, until at last it will burst forth, and cover you with confusion by its pestilential odor. Or it may be, that the tare of the wicked one has just been dropped in your heart. It lies so still and dormant, that you cannot believe that it obtains a place in your heart. Its first germ of life may be beginning to strike its feeble but insinuating roots. Shall God allow it to grow? Would you desire it to be spared until it become a tree and fell upon your own head? No, surely. And neither does the God who loves you. He will send blasts and storms; he will cause the heats of trial and distress to come; he will use the rod of affliction, and the pruning-knife of bereavement—"these things will he do unto you and not forsake you." He will wait for the result. If the growth of evil in you is checked, and good fruit begins to appear, well. If you are roused to inquire why he contends with you; if you are brought to self-examination, confession, and reformation, well. But if not, then what remains after every other affliction has been tried, but that he hide his face from you? "Ephraim is joined to his idols, let him alone" (Hos. 4:17). God is compelled to do so. Your eternal welfare is at stake, and rather than you should perish God will reluctantly, yet certainly, have recourse to this

his last and most painful punishment. Remember, you have yourself rendered this measure imperative. It is the last act to which your heavenly Father desires to have recourse (Deut. 31:17, 18; 32:20). You must be exercised by it for your soul's rescue and salvation. Christ was exercised by it for our sakes, and to prove that he was perfect. Every other trial had been laid on Jesus, and when his dying hour arrived, in order that neither Satan, nor our distrustful hearts, should be able to say that he was not tempted in all points like we are, even this was brought upon him.

The trial, though severe, is a mercy and a blessing to you, and on God's part it is an act of kindness. Rather than die, you would submit to the removal of one or more of the members of your body. Rather than perish, be willing to suffer any trial, if so be that you may thereby be kept from the slavery of sin, the lusts of the flesh, and the slumber of spiritual apathy.

As we do not know from what and how many unseen dangers the intervening providence of God has delivered us in our progress through life, so we cannot understand from how many sins and crimes the trials we have experienced may have kept us back. The light of eternity will make strange revelations, and show ail things plain. What we had deemed our greatest evils, shall then appear to have been our richest blessings; and what we now prize with avaricious fondness, we may then see would have proved our destruction, had it not been snatched away. Regard, then, the hiding of God's face as intended to bring you to serious and impartial self-examination; to make you watchful, prayerful, humble, and diligent; to teach you to hold fast your first love; to strengthen the good things that remain in your heart, and which, perhaps, may be ready to die (Rev. 2:4; 3:2); and to lead you to cut off and mortify the evil things that are ready to live; and to bring you with an innocent mind to your Father, and like a child say, "Teach me what I do not see; if I have done iniquity, I will do no more" (Job 34:32).

Let the desponding and deserted Christian remember, however, for his comfort, that there are two other reasons on account of which the Lord in wisdom and in love may now be hiding his face from him. Those already mentioned are for the detecting, punishing, and removing of evil. These to which we would now call your attention are for the strengthening, improving, and increasing of your graces; to make you conquerors over your spiritual enemy, and to teach you all obedience by the things which you suffer. Remember, there might not be any particular sin which brings this trial upon you. Therefore do not let your conscience be burdened, where, perhaps, there may be no just cause. The disciples in their ignorance inquired, "Rabbi, who sinned, this man or his parents, that he was born blind?" Jesus answered, "Neither this man nor his parents sinned, but that the works of God should be revealed in him" (John 9:2, 3). This may be your case, O Christian. You may now be walking in darkness, in order that God may be glorified in you. As members of Christ's church, we are to show to principalities and powers in the heavenly places the manifold wisdom of God (Eph. 3:10). We are to glorify God even in the fires. Angels are to learn in us what patience, resignation, and submission mean. Even the highest archangel who basks in the sunshine of eternal glory is to look down upon a poor despised Christian, and learn what it is to live by faith and not by sense; to hope against hope; to rejoice in tribulation; to follow hard after God even when he turns away; and to be actuated at one and the same moment by two wills, the one conscious of its own desire, yet checking itself by another, even the will of God, turning wherever it leads and crying, "Not my will, but Yours be done." *These are lessons which cannot be learned in heaven.* Angels are desiring to look down upon our earth to read them. And where but in the church of Christ can they be found? Where but in your heart, O Christian, and in your brethren that are in the "midst of this evil world?" The various crosses and losses of time are common, every day lessons. The most intensely interesting, the highest lesson, which these bright intelligences can obtain, is from a Christian under desertion. That lesson, as indeed every other, was perfectly taught by our great Master. Yet even our imperfect exhibitions of it, impart wisdom as well as astonishment, to these superior beings. They delight to see a Christian bearing with patience and resignation the loss of fortune, the removal of friends, the decays of strength, the other trials and sufferings of life. But when an angel beholds a Christian under the hidings of his Maker's countenance, his whole attention is riveted. He may indeed exclaim, "How will this creature act?" And he may well think within himself, "What would I do if that blessed countenance were turned away from me? What would I become? Would I not be driven to despair?" When then, this angel looks upon the deserted Christian, and beholds him mute and silent, not uttering one murmuring word; when next he perceives that tears begin to flow—sees him fall upon his bended knees in the seclusion of his closet, and hears him say, "Have mercy upon me, O God, according to your loving-kindness: according to the multitude of Your tender mercies, blot out my transgressions. Against You, You only, have I sinned. Do not cast me away from Your presence, and so take Your Holy Spirit from me. Restore to me the joy of Your salvation, and uphold me by Your generous Spirit" (Psa. 51). When he beholds this, he must exceedingly bless and praise the Lord, who has given such grace to men. And further, when he observes, that instead of becoming fretful or sullen, instead of running on in a reckless course, and becoming as forgetful of God, as God appears to have become of him, the Christian acknowledges the justice of God's treatment, often pleads and intercedes for reconciliation, and becomes more and more scrupulous in all his thoughts, and words, and works; leaves nothing undone by which he can serve and please God, and pants and desires with an increasing earnestness of heart after the light of his countenance; that angel, from the contemplation of this scene, will surely turn towards the throne of glory, prostrate himself in adoring admiration, and exclaim, "Great and marvelous are all Your works, Lord God Almighty; just and true are all Your ways, O King of saints."

But there is yet another high purpose to serve, The Christian under desertion must not only furnish a song of praise to the angels of light, but also a lesson of instruction and humiliation to the angels of darkness. These "adversaries" are always insinuating some foul and lying charge, both against the Lord and against his people. Therefore, in his matchless wisdom, Jehovah sometimes takes the "wise in their own craftiness" (Job 5:13), and permits them to carry out their insinuations to their own confusion. Witness the case of Job. The Lord delivered him into the enemy's hand, in order that the lie might be detected by all the "sons of God" in whose presence it was uttered. Trial and trouble, deprivation and loss, one upon another, were brought in rapid succession against that chosen servant. Satan desired to have him. But the great Advocate prayed for him, that his faith might not fail. And though all the means and instruments of Satanic malice were brought to bear upon that lonely man, yet he could not be driven to curse the Lord. The bitterest blast only caused his faith to burn brighter out of the ashes of his earthly hopes; and all the spiritual spectators of that mortal combat beheld Satan's scowl of dismay, and the gleam of triumph in Job's sunken eye when he exclaimed, "Though he slay me, yet will I trust him" (Job 13:15).

It may be so with you, O Christian! Take courage from the consideration. Be faithful unto death. Never give up your claim, through Christ, on a covenant God. To such as you the prophet speaks, "Who among you fears the LORD? Who obeys the voice of His Servant? Who walks in darkness and has no light? Let him trust in the name of the LORD and rely upon his God" (Isa. 50:10).

"The name of the LORD is a strong tower; the righteous run to it and are safe" (Prov. 18:10). Call upon that name; appropriate it to yourself; do so once and again; say, even more, cry like Jesus even in the deepest gloom, "My God, my God." Beware of distrust; beware of unbelief; it leads to despondency, and despondency to despair. Always look upwards. Think of your Master on the cross. He was, forsaken; he had no one to plead on his behalf; he felt the bitterness of desertion infinitely beyond what you experience, for he fully knew the blessedness of near and intimate union and communion with God. Stay yourself, then, on him, and through him, on God, as your Lord and your Father. Cry earnestly, "Restore to me Your generous Spirit." The Comforter will come. He alone can impart life, and light, and peace. And though he tarry, wait for him, wait in prayer, and still hang upon him in earnest longing expectation.

THE COMPLAINT

VERSE 2— *O My God, I cry in the daytime, but You do not hear; and in the night season, and am not silent.*

HAVING given utterance to his anguish with a loud voice—having called upon God in the first part of the verse which we have just considered, we suppose it highly probable that the remainder of that verse, and also of the whole Psalm, was inwardly prayed by our blessed Lord while hanging on the cross. That great cry attracted the attention of men, but now these inward breathings of supplication are intended for the ear of God.

What strong faith is here exhibited! Deserted and forsaken as Jesus was—left alone in the midst of his enemies—throbbing in every limb, with the most intense agony—and surrounded by an oppressive and appalling darkness, he could still cry, "My God, my God," and still uses, in this verse, the same term of relationship and assurance. It is as if he would say, "However much I may be tried, I will not forego my claim. I will acknowledge no other Lord. You have all right and all authority over me. You are my God, and whether it please You to regard or to disregard my cry, I will not believe that I no longer belong to You, or that I shall always be cast off. O my God, allow me to speak; I must unburden my breaking heart; I want no one but, You; I will complain to no one against You—to Yourself alone I will tell my grief's. 'I cry in the day-time, but You do not hear; and in the night season, and am not silent.'

How like the protest of a human child with an earthly parent! It proceeds on the ground of relationship—"I am yours; I cry day and night, yet am not heard. You are my God, yet nothing is done to silence me. In the daytime of my life, I cried, in this night season of my death I entreat. In the garden of Gethsemane I occupied the night with prayers; with continual petitions have I passed through this eventful morning. O my God, you have not yet heard me, therefore am I not yet silent; I cannot cease until you answer." Here Christ urges his case in a manner which none but filial hearts adopt. The child knows that the parent yearns over him. His persistence is strengthened by confidence in his love. He does not keep silence; he gives him no rest, because he confides in his power and willingness to grant the desired relief. This is natural; it is the argument of the heart—an appeal to the inward yearnings of our nature. It is also scriptural, and is thus stated, "If you then, being evil, know how to give good gifts to your children, how much more will your heavenly Father give the Holy Spirit to those who ask Him!" (Luke 11:13).

Our Lord seems to refer to Gethsemane, "I cry in the night season." Many a night had he spent with God in prayer, but never one like this. Here on the cross, he identifies the subject of his petition with that which he three times presented there in his agony. He complains to God that he is not yet silenced, and that what he there asked has not yet been granted. If this view is correct, it enables us to understand the cause of that great agony, and explains the bitterness of that mysterious cup. We know what the subject matter of his prayer is on the cross, and we now learn on what his holy human will was fixed in his threefold prayer. It was neither relief from fear of death, nor deliverance from the expected cross; it was not mitigation of pain—nor escape from his persecutors—nor safety from Satan's assaults, for which he prayed—all these were as nothing to him. To be under such oppressive sorrow because of any one or more, or all of these causes, was unworthy of the Captain of our salvation, completely unlike him who said, "I delight to do Your will, O my God." But here is a noble and worthy reason—here is a matter in every sense becoming the "will" of him who never felt, or thought, or spoke but in perfect harmony with the "will" of his Father. Here is a prayer in which even Christ may possess, as assuredly he did, *two wills,* and yet be free from sin. That prayer is, that he may enjoy the light of his Father's countenance. What language can be conceived to be more appropriate in the mouth of a son? What prayer more agreeable to the ear of the Father? This was the prayer which Jesus presented in the garden and on the cross. In the one he deprecated a trial to which he was looking toward; in the other he prays under its pressure when already come. We all know how dreadful the apprehension of evil is. It is magnified by distance. We have time to think of its worst aggravations, and all the others appear larger by being dimly discerned. When, too, the trial is of a strange and unexperienced nature; of a kind which we have never yet passed through; its strangeness invests it with exciting and mysteriously fascinating power over us, which engages the whole mind, and often overwhelms it. Such, in some measure we apprehend, was that sensation which made our blessed Savior "exceedingly sorrowful even unto death," when in the garden of Gethsemane. Such was that which, with the excruciating reality and intensity of its presence, made him forget even death itself when he was hanging on the cross. It is something, which before it came, Christ can liken to nothing but the last and greatest evil which humanity contemplates. No greater comparison, as to this world, can be employed. But when it is come, it proves, like death, to be enough of itself, and swallows up every other consideration. Therefore, throughout this psalm, and in all his words on the cross recorded in the Gospels, there is not the slightest allusion to, or the remotest suggestion of desire for, deliverance from death. Oh no: it was something infinitely beyond mortal death which our Immanuel dreaded, against which he persistently prayed, and for the obtaining of which he would never rest. Exclusion as our Surety, from a sense of his Father's presence was the last and most bitter affliction which Christ was called to endure; and it was the only trial which his holy filial heart must wish, and rightly wish, to be shortened—to be removed. To be passively contented in such a condition, is as sinful as it is fatal. It proves that we care not for Him from whom we are excluded;

that we are indifferent whether he is pleased or angry with us. To the Father who orders the infliction, such an exhibition must be even more wounding and hateful than the original offence. That parent can answer who has been tried by a willful and rebellious son. What cut deepest into your wounded heart? Was it not this, that when ordered to leave your house and see your face no more, he was still hardened, and seemed as well satisfied with banishment, as if he were abiding under a father's blessing? That revolting picture which a prodigal thus presents, is the very reverse of what Jesus exhibited. His heart burned with love to his Father; his whole soul was occupied with an intense desire to please him, to be with him, to be near him. Christ was, to the utmost point of perfection, what a son, what every son ought to be. His happiness lay where his duty lay, his desires and delights were all centered in obedience. He had no separate interests, no selfish considerations, no personal gratifications, to further and attend to. His will was entirely one with the will of his Father; and that single passage in his history which discloses the identity, by the working, of his own separate and personal will, divulges, not only its holiness by the object on which it was fixed, but also its full acquiescence and harmony therein with the Father's will.

The vast importance of this subject demands the fullest consideration. It opens a path to the removal of all, or most of, those difficulties which encompass the mysterious scene in the garden. It presents the Savior in an attitude which must have exceedingly endeared him to his Father, at the very moment when he was pleading for the removal of that cup, which the Father had determined should not be altogether withdrawn. What was that cup? It was the last, the most bitter which the law had sentenced him to drink. Its dreadful ingredient was exclusion from the Divine presence. It was not put into his hand till he had hung some considerable time on the cross. The sun hid itself in darkness while this cup was administered. If such a darkness and horror spread itself over the whole land at the solemn and awful period, no wonder that an exceeding and overwhelming sorrow came upon the soul of Jesus, when he contemplated it in the garden, on the night previous to its execution. As the last sentence of the law, there was every reason for him to suppose that he was to die under it. Justice seemed to require this. As the Surety of sinners, he must undergo their sentence. The humiliation of the cross, the pains of body, the assaults of devils, and the curse of the law, are to be continued till death ensue. Is the remaining part of the sentence—even exclusion from the Divine presence—to be similarly executed? No reason appears why it should not. Awful thought! Die under the hidings of my Father's face? O dreadful sentence. The more he thought of it when he retired into the shades of Gethsemane, the more horrifying it appeared. No wonder, then, that it is recorded, "He began to be troubled and deeply distressed" (Mark 14:33). He began to think of it with renewed attention, and consequently to feel it with greater acuteness. His sensations correspond with the nature of their cause. That cause is of a most strange and inexperienced kind, therefore he is "troubled." It is also dreadful, therefore "He began to be very sorrowful." It is awfully oppressive, therefore is he "deeply distressed." Must I be separated from my Father? Am I to die without the light of his presence? Is this the irrevocable sentence? I cannot bear the thought. "O My Father, if it is possible... Abba, Father, all things are possible for You. Take this cup away from Me; nevertheless, not what I will, but what You will," (compare Matt. 26:39, with Mark 14:36). The "troubling" of his spirit is exhibited in his actions. He rose from his knees—he went to the disciples—he returned a second time to pray. Again he rose—again he came to the disciples—a third time he returned to pray. The amazement increased, "He fell upon his face." His "sorrow" became "exceeding;" "being in an agony, he prayed more earnestly." The oppression had become so great—the mental pressure so "troubling," that "His sweat became like great drops of blood." But what is the subject of this last, this agonizing prayer? Is it not the same as the first? Does he not use the same words? Does he not deprecate the same cup? Yet he never names it. So sensitively does he recoil from it; so abhorrent is it to his nature, that he seems as if he cannot bear to mention it. Never till the darkness actually enveloped him on the cross, could its dreadful name be wrung forth in words; then he gave utterance to it. "My God, my God, why have You forsaken me?" is a cry which burst from the inmost heart of the Savior, and divulged the secret that oppressed it. What else was worthy to affect that sacred heart to such a degree? What else became the holy will of a Son, either while differing from, or acquiescing in, a Father's will? On what other subject could Christ have a will of his own, which should yet gain the warm approval of him before whom he stood? That Christ set his mind on an object, and prayed for it with threefold earnestness, yet never obtained it, is no pleasing thought to the Christian mind. That he desired that for which he ought not to have asked, is not for a moment to be believed. We conclude, then, that our Savior "in the night season" in Gethsemane, entreated that he might not die under the hiding of his Father's countenance; but if it were the Father's will that he should depart out of this world under it, his love and obedience were so great, that even in this he would submit; that God, acting towards Christ as a Judge, did not then answer his petition, but was so well pleased as a Father, with his earnest desire to be admitted to his presence, that he sent an angel to strengthen him: and that here on the cross, the Savior renews this supplication, and continues in this psalm to pray with the most determined persistence, until he succeeds, and is able to expire in light, and peace, and triumph.

Having now considered the subject of that prayer, let us consider the argument—it is based on OMNIPOTENCE. "Abba, Father, if it is possible; all things are possible with You." This is an ultimate point. The creature's adversity can never reach beyond the help of Omnipotence. But how shall we bring it to our aid? The answer is ready, "By trusting in it." Therefore, the Scripture declares, "all things are possible to him who believes" (Mark 9:23);

and again, "whatever things you ask when you pray, believe that you receive them, and you will have them" (Mark 11:24). It must be previously supposed that no creature will presume to ask any thing contrary to the holy character and revealed will of God. And then, when the object is such as the Scriptures warrant, there is not only clear ground for the strongest confidence, but also a consequent duty to exercise faith, and a sin in not believing. As then, the Savior desired re-admission to the light of God's countenance, the desire was holy, just, and good. His earnestness and persistence regarding it must consequently be the same. Whether, therefore, we behold him several times pleading for his own will, or as often again submitting to the Father's will, we perceive that he is equally holy, just, and good in both: and we do not know which to admire most highly, his perseverance in seeking this blessing, which he acknowledges it may not be the Father's will to give, or his filial submission to that will, even should it continue to deny his request! How did Christ, as a man, setting the example for his church, accomplish this? First, he knew that his petition was right in itself. Secondly, he knew that, being right, God certainly approved of it. Thirdly, he knew that however apparently impossible, nothing was or could be impossible with God. Fourthly, he knew that prayer is God's own appointed means for the bestowment of blessings. Fifthly, he therefore employs this means to make known his will to his Father, and uses the argument of his omnipotence, to show that there is no difficulty in the way, only that which lies in the Father's will. Sixthly, to that will, whatever it may be, he then submits. He holds it too sacred to be intruded on—he stops at this point—he rises from prayer rather than proceed further—he returns to pray a second time—uses however only the same means, presents the same argument, reaches the same point, and again pauses in submission—retires a second time, but soon returns; yet it is only to do as he had done before, and though with increased vehemence and energy, yet still he stops at the same point; and having laid his petition at the threshold of the presence chamber of the Divine will, leaves it there, and submissively retires.

Such is the manner in which Christ acts in prayer. He carries all desires, distresses, enemies, and impossibilities, even omnipotence itself, before him, and along with him, to the throne of grace. He yields to nothing that opposes his progress towards it. Even the might and power of God, which naturally terrify and keep the soul at a distance, faith interprets in its own favor, and presses forward with greater alacrity. To the Supreme Will alone does it submit. What it does not yield to Almighty Power, it concedes at once, with fullest resignation, to the Almighty Will. Never does it venture further. It does not seek to interfere with the Divine volition; it does not presume to inquire what reasons influence, what motives actuate. Concluding that all the determinations of the Most High are, and must be, in and of themselves, immutably and eternally right, it rests in calm submission with the disappointment of its fondest wishes, the blasting of its fairest hopes, and destruction of all its present happiness, believing that the Will which orders it is, and must be, right.

Such is the blessed position of our resigned submissive Savior in the garden of Gethsemane, and on the cross on Calvary. But yet, in his experience, there is another point, even deeper, and more blessed, than this. It is, that Christ rested upon the will of God, not only as to whatever it might be, but also, as knowing what it could *not* be, in reference to his petition. He knew that God's will was *not* that he should be excluded forever from the Divine presence. He therefore willingly submitted to endure the darkness of exclusion, so long as his Father pleased, even to die under it, if he had so determined; accounting the most protracted period as but a moment, compared with the eternity of union and communion in light and bliss, from which he knew it could not be the will of God to sentence him to everlasting banishment. This enables the heart to add to submission patience, and to patience satisfaction, and to satisfaction approbation. Christ did not only submit to the will of God; he approved of it as wise and good. To be for hours or days, in life or death, separated from the presence of his Father, he could and would patiently endure, if such were his holy will for the salvation of men; but he knew that his Father's heart was as much opposed as his own to eternal separation; therefore, with a satisfied and approving heart, he could rise from that prayer of blood, and, calm and strengthened in spirit, could deliver himself quietly into the hands of the traitor and his band, not yet knowing, by direct communication, what the Father's will was in reference to his petition, but well knowing what it was not.

Such appears to have been the state of mind in which the Savior left Gethsemane. The same holy calm of soul was exhibited in all his words and actions before his judges. On Mount Calvary, too, and on the way there, how beautifully does this self-possession characterize the Redeemer! Cheering his inconsolable followers, we hear him say, "do not weep for Me, but weep for yourselves and for your children" (Luke 23:28). When arrived at the place of execution, the first words he utters is a prayer for his murderers, "Father, forgive them, for they do not know what they do" (Luke 23:34). Hanging on the cross, his filial heart forgets its own woes to provide for a mother's comfort, "Woman, behold your son," and to a disciple, "Behold your mother" (John 19:26, 27). Unmoved to reply by all the taunts and insinuations that were heaped upon him, no sooner does he hear the voice of the pleading thief, than he administers consolation to his penitent heart, and says, "Today you will be with Me in Paradise" (Luke 23:43). But a long interval occurs before he speaks again—an awful interval it was of darkness and desertion. From midday till about three o'clock the gloom enveloped the land. For three hours Christ was speechless. During all this time he was drinking of that cup of desertion, against which he had prayed in the garden. Its bitterness was even greater than he had feared. So dreadful was this new sensation, that he could no longer be silent under it: and the next utterance which the evangelists record, is the doleful cry which this Psalm supplies, "My God, my God, why have You forsaken me?" This is the only expression of sorrow which our Savior uttered on the cross. The three remaining sentences are individually dictated by a sense of duty, a consciousness of victory, and a filial confidence in his Father's care over his departing spirit. How thankful, then, ought we to be that the same psalm which supplied an outlet to the Savior's anguish, affords us a clue to the state of his mind, gives us an insight into the progress of his thoughts from desertion to deliverance, and puts us in possession of his arguments in prayer, and of his grateful acclamations of praise!

This verse is a continuation of that cry. It carries on the petition, gives it fresh force, by presenting it in a new form, and urges the suit with greater liberty and boldness, by complaining that it is not yet regarded, "O my God, I cry in the day-time, but You do not hear, and in the night season, and am not, silent." In the margin it is thus translated, "and there is no silence to me." The original literally signifies, "There is nothing done to cause me to be silent." It thus expresses a twofold sentiment, that God had not granted his prayers, or done anything for his relief, and that he will not cease to pray till he has obtained an answer.

Remember this blessed example, this instructive lesson, Christian reader. Imitate the pattern which the psalmist here sets before you, and which your Savior has left for your guidance. Learn, like Jacob of old, to say, "I will not let You go, unless You bless me!" Whatever trials beset you, though walking in darkness and having no light, complain to God, but never of him. Pour out your whole heart before him, Jehovah is a refuge for you. He who petitioned for himself on the cross, is now interceding on your behalf at the throne. Do not faint. Bring forth your strong reasons. Do not be dismayed. He will not plead against you with his great power—no; but He will put strength in you (Job 23:6). It may be the night season of your experience. The gloom of midnight may surround you. Remember Christ under the darkness, and take courage. His sorrows were deeper than yours; he opened them all to his Father—he would take no denial. You do the same; confess fully, unreservedly; enumerate each failing and transgression; deplore your condition; beg for pardon, peace, and purity again; add tears to sighs and words to groans; fear nothing but silence, and you shall soon have no silence to fear.

Painful and most distressing, however, is the experience of apparently disregarded prayer. How often has God called on us, and we have turned a silent ear! This experience, therefore, enables us to sympathize with Him who says, "All day long I have stretched out My hands to a disobedient and contrary people" (Rom. 10:21); and with Him who wept over Jerusalem and said, "How often I wanted to gather your children together, as a hen gathers her chicks under her wings, but you were not willing" (Matt. 23:37). The deep purposes of our Father in heaven, by these sad experiences of his children, are to bring them by a way which they do not know, to be of one mind with himself. The more we are tried and exercised, the better are we prepared for a high seat in glory. Remember therefore, deserted Christian, that even though no cause is apparent to you, God has a high and heavenly design in you and for you, which nothing but your present experience can accomplish. Wait but for a few days, and the glass through which you now see darkly shall fall from your hands, and in the bright mirror of eternity you shall see all things plainly, and know even as you are known. You know the hand that afflicts, but you are ignorant of some of the reasons that direct that hand. Do not press to know them all; submit to the will of your Father, whatever it may be; but O do not live in ignorance of his will, so far as it is revealed. In Jesus such a declaration has been given of that will, as may suffice to cheer the most discouraged heart. The angels sang it at his birth, "GOOD WILL TOWARDS MEN." That one term is enough, "good will!" What more can we desire? The good will of our Creator towards us, is enough to put to flight all doubts and fears of heart, all suggestions and surmises of darkness. Thus, like our blessed

Savior, we can rest even on the unknown will of Jehovah, and believe that it is "good." But if through the power of temptation, we may not be able to gain stability for our tempest-tossed thoughts, on this general declaration, there is further revealed for our encouragement this positive assurance, "this is the will of God, your sanctification" (1 Thess. 4:3). Lean, then, on this truth, that even your present darkness and desertion of spirit, is accomplishing the gracious will and purpose of the Lord in the purifying of your nature. Is it not a strong support to patience and submission, to know that even the most painful of all trials is working out for you and in you, the most blessed of all ends? Do you feel the temptations of sin—are you harassed by the suggestions of Satan—have you no light to cheer, no comforting promise to support you—no answer to your many earnest prayers for deliverance? Stay your mind on this blessed truth, that God cannot, and does not will, that sin and defilement should pollute his creatures. It is not the will of God that any one should be unholy. Here, then, is an everlasting basis. It cannot fail. God is unchangeable. He never will choose, or appoint, or approve, anything connected with sin. Behold, then, on what an indestructible foundation you may build your hopes, when you sigh and cry for freedom from every plague of the heart. Your prayer is acceptable to the Lord God of Sabaoth (Jas. 5:4). He will assuredly answer it; but in his own time, and in his own way. That *time* you will one day acknowledge to have been right and seasonable—not a moment sooner, nor a moment later, than it ought to have been. That *way* you will recognize to have been the best and safest by which *you*, with your peculiar temperament, and in your particular circumstances of life, could have been conducted from sin to holiness, from earth to heaven.[3]

---

[3] Read, "I asked the Lord that I might grow."—By John Newton.

But should you, in a long-continued storm of spiritual trouble, require another anchor to prevent your being driven on the rocks of despair, the Scriptures graciously provide you with this declaration, "The Lord is not willing that any should perish" (2 Pet. 3:9). This enables the soul to outride the fiercest tempest. We do not know through what, and how many, trials we must be brought, in order to the accomplishment of that "will" which desires our "sanctification." At the thought of this we may be often cast down, but whatever trials result from the "sanctifying will," that other "will" which does NOT desire that we should "perish" affords us support and consolation; so that, though cast down, we know that we shall not be destroyed; though perplexed, we know that we need not fall into despair. Driven, then, from one position to another—falling deeper and deeper into doubts and despondences, and utter hopelessness, here is a point beyond which the Christian cannot fall—cannot be driven. Even on the very verge of despair, he might argue thus, "Scripture compels me to believe that God is not willing that any should perish; I must therefore conclude, that he is not willing that I should perish. Here I will take my stand. I will not give way to despair." No sooner does the Christian thus rest on this scriptural ground, than the light of hope begins to rekindle within his heart. It increases: it imparts warmth and life to his benumbed heart. Vital action is exhibited in cries, and prayers, and supplications. He draws nearer and nearer to God as a father and a friend. He trusts him more fully; he loves him more ardently; he serves him more diligently. The weight that crushed him is removed. He runs with alacrity in the path of obedience. Before long he enters where no more weight can fall, no more pressure be felt; but "the far more exceeding, even the eternal weight of glory," and the pressure of love and gratitude and adoration, forever and ever.

THE ACKNOWLEDGEMENT

VERSE 3—*But You* are *holy, enthroned in the praises of Israel.*

WHEN the Savior of the world hung upon the cross, the whole universe of intelligent beings appeared to be against him. The very elements seemed to have joined his enemies. The friendly light of day suddenly became like the darkness of night. Disciples, too, had fled and left him alone. Jews and Gentiles were assembled in one hostile band. Spirits of evil, headed by the prince of darkness, were marshaled against him. The angels of light did not come to his help. Sent forth, as they were, to be ministering spirits to others, they were not so then to him. The law of God sounded forth its voice against him, and enveloped Calvary with the terrors of Mount Sinai, by its awful declaration, "Cursed is every one that hangs on a tree." And, above all, his own God and Father had forsaken him. No light, no gracious communing's, no smile of love, came now from their customary source. This was the most severe trial of all. Were God but to cast one look of approbation upon him, its blessedness would nullify the curse of the law, and the desertion of friends; its sanction would give wing to angels, strike devils with dismay, and confound all his persecutors. But though that approbation filled the bosom of the Most High, every exhibition of it was restrained. No manifestation of love was granted. All was darkness; all was silence. Christ prayed, but there was no answer. Christ cried, but there was no reply. The Son earnestly entreated the Father, but was not regarded. Night and day he offered up his fervent petitions, but they brought no return, save their own cold echo, to his heart. What then does he now think of God? Does he still trust in the Hearer of prayer, even though he does not hear him? This is the momentous question. In this all the anxieties of devils are centered; on this hinges the salvation of men. To decide this great question, Christ is brought to this narrow crossroads. To demonstrate to the glory of God, and the confusion of the "father of lies," that a human soul can trust in the Lord even when he appears to frown, Christ placed himself in his present unparalleled position. Nay, to prove that a human soul can not only trust for future deliverance, but even justify God in regard to present inflictions, and acknowledge his righteousness in the most severe of trials, Christ here adds, "But You are holy, You who inhabit the praises of Israel;" or, as it is rendered in the Prayer-book version, "But thou continuest holy, O thou worship of Israel." Here is the triumph of faith. The Savior stood like a rock in the wide ocean of temptation. High as the billows rose, so did his faith, like the coral rock, grow greater and stronger, until it became an island of salvation to our shipwrecked souls. "You are holy." It is as if he had said, "It does not matter what I endure. Storms may howl upon me; men despise; devils tempt; circumstances overpower; and God himself forsake me; still God is holy, there is no unrighteousness in him."

The Savior painfully experienced on the cross that the dealings of Providence were altered towards him, but he never conceived that the paternal heart was changed. He felt that an awful burden lay upon him. He was conscious that the "thick cloud" of the world's transgressions had come between him and God, so that his prayer had not yet passed through (Lam. 3:44). His soul was overwhelmed with horror at the strange sensation of being unable to discern a Father's face, or feel his all-pervading presence. A mere man in such a situation would have murmured, would have ceased to pray to one who hid his face. But not so the "God of patience" (Rom. 15:5). He neither broke forth with repining's, nor sunk back into sullen silence. The contradictions of sinners, the insinuations of Satan, the piercings of the flesh, the anguish of desertion, extorted from the immaculate Redeemer, no other than this most blessed testimony regarding his Father, "But you are holy."

This is the highest testimony which human thought, or language, can render. "Holy" is an unrivalled, unexampled, term. No equivalent word can be substituted. It signifies not merely a righteousness which law has not condemned, and a purity which sin has never sullied; but a righteousness which law *cannot* condemn, and a purity which sin *cannot* defile. God is holy. This expresses the highest idea we can form of ABSOLUTE PERFECTION. It includes both a negative and positive sense. It denotes the absence of whatever is weak, selfish, sinful, and polluted; and the presence of essential purity, goodness, love, and every excellency. God is holy. "He CANNOT be tempted by evil; NEITHER does He Himself tempt anyone" (James 1:13). This sets before us a two-fold view of the Divine holiness. First, as it refers to God himself; and, Secondly, to ourselves. The nature of God is such that it is utterly impossible he can be tempted by Satan, or man, to form an uncharitable judgment, utter a rash sentence, or do an unkind or unjust act towards any of his creatures. Sin CANNOT present itself in any form so as to gain his approval or consent. He is immaculate in holiness. Like the pure light of heaven, he can no more be affected by the sins of the world, than can the sun by the vapors of our earth. Like the sun too, in its own light, GOD IS GLORIOUS IN HIS OWN HOLINESS (Exod. 15:11).

Secondly, in reference to us, it is said, "nor does He Himself tempt anyone." God CANNOT be tempted, NEITHER CAN he tempt. This latter assertion refers not to the power of God, as if he were incapable; but to his nature, whereby he is unwilling; and it is stated in this positive form in reference to all his outgoings towards man, HE DOES NOT TEMPT. The nature of God is such that he never did, never will, never can, do anything to induce man or angel to deviate in the slightest degree from moral rectitude. Neither storm nor sunshine, prosperity nor adversity, are sent by God on his creatures, to lead them into sin. He CANNOT do so, any more than the sun can send forth rays of darkness.

The Divine nature is holy. Holiness in God is essential and underived. It is not merely one of the attributes of the Godhead. It is the foundation and perfection of them all. Therefore, says an old divine, "Holiness is the beauty of all God's attributes; without which his wisdom would be craftiness, his justice cruelty, his sovereignty tyranny, his mercy foolish pity."

The holiness of God, therefore, is the perfection of his perfections, the excellency of his excellences, and the glory of all his attributes. God the Father is holy; God the Son is holy; God the Spirit is holy. The anthem therefore of eternity which angels sing is, "Holy, holy, holy, Lord God Almighty." They behold continual displays of the wisdom, power, justice, truth, and goodness of Jehovah; these attract their admiration and excite their praises. But when they look to him who, "sits on His holy throne" (Psa. 47:8), they are dazzled by the glistening brightness of ETERNAL PURITY; and instantly conscious how in his sight the heavens are not clean (Job 15:15), and themselves chargeable with folly (Job 4:18). The seraphim cover their faces and their feet, as they fly in adoration around it; and not venturing directly to address the High and Holy one that inhabits eternity, they cry one to another, "Holy, holy, holy, is the Lord of hosts" (Isa. 6:2, 3).

If such is the high and heavenly glory of the Godhead, ought it not also to be our distinguishing theme of praise on earth? The gods of the nations were proverbially patterns of impurity, yet they worshipped them. Herein consisted the glory of the Hebrew nation, that they alone venerated the pure and holy Jehovah. His name is The Worship of Israel. He inhabited the praises of the chosen people. The remembrance of his name was kept alive by their tabernacle and temple. He declared of them, "This is my rest; here will I dwell." He exhibited himself among them by a dark cloud and a shining glory; and he gave them his blessing from the mercy-seat. Their nation[4] is done away, but the Holy

---

[4] When this was written, Israel was not a nation in their land- *Ed.*

One is still worshipped by the Israel of God. That name is applied in Scripture to all who partake of Jacob's spirit, who prevail in prayer with God; "for they are not all Israel who are of Israel" (Rom. 9:6). Every true Israelite, then, everyone who through prayer has obtained this new name, is sure to offer up praises and thanksgivings. These are acceptable to the Most High, they ascend before him as clouds of incense. They encompass his throne. He dwells in the midst of them. The false gods possessed the praises of the heathen, and their polluted names occupied their songs. But the holy Jehovah exclusively possessed the prayers of the Hebrews. His name alone is celebrated in the hymns of the spiritual worshipper, the Israelite indeed. Wander wide over the earth, enter wherever two or three are gathered together in the name of Jesus, listen to the prayers and praises of those who worship Jehovah "in spirit and in truth," and none other but the name of the one living and true God shall be heard praised for his holiness, extolled alone as excellent. How admirably the praises of the church below accord with those of the church, and the angelic hosts, above! The highest note we raise on earth harmonizes with the three-fold chord which is struck in heaven. We sing in feeble, broken strains, "The Lord is righteous in all his ways, and holy in all his works" (Psa. 145:17). They fill eternity with their swelling symphony, "Holy, holy, holy, is the Lord of hosts" (Isa. 6:3).

Meditate frequently on the holiness of God. This will beget holy desires in your soul, which, by the Spirit of grace, will ripen into the fruits of righteousness, which are by Jesus Christ unto the praise and glory of God (Phil. 1:11). Remember that it is only by the help of the Lord the Spirit, that your mind can reach this transcendent theme. He is eminently called the Holy Spirit; not because he is more holy than the other persons in the sacred Trinity, but because he is known to us as the revealer, the communicator, and the preserver of holiness. It is a high and God-like desire to be holy. The most debased of men often wish to attain heaven, because they think they shall be happy. But to pant after an unsullied purity of nature, and to disregard the safety of our condition as nothing in comparison with restoration to holiness, is not a mortal man's suggestion, but an inspired thought which proceeds from the "Spirit of holiness." Heaven is not a mere place of safety; it is a paradise of purity. The happiness of heaven is based on the holiness of its inhabitants. God is holy, and his angels holy; the Redeemer is holy, and his people holy: there are none in heaven beside. That word which sinners refuse to hear on earth, "Be holy; for I am holy" (1 Pet. 1:16), is a word which gladdens heaven, and imparts fresh feelings of unity to the whole family of glory. Therefore seek after the attainment of holiness as the first point of earthly duty, the highest of heavenly privilege. The mind of the infinite God is occupied by this desire; therefore he sends mercies to gain our affections. He delivers us from the hands of our enemies, that we may serve him in holiness all the days of our life (Luke 1:74, 75). Therefore also he administers the rod of correction, that we may become "partakers of his holiness" (Heb. 12:10). Mark that scripture. Let it be engraved on the heart of every afflicted Christian. Here is unfolded the great secret which motivates the Most High in the severest of his afflictions. Fathers according to our flesh corrected us after their own pleasure. The infliction, perhaps, was more frequently proportioned to the amount of their own anger, than to the magnitude of the offence. The destruction of some trifle which they valued might draw down the severest correction; while, perhaps, some flagrant violation of the holy law of God was overlooked or feebly reproved. Of none, but the heavenly Parent, can it be said that his inflictions were invariably intended for our profit. In him there can be no caprice of feeling, no error in judgment, no mistake as to the object, the cause, or the motive of the correction. The *objects* of his fatherly chastisements are his own sons and daughters, whom he is preparing for glory. The *causes* are their omissions of duty, their short-comings in love, their willful transgressions, and their dullness in spiritual learning. The *motive* is their true and eternal benefit. The Scripture here calls it their *"profit."* What heart can sufficiently rejoice at eternal gain? What power of calculation can estimate its amount? This *"profit"* is that we might be "PARTAKERS OF HIS HOLINESS." Not the holiness of angels, but that of God himself. Afflictions, therefore, are designed to accomplish the same end with "the exceedingly great and precious promises." What St. Paul declares to be the object of the former, is identical with what St. Peter tells us is the intention of the latter, "that through these you may be partakers of the Divine nature" (2 Pet. 1:4).

Who will then complain? Who will not rejoice at the amazing disclosure of this God-like purpose? To what an elevation of sentiment does this exalt us! We can look with calm countenance on an ocean of trouble, and say to the fiercest waves, "You are servants for our good." More so, with the apostle St. Paul, even if the "outward man perish," we can call it a "light affliction," which "is working for us a far more exceeding and eternal weight of glory" (2 Cor. 4:17). Because of this too, we are enabled to see and estimate the suitableness of that, to carnal sense, unintelligible injunction of the apostle, "Count it all joy when you fall into various trials" (James 1:2). We feel that we are put in possession of a principle which shall subvert the workings of the powers of darkness, and "survive the crash of worlds." Therefore we cling to it in every storm. When every other support is gone, we cast ourselves upon the holiness of God; when racking pains, and alarming fears, render the spirit mute with anguish; so that we cannot, for the moment say, that God is love, or merciful, or gracious, still we can cry out between every pain, "But—you are holy."

Christian reader, does your Christianity possess a sanctifying power over your heart? Is it a service of "profit" to the soul? Are you advancing in holiness of heart and life? This is the one grand question. The minister and his flock must be holy. When Aaron entered the inner sanctuary, "HOLINESS TO THE

LORD" must be engraved in golden letters on the forefront of his turban (Exod. 28:36).

Are you consecrated by the laying on of hands to be a minister of the Gospel? See that your heart is wholly consecrated to the Lord. Preach to others, but see to it you yourself are not a castaway (1 Cor. 9:27). God has made you a keeper of the vineyards, but does conscience whisper, that the vineyard of your own heart, you have not kept? (Song. 1:6). Examine diligently; prove your own self. The Habit of teaching others, is most deceitful as to ourselves. We, who are called to minister, occupy a post of two-fold danger. O man of God, who are devout at the altar, and eloquent in the pulpit, what are you in your closet? Is it your earnest desire and prayer to be freed from every inward as well as outward sin? Are your petitions fervent to the Spirit of holiness to "cleanse the thoughts of your heart by his heavenly inspiration?" Is your ministry conducted with daily and special prayer for the Spirit's guidance in wisdom and knowledge, soundness of mind, and integrity of purpose? Is your prayer for the Spirit's blessing on your flock, your household, and yourself, by means of the preached word, the prayers of faith, and the sealing sacraments?

Or are you a hearer of the word? What *"profit"* do you gain? Are you accumulating spiritual wealth? The riches of heaven is the pure gold of holiness. Christ counsels you to buy from him gold refined in the fire, so that you may be rich (Rev. 3:18). Buy it without money (Isa. 55:1). Purchase it by prayer. Ask for it. Seek to be freed from sin. Set yourself against one iniquity after another. Put them all aside. Keep them in check. Do not be afraid to detect them. Learn to count them your enemies. Therefore hate them. Cut off open sins, and heart-sins. Do not allow one willful transgression; and search out all your shortcomings and omissions. Put off evils; put on also virtues. Begin to regard your spiritual needs as of greater importance than your temporal cravings. Hunger and thirst after RIGHTEOUSNESS. This is the food of which the world does not know. Is it the food after which your soul longs? Do you strive to be void of offence before God and man? Is it your study to keep your conscience alert, and tender, and clean? Is your spiritual sensibility increasing? Are you able to say with Job, "I have heard of You by the hearing of the ear, but now my eye sees You. Therefore I abhor myself, and repent in dust and ashes?" (Job 42:5, 6). Are you walking in the light, and consequently able to discern more clearly than before? When your thoughts wander, when desires rise, when love grows cold, are you instantly on the watch? Do you mourn to find it this way? Do you honestly confess it, or do you pass it over as a small thing? Is there a godly jealousy at work within you? Do you strive, with the Spirit working in you mightily, to bring *every* thought into obedience to Christ Jesus? (2 Cor. 10:5). Are you filled with a heavenly ambition to be restored to your original, but forfeited, likeness to the image of God? (Gen. 1:26, 27; Col. 3:10). This is a noble desire. The Spirit of God alone implanted it. Even forgiveness is not in itself to be compared to this. It is easy, it is natural, it is selfish, to long for safety, and wish for happiness, and deliverance from punishment. But to sigh for *holiness,* to pant after freedom, not merely from condemnation, but from the sin that causes it, is the true, the heavenly, the eternal principle of spiritual life. Therefore the Savior pronounces his benediction on all such, "Blessed are the pure in heart, for they shall see God" (Matt. 5:8).

When, then, O afflicted Christian, you are cast down and disquieted—when sin tempts you—when even the Scripture distresses you, which declares that "without holiness no one will see the Lord" (Heb. 12:14): still trust in God, for you will yet praise him for the help of his countenance (Psa. 42:11). Remember your Savior's benediction, to strengthen you. Remember the will of God for your sanctification, to encourage you. Remember the gift of the Holy Spirit the sanctifier, to help you, to work in you, to re-create you after the image of Jesus in righteousness and true holiness (Eph. 4:24). Remember the precious promises are given to make you a partaker of the Divine nature (2 Pet. 1:4). Remember that your most painful trials are sent for your profit, to make you a partaker of God's holiness (Heb. 12:10). Keep steadfastly therefore, in the highway of holiness (Isa. 35:8). It will conduct you to that land, where, in perfect light, you shall see what good reasons you had to triumph over every trial and difficulty, replying to them all, "But—God is holy."

THE CONTRAST

VERSES 4, 5, 6—*Our fathers trusted in You; they trusted, and You delivered them. They cried to You, and were delivered; they trusted in You, and were not ashamed. But I am a worm, and no man; a reproach of men, and despised by the people.*

THE history of a soul's struggle to maintain its conscious dependence upon God, is deeply interesting and instructive. When lively love and gratitude occupy the heart; when conscience does not condemn for any special sin; when faith takes hold of one or more of the exceedingly great and precious promises, such as, "I will never leave you, I will never forsake you;" then indeed our happiness abounds, our joy promises to be perpetual; God appears to be all love, all graciousness. But when these are gone; when a denunciation instead of a promise stands most vividly before the mind; when conscience sounds an alarm in all our faculties—when fears within, instead of love—fighting's without, instead of songs of gratitude—and when perplexity unnerves us on every side, then indeed we feel that our own strength is rottenness, and that the wisdom and righteousness of man are utterly insufficient to bring us into the haven of peace. Like a ship in the storm, the soul loses one support after another. The sails of love and gratitude are torn; the rudder of faith removed from its ship; the anchor of hope broken; and the compass of the word too much neglected. Despair begins to paralyze all exertion. But the Captain was once in as desperate a condition, and was rescued. Or perhaps some obscure individual on board asserts there was once a vessel saved from similar danger. Instantly the feeble crew gains strength, and that rallying word seems like life from the dead. "If others, why may not we be saved?" Just so is it with the soul. When we cannot strengthen ourselves on the promises by faith, we take refuge in

God's providence by sense. When memory fails to recall the deliverances and mercies which we have ourselves experienced, we next endeavor to meditate on those of others. This has afforded seasonable relief to many of God's people in hours of trial; therefore it is highly advantageous to be acquainted with the memoirs of tried and advanced Christians, especially with the narratives of Scripture Saints. See how the apostle James encourages to patience. He does not merely say, "Indeed we count them blessed who endure," but he adds, "You have heard of the perseverance of Job and seen the end intended by the Lord—that the Lord is very compassionate and merciful" (James 5:11). This, then, is a scriptural mode of encouragement. It is an argument of two-fold power. Our Lord here employs it for the double purpose of influencing his Father, and of encouraging himself.

This passage is a continuation of that filial acknowledgment by which he glorified God in the preceding verse. It is as though he would say, "I have declared for myself, you are holy. I further testify that though clouds and darkness be round about you now to my experience, yet our fathers trusted in you in their deepest trials, and found you holy too." He repeats the term in the 4th verse, "They trusted in you; they trusted." He reiterates the same idea in the 5th, "They cried to You; they trusted in You:" as if he would feed his faith on theirs, and increase his own trust by enlarging upon that which they exhibited. Or rather as if he would imply that he also "trusts," and "trusts" as they did; that he still cried, still trusted, and therefore why should there be such a difference between his experience and theirs? It is a powerful mode of pleading our own cause, when we put it into the same form with another that has obtained a successful outcome. Christ here expresses that success in an exquisitely appropriate manner. First, the direct and effectual agency of God himself is asserted, "You delivered them." Next, this fact is stated with double reference, "They were delivered" as to their persons; they were "not ashamed" as to their expectations. What a series of powerful arguments these verses contain. First, "Our fathers," therefore we their children should follow their example. Secondly, "trusted in you," therefore you are worthy to be trusted. Thirdly, "You (powerfully) delivered them;" therefore you can deliver me. Fourthly, "You (willingly) delivered them;" therefore you may be willing to deliver me. Fifthly, "They cried to you;" therefore I will cry and never cease. Sixthly, "They trusted, and were not ashamed;" I too will trust, and surely I shall not be ashamed.

Overcome, as it were, with a sense of God's great mercy to the fathers of old time—painfully conscious of that desertion, under the darkness of which he was hanging upon the cross, our Lord next utters this disparaging contrast, as if in justification of his Father's absence from him, "But I am a worm." This is an expression of feeling, of that strong feeling which must be expressed in strong terms. But assuredly, it was also right feeling. Christ spoke what he felt—he felt what was correct. God the Father, and God the Holy Ghost, with whom his spirit had always enjoyed full and conscious communion, were now absent. The spirit of Christ was thus left to feel its connection with the flesh. As the lonely prisoner becomes more sensitive to the gloom of his dungeon walls, when the friend whose visit cheered him has withdrawn; so the spirit of Christ, having no one now with whom to commune, had its attention powerfully called to its earthly dwelling. Though pressed beyond measure with its own sorrows, it could not be insensible to the sufferings of the companion flesh, quivering in its agony. Fully alive, then, to the weakness of his animal existence, closely pressed by its needs and pains, the Savior felt himself placed by it on a level with the basest of the creatures. "I am but flesh as they are. These pains tell me that I am of the earth—a piece of animated dust—an animal—a worm." Such appear to have been the Redeemer's feelings. He perceived that his flesh was as helpless as a worm—powerless and passive, that creature is crushed beneath the foot of man. Christ now felt his human nature to be void of all energy, or power of resistance, sinking under its own sufferings, and unable to aid his spirit in sustaining the heavy load. This expression therefore is not an exaggeration—not a mere burst of grief, such as we poor mortals use in our calamities. It was not a word weightier than his woe; it was a deliberate utterance; a melancholy but correct exclamation. Christ had become exquisitely conscious of the earthliness of his humanity; and we must carefully note that it is only of his flesh—of his inferior part—of his humanity, that he here speaks; and when he calls it "a worm," we are to understand that he felt it to be nothing but utter weakness.

So little accustomed, however, are we to regard our Divine Master as having really "MADE HIMSELF OF NO REPUTATION" (Phil. 2:7), that we are tempted to turn away from such representations, and deem them unbecoming. How little, consequently, can we appreciate the condescension of our Lord! How unable must we be to sympathize with him when he most requires it! If our Lord were really brought to such a depth of sorrow, and such an extremity of feeling, surely we should not withhold our sympathies from him. He may well exclaim in the words of the prophet, "Is it nothing to you, all you who pass by? Behold and see if there is any sorrow like my sorrow, which has been brought on me, which the LORD has inflicted in the day of His fierce anger" (Lam. 1:12). Should we, then, to gain a fuller insight into the depth of our Savior's sufferings, pursue this inquiry, it may be asked if our Lord could say with truth "I am a worm," how could he add, "and no man?" We answer, that the very same sorrow which suggested the one expression, dictated also the other. He really was to his own sensible and oppressed apprehension, but a piece of animated matter, a worm, and not what man is, or what man ought to be.

Let us consider these two points; they are of essential importance to a clear and full understanding of this momentous subject. We say Christ, to his own sensible apprehension, was not what man is, or what man ought to be. First, he was not what man is. Man is a piece of animated, matter—so was Christ; but man is a piece of sinful matter—not so Christ. His humanity was unstained and spotless; his flesh had the nature, but not the sinful nature of man. Christ, therefore, is not what man is. His humanity, consequently, is not improperly or inappropriately compared to and called, a Worm. Indeed, that despised creature's animal life has a resemblance and affinity to that of Christ, which ours does not possess. All the needs and feelings of its nature exist without the least admixture of sin. Its pain and suffering is simple feeling, unalloyed and unsullied. And though two human beings were now in the same bodily pain as our Lord, yet we would rather compare the agony and writhing's of a worm, than those of these crucified men, to the sufferings of our immaculate Redeemer. In fallen man, there cannot exist a pure, simple, uncompounded feeling. Contemporaneously with every movement of our flesh, there is aroused some unworthy, or sinful, desire or emotion. Self-complacency, pride, contempt, disdain, resistance, defiance, impatience, anger, revenge, are not unlikely, some one or more, to be engendered in the heart of every man, under either deserved, or unmerited, sufferings and reproach. But the bodily sensations of Christ never produced, and were never accompanied by, any such emotions. His words and feelings, under his numerous sufferings, had no more sin than have the writhing's of a tortured worm. He suffered simple unmitigated agony. It is no objection to reply that a worm cannot entertain these sentiments, by the very constitution of its nature; for this only brings to view another and more striking point of the comparison. It was just so with Christ. By the constitution of his nature, he could not entertain these sentiments; no such emotions served to counteract the intensity of his pains. Therefore, the resemblance is more perfect, and the Savior, conscious of its completeness, might well say, "I am a worm and no man"—not what man is.

Secondly, I am not what man ought to be. Man was created in the perfection of his nature, a being "very good," as he came from the hands of his Creator. It may be that he was not only beautiful in himself, but also bright with the reflection of his

Maker's glory. A shining radiance, such as remained on the face of Moses for days after his communion with Jehovah, might well be imagined to have glowed from the whole body of Adam, who lived and moved and had his being in God. If this were so, what a marked and instantaneous loss did our first parents sustain by their transgression! The conjecture serves to account for their immediate discovery of nakedness. But, be that as it may, this we certainly know, that man lost the balance of power amongst his members. The harmony between his spirit and his flesh was destroyed: he became subject to pain and weariness, to hunger and thirst, to toil and sweat, to sorrow, sickness, and death. When, therefore, Christ came into the human nature, he found himself not what man was, or what man ought to be. Born, however, as we are, in the fallen condition, we do not feel its detriments; we possess no means of comparison; we never knew anything better. But it was not so with our Lord and Master. He possessed a previous existence, and knew, not only in what excellent condition Adam was created, but also the glory of his own existence before the world was made. Christ was a real living metempsychosis.[5] The only one that our earth has ever seen. He brought the feelings of another state of being into this. He occupied humanity with recollections of Deity. Though this notion of the heathens, as they explain and understand it, is both false and foolish, yet it has a foundation in truth. Here is an instance of it in the person of Christ. And when Christ came into the human nature, he might well exclaim, "I am no man. I am not such as I made him; nor am I what man ought to be."

Endeavor, O Christian, to enter, as fully as possible, into your Savior's feelings when he dwelt in your flesh. We may illustrate them by this doctrine of the transmigration of souls. Suppose this

---

[5] A heathen doctrine of the transmigration of the soul after death from a human or animal to another human or animal body.

heathenish tenet[6] to be exemplified in the case of a renowned and mighty conqueror. Suppose his soul at death to have passed into the body of a worm. Imagine his lofty and ambitious spirit confined for a time to this miserable house of clay—wriggling his length along where his victorious troops had marched. Endeavor to conceive what must be the feelings of a human spirit in such a condition. With what force must he feel the change! How constantly would he be vexed and agonized with his sluggish flesh! With what emphasis would he exclaim, "I am a worm and no man, a reproach of men, and despised by the people." Life would be a perpetual burden, unrelieved, save when communing with his former self. Imagine, then, this only remaining source of consolation to be closed; all pleasing recollection of the past, and hope for the future, eclipsed; and his attention attracted by nothing but the sensations of his earthly member. What a distressing moment of existence! What a revolting consciousness of his present self must be oppressing him! We will pursue the analogy no further; it is one of the gross doctrines of debasing heathenism! How unlike, our pure exalting Christianity! Yet it illustrates this subject. What we have here supposed of debasement and humiliation in the experience of a human spirit, sunk not only to the level, but to the very identity, of a creeping thing is nothing compared to that of God himself descending into human nature. An insect bears some proportion to man, but man bears none to the Most High. The sensations of a human spirit, pent up in an earthworm, are altogether inadequate to represent the feelings of the Son of God when embodied in human flesh. Confessedly "Great is the mystery of godliness. God was manifest in the flesh." "For as the reasonable soul and flesh is one man, so God and man is one Christ." And that one Christ was now racked as with a double crucifixion—his body on the material, and his

---

[6] Metempsychosis. See previous footnote.

soul on the spiritual, cross. Satan was bruising him with assaults of temptation. Man was bruising him with despising's and reproach. It pleased the Lord to bruise him with desertion and the curse. The odious burden of sin was also bruising him. He himself abhorred the sins he was bearing away. Under this fourfold bruising, the agony of Christ's flesh was intense, and the anguish of his spirit overpowering. He felt his fleshly part sinking rapidly. Instead of aiding the spirit to endure, it was becoming a dead weight. Its sharp, shooting, pangs were like so many barbed arrows to his already wounded spirit. But for his union with the flesh, he could not have experienced these grief's. He had eternally dwelt in unalloyed, and uninterrupted bliss. His birth in flesh brought him into close and painful contact with another form of being. The Godhead was all peace, all glory; the manhood all grief, pain, and dishonor. No wonder then, that he complains against it, calls it a worm, and not what man ought to be.

The original is very expressive. It denotes a wine colored worm—the cochineal insect, from which the bright and beautiful dye is made. Thus it is a most appropriate emblem of the Redeemer. It exhibits him in a threefold respect. First, as covered with the crimson sins of the world. Secondly, as scarlet with his own blood. Thirdly, as yielding by his death, that blessed dye which removes all our stains, and presents us without spot in the presence of Jehovah. The Savior says, "I am as the crimson worm. I stand before God colored with imputed sin. He treats me accordingly. All the fathers trusted in the Lord, and were each delivered. Their expectations were not put to shame; but I am as the worm, more valuable in death than life."

This figure and illustration is not without example in other parts of Scripture. Job was reduced to such a state of suffering and depression that he exclaims, "I say to corruption, 'You are my father,' and to the worm, 'You are my mother and my sister'" (Job 17:14). Every individual of the human race is also represented as unclean before the great God and compared to the same despised creature

(Job 25:6). When God addresses the Jewish church with words of encouragement, he shows how fully he enters into her utter nothingness, and that he does not desire that she herself should forget it, by using this figure, "Fear not, you worm Jacob, You men of Israel! I will help you, says the LORD" (Isa. 41:14).

It may be, and not infrequently is, the experience of the Christian, to be brought into loneliness of spirit—enjoying no sensible communion with God—deprived also of the ordinances of Christianity and interaction with pious friends. Through sickness, or disease, the memory may be weakened, and meditation on the past may have become almost an empty void. Fears and doubts may have closed the eye of hope, and shut out all comfortable prospect of the future. We seem, at such times, to be conscious to little more than the fact that we are alive. We begin to learn the strange lesson that self is a burden. In proportion to that degree of love to holiness which the Christian may previously have attained, so will be his detestation of that burden. He will feel, not only his nothingness but his sinfulness. The one will impart a sensation of depression; the other of self-abhorrence. Should we hear him, while in this condition, giving utterance to his feelings, we might be tempted to imagine that he used terms by far too strong, exaggerated, and excessive. If we have made little progress in the school of Christian experience, our astonishment becomes proportionally greater, and we the more readily conclude, that he does not seriously mean all that he expresses. Not infrequently do we detect ourselves putting the same interpretation on the recorded sentiments of the Scripture worthies. In reading some of the strong expressions of feeling, which, for instance, David, Job, Jeremiah, and Paul, use, we are apt to receive them with considerable allowance; we imagine that they speak with morbid feelings, that they would not *use* such language at other times, and that they are not really such as they describe themselves to be. Not a little also of this feeling accompanies our perusal of the Gospels. We can hardly persuade ourselves that the Savior, being God, *felt* the various emotions of grief and joy, the sensations of hunger, weariness, and pain, the trials of spirit, or tortures of flesh, of which we read; or that if he felt them, they could not make much impression. We have an indistinct conviction, that though there were the outward appearances of all these, yet that there was always a holy calm within, and that *his* heart could not truly be agitated with anything like human sorrow.

This is an insidious and dangerous principle. To establish our own experience as the standard by which to judge that of others, is most destructive to the health of our own souls, as well as derogatory and slanderous of the work of grace in our fellow-creatures. We have no right to conclude that they overstate the case, merely because *we* have not felt the same. It is no objection, that they would not use that language at other times. They might not. But it does not, therefore, follow, that their lowest apprehension of themselves was incorrect or exaggerated. So far from this, truth compels us to assert that the strongest expressions of self-abhorrence and debasement which any fallen mortal has ever uttered, are far short of the reality. God's eye discerns and God's purity abhors, in our sin-tainted nature, far more than any mere man has ever yet discovered. The human intellect can neither scan the height of Godhead glory, nor fathom the depth of human emptiness and pollution. The God-man had both before his eye at one glance. In full contrast He beheld them. And if sin, when merely imputed, could bring his holy and unsullied human soul to such a depth of depression, and such an extremity of anguish, how much more would inherent sin bring each of us, were we only capable of regarding it with correct, that is, *sanctified* apprehension? But it is impossible. A full view of sin, as it appears before the perfect God, could not be endured by mortals. And those of our race who have most clearly discerned it in themselves, who have most bitterly bewailed their condition, and who have employed the strongest expressions of self-abhorrence, have only advanced a little beyond their fellows, but have never wholly learned the awful reality, and, consequently, cannot have over-stated it. None but a perfectly holy being can take a full and perfect view of sin. Those who once were pure, as the angels that sinned, know from what a height they have fallen, but it is impossible, with their evil nature, that they can form a just estimate of their present condition. Much less can we of ours.

Born in the flesh, we know nothing higher, until the Spirit of God implant heavenly desires. Then we begin to know, and feel, and hate, our native condition. And in proportion as the mental eye is fixed on the purity and holiness of heaven, brought near to us in Jesus Christ, so is our knowledge of our sinfulness, and our abhorrence of our pollution. If such are the feelings of a heart sanctified only in measure, what must have been the sensations and sentiments of the Holy One of God, when living amongst men! He came into the world purer than the breath of morning. He shone upon the earth as free from sin as the sun is free from darkness. But the brightness of his holiness only brought to light the universality and corruption of sin. He came from a region where the love of God beat high in every heart, and he now moved in one where love to self was the great ruling principle. Imagine a son living in a territory where his father has been dethroned, and from which he has been banished. He speaks on his behalf, and they will not hear; he tells them of his love, and they will not believe it. He invites them to join his cause, and at last gets only twelve men to attach themselves openly to his person. Imagine his ardent soul chained by a feeble body. With a love that never tires, and a devotion that never slumbers, he has limbs, that fail with weariness, and eyes that close in sleep. His willing spirit finds the flesh unequal to the task. It acts as a perpetual clog. So was it with our blessed Lord. He lived in a camp of rebels, where all were traitors to the Most High. His fervent spirit was ever ready to discharge his great commission. But his human body needed continual rest, refreshment, and attention. And now that it was suspended on the cross in torture, our Lord felt to the utmost the weakness and nothingness of the flesh (2 Cor. 13:4). Sinking under its own sufferings, it formed a striking contrast to the noble spirit, which the most protracted sorrows could not subdue. Therefore, he calls it a worm, a helpless thing, and speaks of himself as not possessing the endurance and energetic vigor of a man.

Let the depressed and sorrowing Christian learn from this how to draw consolation from true and scriptural distinctions. Our Lord marks what is peculiar to the flesh, but never condemns a sinless infirmity of the body. He accepts the homage of the heart, even when the outward posture seems to express the very contrary. Our Lord submitted to learn this by experience, that having been tried in all points as we are, he might be able to sympathize with us. See how in the garden, when shamefully left by his disciples to watch alone, he graciously supplied from his own knowledge the only consideration which could extenuate their conduct. "The spirit is willing, but the flesh is weak." Here is a distinction which the mourning Christian often overlooks. He condemns himself at times in matters which are referable only to physical causes. The state of his health, the tone of the nervous system, the influence of weather, are some of the agents which produce low and desponding thoughts. He charges himself with unbelief and distrust of God, and wishes to resemble others whom he sees calm and cheerful in their demeanor. He forgets that such happy frames of mind may be as entirely owing to the influence of health and good animal spirits, as his own depression is the consequence of the reverse. Therefore, let him learn to distinguish between his flesh and his spirit. While he ought no more to rest contented with a desponding mind, than with a diseased body, yet let him be persuaded that the good Physician understands the cause of his depression. Let him not then shrink back from prayer under a sense of unworthiness. Let him not say, *"When I am in this state I cannot pray."* You may, indeed, not be able to engage in prayer in the same manner as when in health; but remember, the Lord does not now desire you to do so, he only expects you to pray according to your condition. This, indeed, is one of the great fundamentals in prayer. Let every man present himself before the Great High Priest in spirit, as did the diseased of every name in the days of his flesh. They never thought of approaching him as they were not, but as they were. If, then, your prayer must be short, let it be special. Lay open your case as it really is. Confess all you feel, and all you fear. Again and again, do the same. Conceal nothing. The Lord loves an open-hearted worshipper. Deplore the state of your bodily health, and of your mental constitution. He can give you balm for both. Ask, and he will give you a blessing. Return quickly with thanksgiving, and you shall obtain another.

But the desponding Christian may sink still deeper into the waters of trouble. He may be heard to say, "I find so many hindrances without and within. I cannot gain the mastery over my spirit. When I strive to pray, evil is present with me. When I would do good to others, some unworthy thought or motive suggests itself to my mind. I am nothing but sin. I can neither pray, nor love, nor glorify God, as I ought." This is a deep and painful experience; but it is also right and good. The conclusion is quite correct. The individual in himself is nothing but sin. And it is an unspeakable mercy to be so led of God as to have made the discovery. The stirring of the pool does not create, but only manifests its corruption. What you now feel is only a bringing to light that which otherwise you would not have believed. It is no new thing. To God it was known long before. Even now the Holy One discerns in the dark depth of the heart, far more than the most desponding mind can detect. What then is the intention of the good Spirit in opening the eye upon the depravity within? It is to lead the Christian from self to Christ. We are long in the school of the Gospel before we learn our *utter nothingness*. Doctrinally, perhaps, we knew it at the very commencement. But there is a wide difference between theoretical and practical knowledge. It is easy to say, "I am a sinner, and can do nothing good of myself." Even while we so speak, there often lurks within us a secret expectation and desire to find somewhat good in our nature. We trust that after some years passed in a spiritual course, we may perceive such an increase of devout feeling as shall preclude wandering thoughts, unruly desires, coldness of affections, and forgetfulness of God. But we forget that the "old man" is so essentially evil that it cannot be made fruitful of good; that therefore Scripture speaks of it as "crucified;" and that we cannot get rid of it altogether while we live, and can only keep it in check—mortify it. We ought to remember that we are but as wasteland being brought into cultivation by the great Husbandman; and that it is alone by his unceasing care, and regular implanting of good seed, that we yield any increase. Leave the finest garden alone, it soon becomes a wilderness. Who would suppose that in its clean and fruitful beds, lie countless seeds of noxious weeds? The heart of man is like a garden. Should it boast, let the Gardener leave it for a time, that it may learn what it is in itself. This the all-wise God sees it often necessary to do. Then the Christian discovers that the seeds of innumerable evils are in his heart: and after many years of wholesome culture and extended usefulness, he is astonished and grieved to find that nothing but sin is its native produce. All goodness in man is implanted. His righteousness is a reflection of that of Christ. To be at all pure and bright, we must revolve round the great Sun. The moon derives her light from this superior star. In herself she is a dark ball. So is the Christian. He is fair through the beauty which Christ puts upon him; but still he is black in his own nature. When he first discovers this, he feels confounded and paralyzed. Yet he ought to have known and remembered that he was always so. He never should have expected to have found it otherwise. It is good that he should no longer be self-deceived. His eye must be opened to the reality of his natural state, that he may be taught to reckon it as "dead," and so may never expect from it the living fruits of holiness.

But how then shall he obtain peace of mind, if he is always to retain a consciousness of this sin-seeded heart? He must still further learn the art of drawing comfort and consolation from sound scriptural distinctions. Let him mark the difference between the "old" and "the new man" within him. Both live; but the one is under a continual process of mortification, the other of vivification. He must cherish the life of the latter, and hasten the dying of the former. This is the condition, the work, the warfare, of every Christian on this side of the grave. Unless therefore he is able to distinguish the "old man and his deeds," which is to be put off, from the "new man and his deeds," which is to be put on, he must often be reduced to a state of spiritual perplexity, and perhaps despair. But he does not need to be. Let him cease to expect anything good from his old nature, and so "PUT IT OFF," and his perplexity will be at an end. Christ is the source of all within him that is good. In himself he is only an engrafted stock. Let the orchard teach. No man expects the golden fruit from the stock, but from the graft. The growth of the latter we cherish and protect, all the shoots of the former we destroy. The whole tree, then, is a twofold thing, a perfect picture of the Christian. Here is both an old nature and a new. In the former there is nothing good, we therefore describe it, and all that proceeds from it, as radically bad. Though the tree is laden with fruit, yet if the stock could speak it would say, and say with truth, "In me resides nothing that is good." Just so is it with the Christian. He separates himself from himself. He employs the life of the new nature to strive against the movements of the old. Overcome, however, at times by its stubborn and obstinate attempts, he exclaims from the anguish of an inward conflict, that seems to be tearing him apart, "Oh wretched man that I am! Who will deliver me from this body of death?" (Rom. 7:24). Here, then, is the only fountain of his peace and comfort, that while thus wretched he can look away from himself to Christ, and thank God for such a Savior. This he does with the greater eagerness and determination, because he feels compelled to declare, "I know that in me (that is, in my flesh) nothing good dwells" (verse 18). Accordingly, he never expects to derive any peace, or strength, or comfort from it; he never willingly allows it to exert itself; he denies his consent to its suggestions; he frowns with disapprobation upon all its movements; he mourns over every successful dash it may make from its prison; he does not will that it should ever think or speak within him; and is so set against this restless foe that he repudiates its every doing and says, "It is no longer I who do it, but sin that dwells in me" (verses 17-20).

Here, then, is a remarkable and important distinction which the Christian learns to make; and while he makes it, he ought to be as conscious of the existence of the one nature, as of the other. Remember, it is, "IF I DO WHAT I WILL NOT TO DO." There must be two wills, the one working against the other. If not—if we consent to the "deeds" of the old man, we must refrain altogether from this language of the apostle. There must be a desire, and an endeavor, we do not say in what degree; but still there must be an honest, sincere, and continual endeavor against sin, and a cordial desire after conformity to the law of God; otherwise we shall awfully deceive our souls, and be guilty of turning the doctrines of truth into licenses of sin. In this same scripture, the apostle states that he possessed also "a delight in the law of God according to the inward man" (verse 22), and a will intent on doing good. If then, the lukewarm professor of Christianity comforts himself with a partial and perverted view of some of the verses of this remarkable chapter, overlooking these, he handles the word of God deceitfully, turns his grace into licentiousness, and ruins his own soul. The true Christian does not act after this manner. However weak and feeble may be the buddings of the new nature within him, he cherishes them with care. He determines, with the help of God, to struggle against every sin that shall be found lurking in his chest. He resolves, in the strength of the Most High, that he will never cease to fight against the law of sin which is in his members. And while he is persuaded that the strife must continue till death separate the combatants, he is also assured that sin shall not have the dominion. Instead therefore of giving up the warfare in despair, at every fresh appearance of the old nature, at every renewed struggle which it makes, he learns to be more active and vigorous, to rely more on the Strong for strength, and to keep a more watchful eye, that he may not lose the mastery, but retain every thought in subjection to the will of Christ.

THE REPROACH

VERSE 6—*A reproach of men, and despised by the people.*

THESE words form a part of the comparison which the Savior had instituted between himself and the fathers of old time. In the depth of his own affliction, he meditated on their faith, and on their deliverances. The success which attended their supplications proved that God was the gracious hearer and answerer of prayer. But the difference of his experience is painfully trying. He does not enjoy that communion with the Father of all to which they were admitted. He appears to be forgotten. His prayers and cries bring no relief. The longer his trial continues it increases in severity. No mitigation can be obtained from any quarter. Heaven is closed against him; and "I am," he remarks, "a reproach of men, and despised by the people."

Reproach is a peculiarly painful species of trial, and formed a large portion of our Savior's sorrow. It is a keen cutting weapon. Even consciousness of innocence cannot altogether prevent the hurting of its wound. Reproach is a many-barbed arrow. It implies reflection, censure, disappointment, and contempt, on the part of him who casts it; and supposes deception, hypocrisy, detection and disgrace, on the part of him who deserves it. Christ suffered all this; though perfectly innocent, he was treated as if utterly guilty. His tender spirit felt that treatment bitterly; his was no stoic's heart—a hard ball of selfishness. From the purity and perfection of his nature, our Lord must have had exquisite susceptibility and tenderness of feeling. See him at the grave of Lazarus. How full of sympathetic emotion! A philosopher of the world, would have thought only of the stupendous miracle he was about to accomplish. But not so our Lord: when he saw Mary weeping, and the Jews also weeping, he groaned in the spirit and was troubled. The shortest verse of Scripture is the most affecting,

"Jesus wept" (John 11:35). While enduring the daily trials of life, and the attendant afflictions of death, his knowledge of the glory that should follow, did not render him insensible to any of the sufferings that went before. Reproach formed a large part of these sufferings.

Many of our Lord's countrymen vainly expected that he would assume the power and glory of an earthly king. His miracles made them regard him as some great one, if not the Messiah. Now, therefore, the bitterness of their disappointment is proportionally increased. Instead of blaming themselves for entertaining hopes which he had never sanctioned, they condemned him for this inglorious termination of their own presumptuous speculations. Of all those who reproached our Lord, it is quite in agreement with our knowledge of human nature to conceive that none would be more forward in this species of persecution, than those who had once professed to be his disciples. Of these, there was a considerable number. The triumphant entrance into the holy city, but a few days before, would naturally tend to swell their ranks, and strengthen their expectations. The active part which many of the citizens took in that affair must have made them marked men to the chief priests and rulers. Conscious of this fact, they would now take care to make themselves conspicuous as his revilers. With cordial ill-will, with blasted hopes, with love turned to gall, would they assail him, on every possible opportunity. We can imagine them waiting until he would come forth from the Hall of Judgment, and then pouncing on their victim with envenomed tongues. As infuriated swarms pursue, and hover round, the object of their hatred, each eager to inflict a sting; so with bitter words and angry gestures, would these attend his progress to the cross. Impatient of his feeble steps, they would urge him forward, crowding, pushing, buffeting—some before, some behind, many on both sides, would pour their malicious insults upon his head. His grieved ear might recognize a voice which formerly craved his blessing; his meek eye might meet the countenance of a former friend turned into fury. A menacing hand which he had once healed, might now be held up against him; and on and on as he advanced, one fresh upbraider after another might step up to his side, and screech reproachfully in his face. But when all were collected together on Mount Calvary, when they beheld him raised on high between the two thieves, then, in one torrent of abuse, would they give vent to their reproaches, "You are the man that deceived us. You called yourself the Christ. Now we have found you out; your miracles were done in league with Beelzebub; your fair speeches and holy words were all hypocrisy; God has not allowed you to escape; you invited us to believe in you; you said you have come from heaven, and would take us there. Now you are where you should be, crucified with thieves, and more vile than they."

This shameful conduct was not confined to the low rabble; to coarse and vulgar men, accustomed to unrestrained language. The narrative of the Gospel informs us that the rulers and chief priests, forgetting the dignity of their position, joined with the mocking multitude, "But even the rulers with them sneered" (Luke 23:35). Here were men of polite and varied attainments, superior in rank and fortune, bearing office in the spiritual and civil government of the holy city—scribes, and Pharisees, and elders of the Sanhedrin, congregated at a public execution, and not only sanctioning the slanderous multitude, but themselves acting as tormentors to the dying. They despised the Nazarene, as they called him; they disdained his lowly background, and humble occupation as a carpenter; they repudiated him as the associate of poor and vulgar persons, even of publicans and harlots. They scouted him as an impostor of the vilest description; a profane and impious individual, who encouraged the people to break the Sabbath, and despise the holy law. Everything that was evil, detestable, and damnatory, in their eyes, seemed to meet in the person of this crucified criminal. They deemed him a traitor to his country, by seeking to make himself a king, refusing to pay tribute to Caesar, and so attempting to involve Judea in the horrors of a civil war. As a worker of miracles, they recognized him only as a dealer with evil spirits, a magician of a superior art of magical incantation, an agent of hell in league with Beelzebub. And lastly, they reviled him as a blasted being, whom Divine Providence would not allow to live, because of his atrocious blasphemies, in making himself equal with God.

Such was the light in which they regarded the crucified Jesus. Obstinately refusing to examine the credentials of his commission, they perverted every fact and argument that seemed favorable to his cause, willfully closing their eyes against the light of truth. And here we behold them giving utterance to all the contempt, hatred, and malice, with which their hearts were filled.

Bitter, indeed, was this ingredient of Christ's cup. In the sixty-ninth psalm, which bears a close resemblance to the twenty-second, *reproach* is the principal sorrow enumerated of our Lord's many sufferings (See verses 7, 12, 19, 20, 26). Five words in the 20th verse, express all that can be said as to the wickedness perpetrated, and its effects on the innocent victim. "REPROACH HAS BROKEN MY HEART." It was so broken, that he could not answer. He ENDURED the hostility of sinners against himself. It is a hard task to continue silent when we are wrongfully accused! To refrain for any length of time from response or objection, when reproached, is more than any mere man is able to accomplish. But our Lord was perfect in patience. He has recourse to God, to whom alone he unfolds his grief, and unburdens his breaking heart. Nor does he pray for the silencing of this reproach as regards himself, but earnestly decries its effect upon his disciples. Hear how he implores his Father's interposition on their behalf, "Let not those who wait for You, O Lord GOD of hosts, be ashamed because of me; let not those who seek You be confounded because of me, O God of Israel. Because for Your sake I have borne reproach; shame has covered my face" (Psa. 69:6, 7).

Christ was accustomed to reproach. It was his daily portion at home and abroad—in the village and in the city—with relatives and amongst strangers. When living in the quiet retirement of domestic life, his brethren, his near relatives said to him, "Depart from here and go into Judea, that Your disciples also may see the works that You are doing. For no one does anything in secret while he himself seeks to be known openly. If You do these things, show Yourself to the world" (John 7:3, 4). To their reproachful insinuations, Christ uttered not an angry word. When, at another time, he was sleeping, during a storm, in the rear part of the ship, his disciples awoke him with this reproach, "Teacher, do You not care that we are perishing?" (Mark 4:38). The great meekness of the Savior rendered him peculiarly liable to suffer from the rudeness, impatience, and insolence, of all who saw him.

This characteristic suffering of our blessed Master must be experienced, more or less, by all those "that desire to live godly in Christ Jesus" (2 Tim. 3:12). If we are faithful to our duty as Christians; if we follow our Lord's example, and "testify to the world that its works are evil" (John 7:7), we shall certainly be partakers of our Master's reproach. It has been so from the beginning. Moses esteemed the reproach of Christ greater riches than all the treasures of Egypt (Heb. 11:26). The apostle Paul declares of himself, "I take pleasure in reproaches for Christ's sake" (2 Cor. 12:10). Our Lord kindly forewarns us to expect, and most graciously encourages us to bear, this painful trial, saying, "Blessed are you when men hate you... and revile you, and cast out your name as evil, for the Son of Man's sake" (Luke 6:22). And Peter, as if remembering the words which the great Teacher had uttered, writes thus, "If you are reproached for the name of Christ, blessed are you, for the Spirit of glory and of God rests upon you. On their part He is blasphemed, but on your part He is glorified" (1 Peter 4:14). Surely then, when we consider the height of glory to which we shall be exalted, and this depth of sorrow, in which our gracious Surety was immersed on our account, we shall not shrink back from an open confession of our gratitude and obligation to him, and shall willingly conclude with the apostle, "Therefore let us go forth to Him, outside the camp, bearing His reproach" (Heb. 13:13).

Consider, O Christian, what the Savior's reproaches were. There is not an indignity that can be named, which was not made a matter of willful misrepresentation against the Lord of glory. Even the most innocent, and inconsiderable, things were made subjects of bitter and vilifying observation. "Is not this the carpenter's son?—How does this man know letters?—Can anything good come out of Nazareth?—You are a Samaritan!—This fellow casts out devils by the prince of the devils—This man is a sinner; he is a Sabbath-breaker; he deceives the people; he blasphemes, he is a friend of tax collectors and harlots; he is a glutton and a winebibber; he has a devil, and is insane."

Such were some of the reproaches that were heaped upon our meek and holy Lord while he lived, and doubtless none of them were forgotten or softened by his enemies when he was dying. Through the goodness of His providence, we are at present exempted from open persecution in our beloved land. There is no cross of nails and wood erected now for the Christian, but there is one of words and looks which is never taken down. It is the will of God that we should be "freed from sin," and be "made perfect" *through sufferings*. Were there no cross, there would be no crown. Our nature must be purged. We never know ourselves until we are tried, consequently, we cannot fight against our besetting sins until we are made acquainted with them. Self must be crucified; but instead of enduring the trial with reluctance, and with many efforts to escape, the Christian should go through it willingly, and esteem it an honor to become a partaker of his Master's sufferings. The apostle Paul strove as for a crown, to attain to the fellowship of Christ's sufferings (Phil. 3:10). He counted it his highest earthly honor; he regarded it as a pledge of eternal glory. Endeavoring constantly to avoid every appearance of evil, as did our Master, we shall yet find, like him, that our words and actions are subjected to the most unexpected misinterpretations. The world does not understand the principles on which the Christian acts, and must therefore interpret all he does according to those by which it is itself actuated. The

Christian, therefore, when tried by any stinging and bitter reproach, should consider it in a fourfold respect. First, *in regard to the reproach itself;* it is only words—sounds that vanish in the air as soon as they are uttered. Secondly, *in regard to those who vilify and misrepresent him;* that it may be from no personal malice, but the unavoidable result of the application of their own worldly principles; that therefore they are to be pitied, and even if evidently malicious, are to be prayed for and forgiven. Thirdly, *in regard to himself;* that it can do him no harm, but much good, if he bears it patiently. And lastly, *in regard to his God and Savior;* that it is a token of his love, a proof of his own discipleship, and a pledge of future honor and glory.

Let him consider also what infamy and dishonor the men of this world willingly endure for the sake of sinful pleasures, and mere temporary profit. Shall the servant of God then, be outdone in zeal by the servants of Satan? They do not care for the disgrace if only they attain their end. They calculate loss of character by the gain it brings, and the happiness by which it is counterbalanced. If they win, they smile, and do not care who despises them. When then, the Christian thus witnesses the power of an evil principle, shall he not be ambitious to exhibit the superior energy of those that are heavenly and eternal? He knows too that however much he may be reviled by others, no one has so much reason to despise him, as he has himself. Lying low, therefore, in his own estimation, and humbling himself in secret to the very depths, he should put it out of the power of the most slanderous enemy, either to sink him lower in his own opinion than he has already cast himself, or to accuse him of a single wrong done to a fellow-creature.

Therefore let the Christian in this trial, as in every other, earnestly pray for the supply of the Spirit of grace. Without His indwelling and sustaining power, we always fail—we cannot but fail. To be despised and reproached, will naturally, and immediately, excite sinful resistance, anger, and perhaps retaliation. But with the in-working aid of the Holy Spirit, the Christian will be enabled to exhibit patience, meekness, and gentleness; and to return kindness for their malice, love for their hatred, and prayers for their reproaches.

THE MOCKERY

VERSE 7—*All those who see Me ridicule Me; they shoot out the lip, they shake the head, saying...*

DURING the three hours in which our Lord hung on the cross, previous to the commencement of the darkness, he observed the conduct of the assembled multitude.

The behavior of the unfeeling crowds who press to witness an execution is nearly the same in all countries, and in all ages. In our own Christian land, there are not lacking disgraceful scenes of tumultuous acclamation, when a miserable fellow-creature is being launched into eternity. The hiss, the scorn, the laugh, the insults, mark not only their indignant feelings at his wickedness, but also their own destitution of that nobleness of pity, and solemnity of heart, which should characterize every rational being at such a moment. But man is a fallen, selfish being—"a strange commixture of good and evil." Prejudice and passion obliterate the stirrings of humanity, and convert us into fiends. What else is a mocker at calamity? God has no pleasure in the sorrows of his creatures. The malignity of Satan finds pleasant food in the most painful torments. But surely man joins in Satan's laugh, only when he has Satan's spirit.

How bitter is the laugh of scorn! How cruel is disdain and mockery! Jesus was here tried to the utmost. All that men could do in this way was done. The women joined the scornful men. The rich took part with the poor. The chief priests demeaned themselves to a level with the lowest of the crowd. Forgetting self-respect, and even decency of manners, everything was sacrificed to the gratification of reviling Christ. Except in the little band of true disciples, there was exhibited one universal mockery over this congregated mass of human beings. The smile of contempt, the jeer of ridicule, the loud laugh of derision, were all employed against the Lord. Instead of sympathizing in his sorrow, they were rejoicing and exulting over his distress. "All they that see me laugh me to scorn." Here there was no mistake. A dejected spirit is apt to imagine evils. But Jesus had experienced this treatment too frequently before to misunderstand it now. When he entered the chamber of death, and comforted Jairus, it is said of the people in the room that, "they laughed him to scorn" (Matt. 9:24). It was needful that the Redeemer should be tried in every possible way; that he should be "tempted in all points as we are." This was doubly necessary. First, that he should be proved to be "yet without sin;" and, Secondly, that he should thus be able from his own experience to sympathize fully in the sorrows of his people.

Ridicule is at all times bad—to all persons painful—and from any individual rude and disgraceful. We dishonor ourselves by employing it. At best it is a punitive weapon, never a healing medicine. If it banishes an offence from the behavior, it sinks one deeper into the heart. Of all retaliatory weapons, it seems most like that which an evil spirit would put into our hands. It defends self, and wounds an opponent, but never does real good to either. The satirist is dreaded, but not loved. We smile at his pictures of others, but we recoil from his company. Yet the smile is sinful, which attends a sinful deed. If we loved our neighbor, as we love ourselves, we would as deeply feel and certainly reprove, the ridicule that injures him, as we do that which is directed against ourselves. So would Jesus have felt. He never listened to a backbiter, or a satirist. The first attempt would have called forth his disapproval. Yet he here endured it in his own person without murmur or complaint. He heard all that the company of mockers could say against him. It is written of the persecuted saints, and may especially be affirmed of the Savior, "He had trial of cruel mockings." Nor were his revilers contented with scornful epithets. Their malevolence was too great to find vent only in words. Signs and gestures, movements and gestures, must increase its emphasis, and assist its utterance. The evangelists give us a full account of their shameful doings. Matthew says, "They that passed by blasphemed him, wagging their heads." Mark adds, "Likewise the chief priests also, mocking among themselves with the scribes, said, "He saved others; Himself He cannot save" (Mark 15:31). Luke informs us that "the soldiers also mocked Him, coming and offering Him sour wine" (Luke 23:36).

Mockery accompanied the Savior from the garden of Gethsemane until he expired on Calvary. Judas set the example with his insidious kiss. The men that apprehended him mocked him. The officers at the various courts mocked him. The chief priests, scribes, and Pharisees, mocked him. The high priest himself, Caiaphas, mocked him. The servants of his house, and others, surrounded the Savior, and mocked him. They struck him with their rods, and with the palms of their hands—they spit in his face—they plucked off the beard—they blindfolded him; then they buffeted him with their fists, and said, "Prophesy to us, Christ! Who is the one who struck You?" (Matt. 26:68). Herod and his men of war mocked him, and treating him as nothing—arraying him in a gorgeous robe, they sent him away as a laughing stock back to where he was brought from. Pilate regarded him as a weak, inoffensive creature, and jestingly asked him, "What is truth?" He then brought him forth, saying, "Behold the man"—and sent him to crucifixion with this mock title, "The King of the Jews." The Roman soldiers mocked him with a most perfect mockery. They acted it to the very life. They procured a crown—it was of thorns; royal garments—they were a cast-off purple vest, and a scarlet robe; a scepter—it was a reed. They paid him homage as a king—it was mock-kneeling, laughter, and derision; they lavished their honors upon him—their salutation was a scoff, "Hail! King of the Jews!" Their gifts were not gold, but blows—not frankincense, but spitting—not myrrh, but mockery. When he was led away to Golgotha, a mocking multitude followed him. His feeble frame, his tottering steps, his ghastly visage, were subjects of entertainment, ridicule, and biting sarcasm, to his enemies. Doubtless, his friends shared this humiliation. The weeping of the women would be mocked, their wailings derided, their gestures of grief pointed at with laughter.

All this too was perfectly gratuitous. The ceremonies of judgment had some show of necessity—the scourging, and the crucifixion, were ordered by the officers of justice. But to make delight and mockery over a fellow-creature's sufferings, was the most shameless piece of cruelty that has ever been heard of. It was altogether without the least pretense of reason. The gratification of their own cruel and malicious propensities—the indulgence of their hatred, and spiteful feelings—and their mad desire to render Christ as miserable as it was possible to make him, were their only stimulants. Therefore they hurry him forward to Calvary, so that they may set him up as their mark—a spectacle to the whole nation that abhors him (Isa. 49:7). There every species of mockery that can be thought of is employed. They wag the head, shoot out the lip, make wide the mouth, draw out the tongue, wink with the eye, point with the finger, utter the jest, break forth with laughter, and jeer at him with the bitterest scorn.

Imagine this dreadful scene. Behold this motley multitude of rich and poor, of Jews and Gentiles. Some stand in groups and gaze. Some recline at ease and stare. Others move about in restless gratification at the event. There is a look of satisfaction on every countenance. None are silent. The velocity of speech seems tardy. The theme is far too great for one member to utter. Every lip, and head, and finger, is now a tongue. The rough soldiers, too, are busied in their coarse way. The work of blood is over. Refreshment has become necessary. Their usual beverage of vinegar and water, is supplied to them. As they each are satisfied, they approach the cross, hold some forth to the Savior, and bid him drink as they withdraw it. They know he must be suffering an intense thirst, therefore they aggravate it with this mockery of refreshment. Cruel Romans! And you, O regicidal[7] Jews! Was not death enough? Must mockery and scorn be added? On this sad day Christ made you *one* indeed! Dreadful unity which constitutes you joint mockers and murderers of the Lord of glory!

Contemplating this scene with feelings of indignation, the Christian may be tempted to say, "Had I been there, I would not have joined this mocking multitude." Do not boast like that. Had you been there, you would, without God's grace, have taken part with that cruel crowd. Have you done nothing to offend your Master since last year? If your conscience would tell you, you have often grieved him, now that he is in heaven, let calm reflection convince you, that without restraining grace, you also would have mocked him in his sorrow upon the cross. All Jews and Gentiles are alike. Both classes equally need the Spirit of God. "As in water face reflects face, so a man's heart reveals the man" (Pr. 27:19). What others did, we would without sustaining grace, do also. Let us remember Peter, and be humble. The hour of trial proves how weak the very strongest are in themselves. Every Christian knows by experience, that he has not in every company, and on all occasions, acted and spoken as a valiant and faithful soldier of the cross. Remembering therefore, how difficult it is, and how impossible in yourself, to stand even for an hour, against the example of those around you; thank God, O Christian, that your sins were there that day, and not your person; lest, being ashamed to join a few weeping women, you would have been led away with the multitude to do evil, and been found with eye, and head, and finger, mocking the meek and suffering Savior of the world.

---

[7] The killing of a king, a person who kills a king or is responsible for his death. From Latin rex -king, and cide.

THE TAUNT

VERSE 8—*"He trusted in the LORD, let Him rescue Him;*
Let Him deliver Him, since He delights in Him!"

HERE are recorded some of the words, in which the scorn and mockery of our Lord's persecutors were embodied. How remarkable to find them in a psalm written so many hundred years before! We should be at a loss how to explain the fact, had not the apostle Peter informed us that "holy men of God spoke as they were moved by the Holy Spirit;" and "the Spirit of Christ who was in them was indicating when He testified beforehand the sufferings of Christ and the glories that would follow" (1 Pet. 1:11). The comparison, then, of this and of similar passages of the Old Testament with the accounts given in the New, affords abundant proofs that it is truly so, and enables us triumphantly to conclude, "Surely these books were written by none other than the finger of the living God."

How exactly is this prophecy from the mouth of David, fulfilled by those who crucified our Savior! Matthew informs us in the 27th chapter, verses 39-44, "And those who passed by blasphemed Him, wagging their heads and saying, "You who destroy the temple and build it in three days, save Yourself! If You are the Son of God, come down from the cross." Likewise the chief priests also, mocking with the scribes and elders, said, "He saved others; Himself He cannot save. If He is the King of Israel, let Him now come down from the cross, and we will believe Him. He trusted in God; let Him deliver Him now if He will have Him; for He said, 'I am the Son of God.'" Even the robbers who were crucified with Him reviled Him with the same thing."

The taunts here enumerated, are bitter and cruel in the extreme. It is a five-pointed dart with which our Lord is pierced. First, "You who destroy the temple and build it in three days, save Yourself!" Second, "If You are the Son of God, come down from the cross." Third, "He saved others; Himself He cannot save." Fourth, "If He is the King of Israel, let Him now come down from the cross, and we will believe Him." Fifth, "He trusted in God; let Him deliver Him now if He will have Him."

To human nature it is always a severe mortification, to be exposed to this species of trial. Grievous indeed is it to have our words distorted to falsehood, converted into jest, retorted against ourselves, and blazed abroad to our discredit. Christ was now enduring this fourfold contradiction. Those very words by which he sought to save their souls, were now repeated only to ruin his own cause. Those kind and healing miracles which he wrought for others, were now mentioned to show, by striking contrast, his own utter weakness. That confidence which he had always exhibited in the Divine love and providential care, were now alluded to only to prove that God would never acknowledge him. And that almighty power which he had exhibited, was now challenged to give one other proof of its existence, that all his enemies might be immediately convinced and converted.

This was a cruel dilemma to invent. Either Christ must now give them the proof required, or else that cause, which was dearer to him than life, must receive its apparent death-blow. The alternative, too, which they presented was of a tempting nature. The chief priests, the rulers, the whole assembled multitude, were ready to acknowledge him to be the Messiah. By descending from the cross, all those who had come up to worship at Jerusalem would be converted, they would carry the account to the remotest corners, and all the Jewish people would embrace the Christian faith. When, too, our Lord could so truly say to himself, "I am the Son of God; I am the king of Israel; I am beloved of my Father; I do possess power to leave this cross;" this must, humanly speaking, have seemed the right moment to prove it, and have formed a strong temptation to exert it. To convert so many souls by a single act, might seem to man a sufficient reason for its performance, and to imply that it would be wrong to withhold it. We say, this must have proved a strong and overpowering temptation to mere human nature. And had Christ been only a man, as the Socinians blasphemously assert, he would have yielded to its influence. It is impossible to conceive how a mere man could have resisted such an appeal for the accomplishment of that very object for which he was now suffering, and by which those sufferings would no longer be necessary. But Christ, being God, "had no need that anyone should testify of man" (John 2:25). He knew that even this great miracle could have no saving effect upon their minds. He had declared before to his disciples, "If they do not hear Moses and the prophets, neither will they be persuaded though one rise from the dead" (Luke 16:31). So hard and unimpressible by eternal things is the natural heart! But had even this great multitude been thus brought over to the new religion, how could that law be satisfied which demanded life for sin? Unless Christ had died, he could neither have overcome death, nor him that had the power of it (Heb. 2:14). That atonement also, which he came to accomplish, would have remained incomplete. No acceptance, consequently, with the Judge, could have been found for the Surety, nor any acquittal for the debtors; and we would have remained outcasts from Paradise— temporary tenants of a sin-bound world, but eternal occupants of that place, where light and bliss are forever absent. But, blessed be God, the faith and hope of the Christian does not hang, like those of the Socinian, on a fallible creature. He who was taunted on the mount of Calvary was GOD OUR SAVIOUR WHO ALONE IS WISE (Jude 25). He knew how inconclusive the reasoning's of his enemies were, how insidious their professions, and how utterly vain the greatest miracle to bring about their conversion.

Our great Redeemer instantly repelled the temptations presented to his mind in these five taunts, but did not put aside the pain and suffering which they occasioned. Doubtless, there was a vast variety of reproachful epithets and accusations used on this occasion which are not recorded in the Gospels. But these are sufficient, as specimens, to show with what wanton cruelty our Lord was treated; and we can easily conceive, that of all the various taunts, none entered deeper than the last, into his human soul. It stings to the heart to be taunted with the futility of our confidence in God. Indeed, the Holy Spirit seems to have marked *this* as the most painful of all our Lord's reproaches, by causing it to be specifically recorded in this prophetic psalm, "He trusted in the LORD, let Him rescue Him; let Him deliver Him, since He delights in Him!" Little remembering that these words were prophesied in reference to the Messiah, the malicious revilers on Mount Calvary employed them to torment their victim: "He trusted in God," they said, "let him deliver him, since He delights in Him." This taunt is intended to insinuate, first, that the crucified Jesus did not trust in God; secondly, that he had pretended to do so; thirdly, that if he trusted at all, it was of no avail; and fourthly, that God had quite cast him off, and would never acknowledge him. Such was the fiery dart with which men and devils assaulted our blessed Lord! To every true Christian, trust in God is as the apple of the eye. To Christ, it was his life, his all. To be tried here, therefore, was the most severe stroke of all. And we must remember, that while men were loudly bellowing this temptation in our Lord's ear, Satan and his legions were busily engaged in assaulting him with it, directly and immediately, upon his spirit. When Christ condescended to become a man, he made "trust in God" his refuge and strong tower. The Old Serpent knew this. By undermining the confidence of the first Adam in the Creator, he had procured his ruin, and obtained possession of the world. Now, therefore, he endeavored, the more earnestly, to weaken this stronghold in the heart of the second Adam, that he might retain his dominion, and add a new trophy to his crown. He must also have been aware that this was the last, the decisive, conflict. He was now fighting for victory or death; his all was staked on one blow. While, therefore, his human allies assaulted the Redeemer's body, he assailed his soul. The grand point of attack was incessantly attempted; and nothing was left undone in order to shake the stability of Christ's reliance upon God. The moment chosen for this combined effort was the most appropriate that had ever occurred in the history of Christ. It is important to mark this. Satan is a subtle foe, a skillful leader; he selects choice temptations, and suitable seasons. Christ was now forsaken by his Father; that blissful presence in which he had always lived was now withdrawn. This, then, is the moment to tempt him to think that it is useless to confide in Jehovah any longer. Instantly the spirits of evil press this temptation upon our Lord with inconceivable rapidity, variety, and power. The prince of this world came thus to Jesus, but found "NOTHING IN HIM" (John 14:30). Not a thought, nor a feeling, nor the slightest inclination or desire, could the spiritual adversary excite in him to suit his purpose. All was truth and loyalty to God. Even in that dark hour of his desertion, Christ did not swerve from allegiance of heart, nor did the slightest shade of doubt rise within his heart. Men might declare, and spirits of darkness insinuate, that God had forsaken him, and would never turn to him again, but the heart of the true Son repelled all their suggestions against his Father. He knew as well as they did, that God had forsaken him. Even more, he *felt* it—in his inmost soul he deplored it. But to that part of the temptation he could reply, "The Lord is righteous in all his ways, and holy in all his acts. I bow to his unerring wisdom. I know there must be good reasons for his withdrawal." But to the second part of the temptation, that God would never acknowledge him again, Christ would not give way to for a moment. The first was a matter of fact; this was a lie, and a libel on the character of the Most High. His word had declared that those who trusted in him would never be ashamed. Though every appearance, therefore, was against the promises of God, yet Christ rejected appearances, and clung to the promises.

Imitate this example of the great Master. In the severest conflicts, brace yourself upon the faithfulness of that God who performs all his promises. Never let go your confidence: "which has great reward" (Heb. 10:35). Whatever distress and darkness you experience for the present, whatever fiery darts are shot into your thoughts, by the adversary, still say, "Why are you cast down, O my soul? And why are you disquieted within me? Hope in God, for I shall yet praise Him for the help of His countenance" (Psa. 42:5).

When you witness others tried as to their trust in God, flee to their help. It is a painful and dangerous temptation. Had you beheld your Lord taunted, you would have repelled the insinuations. Do so now in the members of his body. "Strengthen the weak hands, and make firm the feeble knees. Say to those who are fearful-hearted, "Be strong, do not fear! ...He will come and save you" (Isa. 35:3, 4). Reject all taunting language, it is a whisper from beneath. "God gives... without reproach" (James 1:5).

THE APPEAL

VERSES 9, 10— *But You are He who took Me out of the womb; You made Me trust while on My mother's breasts. I was cast upon You from birth. From My mother's womb You have been My God.*

THE bitter severity of all the taunts with which his enemies assail him, has no other effect than to lead the Savior to make a direct appeal to his Father, to that very God who was hiding his face from him; and who was represented as refusing to acknowledge him. That appeal is set before us in these two verses. It is one of an unusual, and remarkable, nature. The argument on which it is founded is most forcible and conclusive. At the same time it is the most seasonable *and* appropriate that can be urged. We may thus paraphrase it, "I am now brought as a man to my last extremity. It is said that God disowns me; but it cannot be so. My first moment of existence he tenderly cared for. When I could not even ask for, or think of, his kindness, he bestowed it upon me. If, of his mere good pleasure, he brought me into life at first, he will surely not forsake me when I am departing out of it. In opposition, therefore, to all their taunts, I can and will appeal to himself. My enemies declare, O God, that you have cast me off— *but you are he who took me out of the womb*. They affirm that I do not, and need not, trust in you; but *you made me trust,* (or, *kept me in safety,* margin,) *while on my mother's breasts.* They insinuate that you will not acknowledge me as your Son; but *I was cast upon you from birth; from my mother's womb you have been my God."*

How closely pressed must our blessed Lord have been, that he should thus fetch his argument from afar. A mind intent upon its object brings forward strong and unexpected reasons. None but invincible and fundamental arguments will stand in such a crisis. Yet it is open to an immediate objection, and nothing but the solidity of truth can stand the shock of this ready reply—"Every human being may say the same. What has been done for you more than is daily accomplished for thousands of infants? Many of these experience even greater providential deliverances." To a mere man, and to weak faith, such a reply is staggering and confounding. The answer is obviously too just and reasonable not to silence and strike us silent. It requires a scripturally enlightened mind, and a strong confidence, first, in the motives, and secondly in the promises, of the generous Creator to stand against it. These motives and promises, too, must be known to be good and gracious, otherwise who can confide in them? Blessed Bible, which communicates to us the otherwise unknown mind and will of the Great Supreme! In your consoling pages the promise is written, "Listen to Me, O house of Jacob, and all the remnant of the house of Israel, who have been upheld by Me from birth, who have been carried from the womb: even to your old age, I am He, and even to gray hairs I will carry you! I have made, and I will bear; even I will carry, and will deliver you" (Isa. 46:3, 4). Jesus as a human scholar, had read that Scripture. His own Spirit had inspired it. He here shows how well he can remember, and apply, the argument which it furnishes.

What an all-sustaining declaration, "I HAVE MADE, AND I WILL BEAR." It founds a promise, on an indisputable, self-evident fact. "You are a living being. God made you such. If he were willing to make you, he will not be willing to forsake you." Such is the argument. It leads us from self to God. His motive in creating was his own glory. The good pleasure of his will brought us into existence. On what simple, but scriptural, and invincible premises, therefore, do we rest our supplications in that beautiful prayer, "O merciful God, that has made all men, and hates nothing that you have made, nor desires the death of a sinner, but rather that he should be converted and live, have mercy." How astonishing, and reviving, to find that our Lord employs the same argument with his heavenly Father. He goes back to the helplessness of infancy. He seems, as it were, to concede the point to his opponents. "I am," he admits, "hanging on this cross in all helplessness. I do not appear to have any power to deliver myself, or any interest with God to do so for me. But I once hung in as helpless a condition. When an infant on my mother's breast, when carried into Egypt, an unseen arm protected me; and as I did not see it, nor consciously felt it then, so will I believe it still upholds me, though I do not see it, nor feel it now."

The force, rather the benefit, of this argument, as of every other, lies in its use and application. The promises are made to faith; that is, given to be believed, and urged, and made use of. A promissory note gives neither food nor clothing while it lies in the desk only as a written document; but when it is regarded as good as gold, and is applied to use, its value instantly appears; its benefits are enjoyed. God's promises, and first acts, of care and kindness, should all in this way be turned to good account. He desires they should. It is because of our sin, our source of weakness and temptations, that we do not do so. See how it is used in Scripture to comfort and sustain the soul (Jer. 1:5; Gal. 1:15; Isa. 49:1; Psa. 71:6; Psa. 139:15).

What a blessed refuge to the creature, to be allowed to go back upon its Creator. How good for the soul to be driven from one experience to another; to be brought down to the babyhood of being, that, finding utter nothingness, it may be forced at last to cast itself entirely upon God! Fallen man naturally regards God only as the last resource, when he can do nothing better. As leaving him, was the first evil committed, so returning to him is the last thing attended to. "My people have committed two evils:" (first) "they have forsaken Me, the fountain of living waters," and (secondly) "hewn themselves cisterns—broken cisterns that can hold no water" (Jer. 2:13). The disappointed hewer, sighing over his broken cistern, thinks only of making another. That he ought to return to the full fountain, does not so readily occur to his mind, as that he must be more careful to construct another that will not so easily break. This figuratively, but truly, represents the conduct of all unregenerate men. When one child dies, they console themselves that others remain. When friends depart, they retain the hope that they shall acquire more. When one object of delight satisfies, they endeavor to invent another, and often fly the whole round of pleasure in pursuit of that contented satisfaction which shall have nothing further to desire. This they never find: yet onward they hurry, and never think of the well-spring of peace and joy. Nor will they. Until the Spirit of the Lord instructs them, and leads them to the Most High, none at all will regard him. Alas! Even in those who have been born again of that great Life Giver, how much more proneness is there to the way of nature, than to that of grace! If our trials increase, how much more ready are we to seek the consolations of our fellow Christians than of God himself! Whenever our prayers fail to yield us relief, we are more anxious to obtain the kind supplications of a friend, than the intercession of the appointed Advocate above! We wish to abound with comfort and peace, and more often seek them from our own pleasant plans, and past experiences, than from the undeceiving and infallible assurance of God's promise. When closely pressed with temptations to melancholy, when doubts and despondency prevail, how prone we are to grope in the dark chambers of our own hearts, searching for evidences, the existence, nature, and uses of which, nothing but the light of God's Spirit can enable us to discern. What an increase of evil arises! We become more confused, perplexed, and miserable. Therefore we make great mistakes, we put darkness for light, and light for darkness. We fall into a spiritual hypochondriasis [8], which leads us to regard everything as against us. We find a good evidence, and imagine it to be bad. We examine a symptom of our spiritual decay, and conceive it to be worse than it really is. We meet with one of an

---

[8] Excessive preoccupation, worry, or talk about ones health.

indifferent nature, and persuade ourselves that it is of the most unfavorable kind. Too often we go on, until we sink down into a settled fear, and dullness of spirit, darkness, and despair. How foolish, how sinful is this conduct! It grieves the Holy Spirit. It assumes that God refuses to give us light, or to impart comfort to our souls. It dishonors him. It seems to say, either "I need not," or, "I will not, go to God himself; since these fail me, all is lost." After continuing for weeks, or months, or even years, in this condition, we are at last brought to say, "I must, after all, trust the bare promise. It is only getting worse and worse with me. I will cast myself on God as I am, and if I perish, I perish." When the Spirit of God has enabled us to do that very thing, which a child ought to have done long before, which ought to be the first, the spontaneous, impulse of its heart, we find an all-sustaining help. God hears the appeal. He honors that confidence which honors him. He takes off the heavy burden. He relieves the sorrowful heart. He pours balm into the wounded spirit. And if the poor despondent soul had come to him at first, he would have found the fountain as full, as open, as living, as now. Learn then, O Christian, to make the Lord your confidence in the first place, not in the last. Begin, and continue, as well as end, all things in him. Always draw near to God as you are. Never wait in hopes to soon be something which you are not now. Delay is dangerous. Satan will take advantage of it. The longer the heart has to cool, the colder it becomes. As a piece of iron in the hand of the workman, so is the Christian in the hand of God. Instantly as it is removed from the fire, the chilling atmosphere around steals its heat insensibly away. It soon loses its glowing whiteness, becomes covered with darkish spots, and at last returns to its native blackness. From being susceptible of impression, and taking the shaping of every stroke, it becomes harder and harder, and the next blow will break it to pieces, or it must be thrust into the furnace again.

Oh do not compel your Maker to deal severely like this with you. He does not desire it. Instead of retreating into self, before the temptations of Satan, or of men, do as your Lord here sets you an example. Make a direct appeal to God himself. Though racked in feeling, as on a mental cross, hanging by spikes of perplexity, cast yourself on God at once as you are. This is what Jesus does in these verses. He does not give way to despondency or unbelief. The moment a temptation assails him, he carries it to God. Here he allows himself to be reduced, as it were, to the last extremity—to the lowest point of creature-weakness—and then places himself in the Almighty hand. As if man had proved the case against him, he leaves that great Friend to answer the charge who had sustained him till now. Even more so, he throws a necessity upon God, and makes it appear as though he were personally concerned, and bound to answer these taunting men. As if he said, "You brought me into this being, you will help me to sustain it."

This argument must prevail. It is founded on what God himself has done. It places him in the position of one who allows his work to be spoiled. It supposes that the same motive which induced him to commence, will lead him to complete. It is argumentum ad Deum; it is an argument which involves the Creator in a matter of duty and interest. It is heavenly logic. The Great Teacher invented it. Everyone must enter the school of Christ who desires to learn how to employ it. Turn to the sermon on the Mount: hear how he exhorts the disciples to take no anxious thought for the sustenance of their life, or for the covering of their body. What is the argument he employs? It is included in this simple question, "Is not life more than food and the body more than clothing?" (Matt. 6:25). Yet how much is contained in that one question! With what force does it urge us to trust all to God! He gave us the great, and will he withhold the small? He supplied life, and will he deny food? He provided the body, and will he begrudge giving it a covering? How adapted is such a mode of reasoning to our condition! What we see, and hear, and feel, to be realities in the world around us, are made the proofs and arguments of an invisible love and care.

We are thus taught to read God's thoughts in his works. Every fowl of the air, every lily of the field, is a witness for the Creator, to confound the distrustful heart of man. The very hair on our head, and the measure of our stature, are made to proclaim not only the futility of our anxiety, but also the minuteness and exactness of the care of God. Those witnesses, too, are daily testifying; these proofs are hourly at hand; they are even a part of ourselves. Our perishing flesh gives the lie to our doubts and fears. If all inanimate nature could speak, it would say, "Trust the all-wise Ruler." "But," responds the desponding Christian, "the immaculate Redeemer may well use such an argument; he may appeal from his birth, from his life, from every thing he pleases, and gain success in all. But my very birth ushered me into the pollution of my nature; I have forfeited my life; my body is corrupt through sin. How, then, can I build any argument upon them? The very birds and flowers, the animate and inanimate creation, are better in this respect than I am; they are free from that sin by which I am overwhelmed." Your words are true, O despairing one, but the reasoning proceeds on premises that are false. In speaking this way you forget two things; first, that Christ has taken your place, and speaks in your name; and, secondly, that you must put yourself on the merits of Christ's righteousness, and present every plea and prayer in his name. This is the Gospel exchange, of which, in the time of temptation, too many lose sight. To this, however, all must come for peace and strength; whether sooner or later, there is the same necessity. To trust in Christ's suretyship, and build all our arguments on his righteousness, is the only source of relief and comfort to the burdened heart. "Come to Me, all you who labor and are heavy laden, and I will give you rest." If the wearied soul comes instantly, it finds rest. If it labors on for many years, and imagines itself not yet weary enough, or heavy laden enough, to come to the Savior, or to be accepted of him, it must come to him at last, for no where else can it find rest. How much better, then, to come at once, and as the sinner is, than to carry so long the heavy burden on his own shoulders. This is a "voluntary humility" which is displeasing to God. How much more like an obedient child, to comply the instant we are ordered to, than to delay long before we submit! Under the appearance of being too afraid of self, it exhibits a degree of ignorance and self-will, which is most dangerous and sinful. Let us learn to receive the kingdom of heaven like a little child. As an infant receives that once doubtful inheritance, which its surety has secured for it, and lives and grows up, in the enjoyment of all its privileges, without ever attempting to cancel the guardian's deed, so must we. Without asking our consent or advice, a Trustee was appointed by our heavenly Father to manage our concerns; he occupied his whole time, and spent his life, to set them right; he conducted them to a successful outcome, and calls on us to enter into the enjoyment of them. Receive the kingdom of God at the hand of your spiritual Surety, as a child receives an earthly estate at the hands of a temporal trustee; do not cancel his act; do not frustrate his work; do not grieve his Spirit. It is true you are a sinner, but your Surety's blood has removed all guilt from between you and your heavenly Father. It is true you have no right to any thing in yourself, but Christ gives over his right to you. It is true you can lay no claim to anything, but Christ prefers one for you. Your life was forfeited, but Christ has paid the penalty; and your present existence is a loan for which you are indebted to the death of Christ. Your body is indeed corrupted, but there is a time coming, when, if you believe in him, Christ will "change your lowly body and conform it to his own glorious body." Pray, then, to the Spirit of Light to enable you to perceive the meaning, and to feel the power, of this Gospel exchange. It is one, remember, which has been already made on Christ's part; he never consulted you before he took your nature, and died in your stead. But on your part, also, this exchange must be made, as well as on that of Christ. As he took your nature voluntarily, so must you accept his suretyship; you must renounce all your own grounds of confidence, and place your whole trust on the merit of what he has done and suffered.

But the discouraged soul may add, "I cannot, like Christ, say 'MY GOD;' he had a right to use this language. I have none!" We answer, True, you have no right in yourself, and what is more, you never can have. A sinful creature can have no inherent right to call God by this endearing and connecting name. And if we must not trust in God until we possess this right, then are we undone. No human being, consequently, dare address the Most High by any other titles than those of Creator and Judge. Yet even here, you possess a right, and are bound to say, my Creator and my Judge. God stands connected with you in these indissoluble relations. He is your Creator, and if you do not trust in him as such, he will be your Judge to condemn you. But consciousness of sin makes us afraid of God. We know that as our Creator, we have violated his laws, and therefore the consideration of this relation to him, with remembrance of our sin, must tend to widen the moral distance which already exists. But, blessed be the Father of all mercies, our bankrupt name is exchanged for that of Christ; our ruined cause is undertaken by a Surety; our forfeited estate is brought back for us by a heavenly Redeemer. A Trustee is provided to take our name and nature, our debts and penalties, and to give over all his rights and privileges to us. In Christ we can call the Almighty Creator and Judge OUR GOD and OUR FATHER. In Christ it is our duty to regard God as *ours*. We sin against Christ when we address the Most High in any other manner. We virtually deny our obligation to obey the commandments, when we do not call God *our God*. The beginning, and basis, of both tables of the law is, "I am the Lord your God." What a blessed necessity is then laid upon us to regard the Great Creator as our God!

What an acceptable knowledge is this which makes us acquainted with ONE whom we can call our own!

Personality of interest in any matter, gives it sure influence over our selfish hearts. We are captivated with the generosity of him, who makes it our first duty to APPROPRIATE his blessings. This one act may be called the beginning, continuance, and end, of a Christian's work. "Christ Jesus... became for us wisdom from God—and righteousness and sanctification and redemption" (1 Cor. 1:30), and our whole duty in regard to him as such, is that of *appropriation*. "Put on the Lord Jesus Christ" (Rom. 13:14; Eph. 4:24), is the injunction of the inspired volume. "Put on," that is, take him as given; use him as made over to you; be wise in his *wisdom;* accepted before God in his *righteousness;* inwardly pure and holy by his *sanctification;* and finally and eternally delivered from all sin and corruption, from Satan, death, and hell, by his *redemption*. This is the glorious privilege to which we are invited; this is the first, last, and constant duty, which the Scriptures direct us to. We are all welcome in this way to apply Christ's fullness to our own use. This work of appropriation is an everlasting employment. Until we are able to know the fullness of the freely-gifted Savior, "which passes knowledge," we are not at liberty to cease. Let the Christian, then, enter on this duty with a brisk and cheerful readiness. Let him be as willing, as he is welcome, to be always putting on the new man, which, after God, is created in righteousness and true holiness; and daily appropriating something more out of THE ALL-FULNESS. This was what the apostle did continually. He laid hold more and more of the things of Christ, and made them his own. At last he was able to say, "all things are mine." So let every Christian appropriate what Christ freely gives. May the Holy Spirit enable you to do so more and more, until you are able, even when looking back on the feebleness of infancy, or when feeling your nothingness of nature, and vileness through sin, to cast yourself on the care of an Almighty Creator, and say, through Christ, "You are my Father and my God."

THE ENTREATY

VERSE 11—*Be not far from Me, for trouble is near;*
for there is none to help.

PERSEVERING urgency of supplication, proves the existence alike, of severe distress and powerful faith. This entreaty gives evidence to both in the heart of our Lord. Having made a strong appeal to God, he seconds it with this earnest entreaty. There is remarkable force and propriety in its expressions. Every syllable speaks. "Be not far, for trouble is near." What a contrast! What an argument! But look at what is added, "for there is none to help." What a conclusive statement! What an irresistible appeal!

Here is the extremity of sorrow in which Jesus was placed. Trouble was near indeed. It was in his body, and in his soul. Yet mark what perseverance in prayer. Observe how he never deviates from the one petition. That presence of God which was first sought, he still seeks, and will never rest until he finds it. Earnest desire after God occupies Christ's whole soul. No suffering of body, no temptation of spirit, ever diverts him from it. His mind is absorbed. His desires are all centered in Him whose "presence is salvation" (Psa. 43:5, margin). The power of concentration of mind must have been fully possessed by our blessed Lord. As a man, we must regard him to have been of powerful intellect, lively imagination, exalted sentiments, and exquisite feelings. This perfect endowment of faculties, necessarily rendered him susceptible of impression, to a degree altogether inconceivable by men of a sinful mold. The conceptions of his mind were clear as light; the pictures of his imagination alive with the realities of both worlds; his sentiments pure as the atmosphere of heaven; his feelings tender as tenderness itself. With such a constitutional temperament, "with an unfathomable susceptibility of anguish," how continually, how sorely must he have suffered in this rough world! He was the "garden of renown" (Ezek. 34:29); the sensitive plant of humanity, recoiling from every touch, and shuddering at every approach of sin, that surrounded him on all sides. With such an intellect, too, whatever object caught his attention, must have obtained a full, undivided, and perfect application of thought. There were no opposite principles at work in his mind. No hesitation of judgment; no debate of choice; no balancing of interests; no calculating of consequences. Perception was immediate; decision instantaneous. His holiness of nature must have rendered every exercise of his mind on earthly things, a source of pain and grief. It is said of Lot that "his righteous soul," was, "tormented from day to day by seeing and hearing their lawless deeds" (2 Pet. 2:8). Had this nephew of Abraham not possessed that "righteous soul," these deeds would have proved rather a gratification. It was his righteousness alone that caused him to suffer in seeing and hearing the Sodomites. If this can be said of a stained sinner, how much more of the spotless Savior? His essentially righteous soul must have been daily grieved with sin that met him at every turn. Christ could not feel indifferent to any thing. Multitudes pass unscathed through life, fully armored in their indifference. Apathy is a coat of mail which nothing penetrates. But Christ never put it on. His only breastplate was righteousness. The sword of justice could not penetrate it, but the transgressions of men pierced it every hour.

When, then, Christ here says, "trouble is near," we must consider that throughout his entire humanity, he felt first the trouble, and secondly its nearness. His intellect perfectly apprehended its nature. His imagination, was alive to its horrors. His sentiments were shocked by its vileness. His feelings lacerated by its nearness. Nor did any thing withdraw his attention. He might look over both worlds, and find no one that could, and would, sympathize with him in his trouble. He was alone in the universe of being. There was a God in heaven, there were men on earth, but there was a God-man nowhere. Christ felt as one left to himself, altogether alone: as one also against whom, at this moment, the whole universe seemed to be turned; therefore he adds, "There is none to help." I look above, around, below, but there is no friend at hand. "Look on *my* right hand and see, for there is no one who acknowledges me; refuge has failed me; no one cares for my soul" (Psa. 142:4). "I am as a sparrow alone on the house-top" (Psa. 102:7), at which arrows are being aimed from every direction. The bird does not use her wings to flee, for she does not see the danger. But here is One whom all the archers wound— who knows, who feels the danger, but who refuses to use his own power to free himself. He waits till God shall help him. Therefore he does nothing but pray. Hear how he perseveres in supplication, as other psalms may be understood to represent, "Attend to my cry, for I am brought very low" (Psa. 142:6). "Save me, O God! For the waters have come up to my neck. I sink in deep mire, where there is no standing; I have come into deep waters, where the floods overflow me. I am weary with my crying; my throat is dry; my eyes fail while I wait for my God. Those who hate me without a cause are more than the hairs of my head; they are mighty who would destroy me, being my enemies wrongfully" (Psa. 69:1-4).

How wonderful and exemplary, O Christian, is this conduct of our suffering Lord! It proves him to have been more than man! His resignation and meekness under trial, his patience and perseverance in waiting upon the expected help of God, are indeed human virtues, but exhibited in him with superhuman, and Divine, power. He could have proved his own effectual helper. A single request in prayer to his Father, would have brought twelve legions of angels to his deliverance (Matt. 26:53, 54). And what mere man, having such resources at his command, would not have availed himself of one, or more, or all of them, for his help? What mere man could leave himself in the hands of his enemies like this, and only exercise against them the voice of prayer? Jesus on the cross is God incarnate. None but himself could have said, "There is none to help," and yet not make haste to be his own helper. He is hanging in death as our surety sacrifice, and he is praying as the high priest of our profession. Imitate, then, his example, O Christian, however forsaken, and forlorn, your circumstances may be. Learn that your strength and safety lie in Jehovah. Learn that there are periods in which you can only leave yourself to him, by leaving yourself to your enemies. He that believes will not act hastily (Isa. 28:16). He that believes will not be put to shame (Rom. 10:11). He that believes shall not be confounded (1 Pet. 2:6). Why? Because he that believes will pray; and to him that prays and believes "NOTHING SHALL BE IMPOSSIBLE" (Matt. 17:20). How? Because the omnipotence and faithfulness of Jehovah, Father, Son, and Holy Spirit, are immediately engaged, and expressly covenanted, to aid him, by this promise, "Call upon ME in the day of trouble; I will deliver you, and you shall glorify Me" (Psa. 50:15).

THE ASSAULT

VERSES 12, 13—*Many bulls have surrounded Me; strong bulls of Bashan have encircled Me. They gape at Me with their mouths, like a raging and roaring lion.*

IN these and a few of the following verses, our Lord more particularly specifies the enemies that surrounded him, and the miseries which he endured. He spreads his trouble before the Lord, as if he would arouse the attention of Heaven by the minuteness of detail, and prove the reality of his distress, by enumerating its various and most prominent features.

He begins with his enemies; he compares them to "bulls," to "strong bulls of Bashan." In that fertile country, this animal was nurtured to its greatest perfection; there it attained its full power and vigor. The characteristics of various animals have been figuratively applied, in every age and country, to represent those of man. The pen of inspiration has here represented the enemies of our Lord, by the significant emblem of strong bulls. These animals are remarkable for the proud, fierce, and sullen manner, with which they exercise their great strength. Such were the persecutors who now beset our Lord. These were, first, human, and secondly, spiritual foes; and both were alike distinguished by that proud, fierce, and sullen manner in which they assaulted him.

When contemplating the crucifixion of our Savior, it is difficult to keep at all times before the mind the fact that spirits of darkness were as truly, and as busily, engaged there, as were human beings. Indeed, we must suppose that the latter, before they could reach such a height of malicious cruelty and wickedness, must have been actuated by evil spirits; their wickedness was fostered and directed by a power superior to themselves; their pouting lips, their wagging heads, their pointing fingers, and their taunting tongues, were animated by Satanic influence. The spirits of darkness had thus a double advantage in their assaults. Their own attacks could only be directed immediately on the spirit of our Lord. But whenever they desired to bring any particular temptation to bear with all possible force, they would avail themselves of the members of these men's bodies, to give it human utterance, and to assail the outward senses, at the instant they assaulted the inner man. Such was the difficulty in which our Lord was placed. Many bulls and strong, had beset him all around. He feels the helplessness of his condition—he tells it to his God.

Imagine you see a fellow-creature closely pursued; not only one enraged animal, but a whole herd fall upon him; they trample him under foot; they surround him on every side, and bellow against him; they strike him with their horns; they toss him to and fro; they rush upon him with one accord. What horror, what fearfulness, what helplessness, is pictured in this condition! It was just like this now with our Lord upon the cross. We may well imagine him to say with the Psalmist, "My heart is severely pained within me, and the terrors of death have fallen upon me. Fearfulness and trembling have come upon me, and horror has overwhelmed me. So I said, "Oh, that I had wings like a dove! I would fly away and be at rest" (Psa. 55:4-6). Great, indeed, was that trouble in which our Lord was placed upon the cross. On all sides he was surrounded, from all sides assailed. With persevering and desperate fury would the various powers of darkness press our Lord with their different temptations, throwing themselves, as it were, upon his spirit. The trouble was near indeed. Christ was alone. At every instant he had to repel innumerable temptations. This is done by men, as well as by unembodied spirits, by a direct effort of the will. Christ's human soul was incessantly called upon to exercise its holy will in the rejection of these temptations; and it needs to scarcely be added, that a temptation, whether presented audibly, visibly, or mentally, cannot possibly leave any stain when rejected by the will. Let this be pondered. Many individuals feel averse to think that Christ was directly tempted by Satan, not distinguishing sufficiently the difference between the suggestion, and the reception, of evil. It is important to clear this point. Every person may readily perceive, that no guilt could result from our Lord's hearing a temptation uttered by the mouths of these taunting men. So, likewise, no moral stain could be left, when, without human instrumentality, the wicked spirits darted their suggestions into the Savior's mind. In the one case, the evil word he heard was rejected, and in the other, the fiery dart he felt was cast off, by the instantaneous activity, and holy energy, of our Savior's will.

The apostle exhorts us to take the shield of faith, with which we shall be able to quench all the fiery darts of the devil (Eph. 6:16). It was this shield that our Lord held fast. Pressed on every side, pinioned in his body, wounded in his soul by that sharpest of all spears, the curse of God, Christ was now placed in the greatest crisis that ever any immortal spirit knew. The sons of pride stood round his cross. Well fed and clothed, pampered with all luxury, stout and strong, like bulls from the rich pastures of Bashan, they stood and bellowed against their crucifying victim. Relentless and sullen, never once did they show him the remotest pity; fierce and proud, their words and taunts were selected with most bitter and cruel ingenuity; savage in their malice, they left nothing undone which could wound and lacerate his feelings. What these human foes did visibly, and audibly, was an outward picture of what proud, fierce, and sullen spirits were doing inwardly. Wrestling in their great might with the spiritual energy of our Lord, they gave unceasing vent to their malicious insinuations; thrusting themselves close upon his spirit with fierce fury, they endeavored to obtain an entrance into the inner chambers of his will. Incessant and innumerable were the temptations with which they besieged him; but all in vain. An Almighty and immaculate Will resided in the crucified frame of Jesus of Nazareth.

So wild, impetuous, and furious, was this assault of men and devils, that our Lord adds, "They gape at me with their mouths, like a raging a roaring lion" (verse 13). The deceitful couching, the sudden spring, the fearful roar, the tearing power of the lion, give another representation of the enemies of the Redeemer, and of the nature of their assaults. Hear how he speaks of them in the 57th Psalm, 4th verse, "My soul is among lions; I lie among the sons of men who are set on fire, whose teeth are spears and arrows, and their tongue a sharp sword." The cunning and treachery of the feline species, may be fitly chosen as emblematic of our Savior's enemies. The Pharisees and scribes had often laid wait for him; they sent people pretending to be righteous men, who should entangle him in his talk. Now then, that they had laid their paw of power upon their prostrate victim, they were ravening in his blood, and satiating their glaring eyes with the sight of his mangled and quivering body. "But in my adversity they rejoiced and gathered together; attackers gathered against me, and I did not know it; they tore at me and did not cease; with ungodly mockers at feasts they gnashed at me with their teeth. Lord, how long will You look on? Rescue me from their destructions, my precious life from the lions." (Psa. 35:15-17).

THE FAINTNESS

VERSE 14—*I am poured out like water, and all My bones are out of joint; My heart is like wax; it has melted within Me.*

THE most strenuous efforts of the combined Powers of Darkness—the most cruel taunts and angriest torments of men—could make no unholy impression on the spirit of the great Redeemer. His flesh, however, felt the effects of their assaults. His blessed body was exquisitely susceptible of impression. It could suffer, it could languish, it could die.

Our Lord shows, by the words of this verse, how intensely he feels the weakness of his earthly vessel. What expressive terms convey the knowledge of it to our minds! We can more readily sympathize in the physical sensations which our Lord experienced, than in the mental and spiritual anguish which he endured.

HE WAS STRETCHED. We know what pains ensue to a limb or a finger that is kept in one unvarying position, even for a few minutes. Christ had now been stretched for nearly, as some think, six hours.

HE WAS PIERCED WITH NAILS. The most tender parts of his body, the hands and feet, where the nerves of sensation are most numerous, and close together, were pierced with large strong nails. We know what we feel when a thorn, which we can scarcely discern, lodges in our skin.

HE WAS RACKED TO DISLOCATION. When the elevated cross settled into its socket, the jerk must have shaken the crucified person with great violence. A racking jolt must have been felt throughout the entire frame. Every muscle would be stretched, and the ligaments of the joints strained. From what we must conceive to have been the previous enfeebled state of our

Lord's body, we conclude that its muscular power must have been greatly diminished. It is not improbable but that, with the shock, the ligaments would not only be strained, but also would give way, so that partial or entire dislocation ensued, especially in the wrist, elbow, and shoulder, of each arm. The text informs us that it was so. "All my bones are out of joint." Not one was broken, but most, or all, were dislocated.

HIS BODY WAS BURDENED WITH ITS OWN WEIGHT. Having hung for so many hours, the strain on every part of the frame would increase with every succeeding moment. The gradual elongation of the muscles must necessarily weaken them. Strong spasms, incessant aches, and shooting pangs, would still further incapacitate them for the office of sustaining. The depressed body, dragging thus from the arms, would sink upon itself. It is uncertain whether there was any projecting pin in the center of the cross, to sustain part of the weight of the body. If there were none, as some think, then the entire weight must have been suspended from the hands. The loins, loosened by intense agony, would be incapable of yielding to the limbs that strength which was necessary to maintain them in an upright position. The knees therefore would be bent forward in utter weakness. The wounds in the hands would consequently be torn, and greatly enlarged. The heel also, and that part of the foot which was above the nail, would be pressed with painful force upon the iron.

HE WAS FAINT. Such a feeling of languor and faintness ensued, that language fails to express it, and the emblem of "water poured out" is used to represent it. As the water falls from the vessel to the earth, see how its particles separate farther and farther from each other. Its velocity increases as it falls. It has no power to stop itself mid-way, much less to return to its place. It is the very picture of utter weakness. Such was our Lord's experience. The sensations we feel when about to faint away are extremely distressing. We appear to our own consciences to be nothing but weakness—as water poured out:

every bone feels relaxed and out of joint; it seems as though we had none; the strength of bone is gone, the knitting of the joints loosened, and the muscular vigor has fled. A sickly giddiness overcomes us. We have no power to bear up. All heart is lost. Our strength disappears, like that of wax, of melting wax, which drops upon surrounding objects, and is lost. Daniel describes his sensations on beholding the great vision in this way, "no strength remained in me; for my vigor was turned to frailty in me, and I retained no strength" (Dan. 10:8). In regard, however, to the faintness which our Lord experienced, we ought to notice this additional and remarkable circumstance, that he did not altogether faint away. The relief of insensibility he refused to take. When consciousness ceases, all perception of pain is necessarily and instantly terminated. But our Lord retained his full consciousness throughout this awful scene; and patiently endured for a considerable period those, to us, insupportable sensations, which precede the actual swoon.

Let the afflicted Christian, when sunk alike in health and spirits, and passing, it may be, out of one faint into another, endeavor to think of the Savior's faintness on the cross. The elder brother can sympathize with us even in such an extremity of feeling. Remember how meekly he bore his own affliction; how tenderly he feels for the most unworthy of his brethren in their distresses. Call to mind that compassionate consideration which he exhibited in the days of his flesh, towards the multitudes that followed him (Matt. 9:36). Hear how he speaks to his disciples, "I do not want to send them away hungry, lest they faint on the way" (Matt. 15:32). Now that he is ascended to the highest heavens, his heart is as full of sympathy as before. While, therefore, you would desire that he should regard your present trial, direct your own attention in like manner to his former affliction. The sympathy between Jesus, the head, and your soul, as a member of his spiritual body, will in this way be consummated. The very lowest depth of your experience, shall find that of Christ beneath it. Sink, then, and fail, as may both heart and flesh, the sympathy of Jesus-God will never fail you. Therefore, let all afflicted Christians attentively, and fully, and unremittingly, "CONSIDER HIM THAT ENDURED," lest they become "weary, and discouraged in their souls" (Heb. 12:3). Though faint, let them be still pursuing, under the Captain of their salvation, against all their enemies (Judges 8:4). Yes, even though the outward man perish, there is no cause to faint (2 Cor. 4:16). Even though darkness envelopes them, let not their hearts despond. "Why do you say, O Jacob, and speak, O Israel: "My way is hidden from the LORD, and my just claim is passed over by my God"? Have you not known? Have you not heard? The everlasting God, the LORD, the Creator of the ends of the earth, neither faints nor is weary. His understanding is unsearchable. He gives power to the weak, and to those who have no might He increases strength. Even the youths shall faint and be weary, and the young men shall utterly fall, But those who wait on the LORD shall renew their strength; they shall mount up with wings like eagles, they shall run and not be weary, they shall walk and not faint" (Isa. 40:27-31).

If then, O Christian, you faint in the day of adversity, may we not say, "your strength is small?" (Prov. 24:10). Christ is given of God to be our strength. Lay hold on him, and you shall be invincible. Pray fervently to the Holy Spirit to inspire you with the mind that was in Jesus; to impart to you the same desires and earnest longings which filled his heart. It was not with mere pain, that he was faint. It was not with anxiety to be freed from affliction that his spirit melted. It was with intense desires after God, with unutterable emotions under his Father's withdrawal that Christ's heart was poured out like water. We may suppose these to be his words, "My soul longs, yes, even faints for the courts of the LORD; my heart and my flesh cry out for the living God" (Psa. 84:2). "O God, You are my God; early will I seek You; my soul thirsts for You; my flesh longs for You... My soul follows close behind You" (Psa. 63:1, 8). This was the "one thing" which Christ desired, which he sought after. Is this also the chief happiness of your heart? Is the enjoyment of God's favor—the return of his presence of light and love—the principal subject of your prayers, the first and last object of your hopes, anxieties, and desires? Then do not fear, neither despair. Weep, and mourn, yet do not despond. Sow many prayers, cast forth your supplications, plant your petitions without ceasing, and in due season you shall reap, if you do not faint (Gal. 6:9).

THE EXHAUSTION

VERSE 15—*My strength is dried up like a potsherd, and My tongue clings to My jaws; You have brought Me to the dust of death.*

THOUGH the faintness, mentioned in the preceding verse, never reached its crisis, *yet* it was followed by COMPLETE EXHAUSTION. This was the natural effect of crucifixion. We have remarked that our Lord's body was stretched, was pierced with nails, was racked to dislocation, was burdened with its own weight, and was oppressed by faintness. We now further observe, that INFLAMMATION must have commenced early, and violently, in the wounded parts—have been quickly imparted to those that were strained—and have terminated in a HIGH DEGREE OF FEVERISH BURNING OVER THE WHOLE BODY. The fluid in the body would as a result be dried up, and the watery particles of the blood absorbed. The skin, parched by the scorching sun till mid-day, would be unable to absorb, or supply, any moisture. The loss of blood, at the hands and feet, would hasten the dehydration. Therefore our Lord says, "My strength is dried up like a potsherd, and my tongue clings to my jaws." The fever would devour his small remaining strength. And THIRST, that most intolerable of all bodily privations, must have been overpowering. His body appeared, to his feeling, like a potsherd that had been charred in the potter's kiln. It seemed to have neither strength, nor substance, left in it. So feeble had he become, so parched and dried up, that CLAMMINESS OF THE MOUTH, one of the forerunners of immediate termination, had already seized him. "My tongue clings to my jaws; You have brought me to the dust of death."

"For our sakes Christ yielded himself like 'water' without resistance, to the violence of his enemies; suffering his 'bones,' in which consists the strength of the frame, to be distended and dislocated upon the cross; while, by reason of the fire from above, to the burning heat of which this paschal lamb was exposed, his heart dissolved and melted away. The intenseness of his passion, drying up all the fluids, brought on a thirst tormenting beyond expression, and at last laid him low in the grave. Never, blessed Lord, was there love like your love! Never was there sorrow like your sorrow! Your spouse and body mystical, the Church, is often in a degree conformed to you, and as you were, so is she in this world."—*Bishop Horne on the Psalms.*

The statement of this verse may be illustrated, by the situation of a soldier expiring on the field of battle.[9] Of a late excellent officer, and exemplary Christian, it is recorded, that he "lay wounded, naked, bleeding, and helpless, for two days and two nights, exposed to the intense heat of a burning sun, and, what every soldier, whose lot it has been to lie wounded on a field of battle, knows to be more dreadful than any or all circumstances of suffering united together, TO THE LACK OF WATER." He says, "At this dreadful period of pain and destitution, I was lying naked on a bank of scorching sand, fainting from time to time with loss of blood, and, from the severity of my wounds, unable to move, I was assailed with the rage of intolerable thirst. Mere weakness, approaching to insensibility, induced at length a kind of resignation, and even a hope that a few hours would put a period to my sufferings."— *Governor Melvill's Memoirs.*

Such is the natural human feeling under protracted sufferings. But the grand desire of our Lord was not their mere termination, but the return of the light of his Father's countenance. However severe were his bodily pains, they appeared to him as nothing in comparison with this, that the consolations of God's presence should be absent from him, when he was on the very point of expiring. He therefore complains of it, sets it forth as an argument, "You have brought me to the dust of death;" as if he would say, "And do you still leave me, when I sink exhausted under the last enemy?"

---

[9] Poole's synopsis.

Sad and sorrowful condition to which the Savior of the world was reduced! Grievous, indeed, is sin, when we see what it cost the Savior! Your sins, O reader, brought Jesus to this extremity! He endured the agony of a raging thirst, so that you might drink of the river of God's pleasure. Go down, then, deep into the fountain of your heart. Let the wounds of Jesus open all the springs. Bring forth the tears of true contrition and penitence, to satisfy the longing desire of him who thirsts for your soul's eternal welfare. Do not be like the unfeeling potsherds of this world, who strive against their Maker (Isa. 49:5). Do not say your sins are few in number, and not aggravated in their nature. One sin thrust Adam out of paradise. Your one sin, either brought Christ to this cross, or will bring you to perdition. Repent! Repent! Shall Jesus thirst, and thirst for you, and will you begrudgingly give him a tear? Shall His tongue be powerless, and will you not speak for it, and say, "Sad, sad day in which I sinned! Cursed be the guilt with which I crucified my Savior!" Fall upon your knees, and pray, "Lord, make me to weep over myself and you. Help me to learn the atrocity of my sins, in the severity of your sorrows." This is both your duty, and your privilege, fellow-sinner. Weep with your dying Lord, lest angels weep over your death-bed. His stripes will heal you. His wounds will cure you. His sorrows will comfort you.

Blessed Balm of Gilead! Bruised to be our medicine! I feel your bruises as my own. They are mine, and they are yours; for I inflicted them, and you bore them. Amazing partnership of sin and sorrow! The sin is mine, the sorrow yours. Yet mine you take, and yours, mine make. So now your sorrow's mine, and all my sins are yours. O wonderful exchange of love and grace, with gratitude and sympathy!

THE PIERCING

VERSE 16—*For dogs have surrounded Me; the congregation of the wicked has enclosed Me. They pierced My hands and My feet.*

SO varied, and so great, was the malignity exhibited by the enemies of our Lord, that the characteristics of two species of ferocious animals, were not adequate to describe it. Another emblematical figure is therefore introduced. The assembly of the wicked is compared to that of dogs, who haunt about the cities, prowl in every corner, snarl over the flesh, and devour it all with greediness. Like the wild cry of dogs in pursuit, with unfailing scent tracking their victim, vigilance of eye on all its movements, and a determination which nothing can falter, they run it on to death. The oriental mode of hunting, both in ancient and modern times, is murderous and merciless in the extreme. A circle of several miles in circumference is beat around; and the men, driving all before them, and narrowing as they advance, enclose the prey on every side. Having thus made them prisoners, the cruel hunters proceed to slaughter at their own convenience. So did the enemies of our Lord. Long before his crucifixion, it is recorded that they used the most treacherous plans to get him into their power. The scribes and the Pharisees began to urge him vehemently, and to provoke him to speak of many things; laying wait for him, and seeking to catch something out of his mouth, that they might accuse him (Luke 11:53, 54). And they watched him, and sent forth spies which pretended to be righteous men, in order that they might take hold of his words, so that they could deliver him into the power and authority of the governor (Luke 20:20). Having marked their victim, having chosen their opportunity, having tracked him to his usual place, the dogs surrounded him, the wicked enclosed him. Judas, who "knew the place," came, "with a great multitude with swords and clubs" (John 18:2 and Matt. 26:47), and they laid hold of him and led him away. "As soon as it was day, the elders of the people, both chief priests and scribes, came together and led Him into their council" (Luke 22:66). "For truly against Your holy Servant Jesus, whom You anointed, both Herod and Pontius Pilate, with the Gentiles and the people of Israel, were gathered together" (Acts 4:27).

In this way our Lord was pursued to death—surrounded on all sides—by wicked hands taken, and crucified, and slain. Like a stag in the midst of the hunters, he saw no way to turn. "The archers have bitterly grieved him, shot at him and hated him" (Gen. 49:23). So that he could not escape, they pierced his hands and his feet. They did not expedite his death. His wounds were in the limbs, not in the vital parts, lest he should too soon be gone. The wicked Lords of the Philistines said, "Call for Samson that he may perform for us" (Judges 16:25). The cry in Pilate's court was, "Crucify him, crucify him;" not merely "Away with him from the earth," but "Away with him in the most shameful manner, and with the most excruciating torments, that the laws allow." Notwithstanding the infatuated madness of the moment, the Jews remembered that it was not lawful for them to put any man to death. Nor, indeed, would the most severe of their own legal punishments have satisfied their malice. They appear glad for once to be under Roman law, that they may ensure for their victim a Roman punishment. Herod and Pilate dismissed their enmity, and the hypocritical mob cried out, "We have no king but Caesar." The objections of the relenting governor only incensed their rage. His attempt to deliver himself from the guilt of pronouncing condemnation on the innocent, made them only the more eager to take it upon themselves, "His blood be on us and on our children." Awful legacy of a spoken curse, which their posterity to this day inherit! The outrageous clamor of the priests and of the people prevailed; the wavering judge gave sentence for the humiliating and cruel execution. On Calvary they had, at last, the satisfaction to behold him, firmly grasped in the lingering death of the Roman cross. Of all sanguinary punishments, that of crucifixion is one of the most dreadful. No vital part is immediately affected by it. The hands and feet, which are furnished with the most numerous and sensitive organs, are perforated with nails, which must necessarily be of some size to suit their intended purpose. The tearing apart of the tender fibers of the hands and feet, the lacerating of so many nerves, and bursting of so many blood-vessels, produces intense agony. The nerves of the hand and foot, being the terminations of those which occupy the arm and leg; and these being intimately connected with the nerves of the whole body, the laceration of the former are felt over the entire frame. Witness the melancholy result of even a needless puncture, in any one of these remote parts, that a spasm is not infrequently produced in the muscles of the face, which locks the jaws inseparably. When, then, the hands and feet of our blessed Lord were pierced with nails, he must have felt the sharpest pangs shoot through every part of his body. Supported only by his lacerated limbs, and suspended from his pierced hands, our Lord had nearly six hours' torment to endure.

Our Jesus is thus THE PIERCED ONE. He was pierced in his head by the thorns, he was pierced in his back by the scourge, he was pierced in his hands and his feet by the nails, and he was pierced in his side by the spear. This forms one proof that he is the true Messiah. O Jew, reach your finger here, and behold his hands; and reach your hand here, and thrust it into his side, and do not be faithless but believing. The promise is sure; the time is approaching, (may it not be far off!) concerning which he has declared, "And I will pour on the house of David and on the inhabitants of Jerusalem the Spirit of grace and supplication; then they will look on ME WHOM THEY HAVE PIERCED. Yes, they will mourn for Him as one mourns for his only son, and grieve for Him as one grieves for a firstborn" (Zech. 12:10). Our New Testament testifies the same truth with the Old Testament which the disciples of Moses venerate. They were written by the same Spirit of inspiration. The light which guided the pen of Zechariah, directed that of John; and because the time of the accomplishment is so much nearer, the latter proclaims, "Behold, He is coming with clouds, and every eye will see Him, even they who pierced Him. And all the tribes of the earth will mourn because of Him. Even so, Amen" (Rev. 1:7). Oh that multitudes of Jews and Gentiles may be prepared for that day! May the Spirit of life come into the dry bones, and may an exceedingly great army be raised up, who, as faithful soldiers of the cross, will not be ashamed to confess the faith of Christ crucified, but will fight manfully under his banner against sin and the world, Satan and the flesh.

Look here, also, O Christian! The bleeding Savior is raised up, that whosoever looks unto him may be healed. As the Israelites of old were saved from instant, and painful destruction, by turning their weeping eyes to the bronze serpent; so now by the eye of faith, when you look to Jesus exalted on the cross, you shall be delivered from spiritual and eternal death. "Look unto ME, and be ye saved, all you ends of the earth." As it is a spiritual or moral looking, so is it a spiritual or moral salvation. We behold in Christ's body the effects of sin, and we learn to hate it, as the cause of evil to our BEST FRIEND. We see the nails driven through his quivering flesh, and we would eagerly pull them out again, and cast them away. But we learn that our sins were the sharpest piercings which our Savior felt, and we hurry to remove them. As we would turn, with dismay and abhorrence, from the sharp spear, and bloody nails, that pierced the Savior's body, so should we turn from our own sins and transgressions. This is the healing of the soul by the wounds of Jesus, when the piercing of his body affects our heart with hatred against sin. It is for this reason that he is named JESUS, for he saves his people from their sins (Matt. 1:21). The safety of heaven is not only secured to them at last, but the salvation of holiness is imparted to them at present. They are saved from the dominion of sin, saved from the practice of sin, and saved from the love of sin. The sight of a crucified and pierced Savior, accomplishes this great work in their hearts. When the Spirit of Light opens their naturally darkened understanding to apprehend what Christ the Lord has suffered on their behalf; when they in this way "look on him whom they have pierced," they begin to mourn indeed, and to be in bitterness, because their best friend should suffer to such a degree, and that their sins should be the cause. A full and generous grief takes possession of their hearts. They feel as if they had a right to weep over one whom they have slain, who loved them. Like Mary, his mother, a sword now pierces through their own soul also (Luke 2:35), when they think of their torn and pierced Savior. Every one mourns alone. In the secret of the closet, when no eye sees them, they bitterly mourn over the sins by which they have pierced their Lord. And in proportion as the Spirit of grace and supplication is received, so is the depth of their sorrow, and the bitterness of their lamentation. In this world alone do they weep. The days of their mourning terminate when they behold the Savior in his glory; therefore they will not now restrain their tears, since God himself is to wipe them away forever. And though they would gladly rather depart and be with Christ, which is far better, yet they do feel a sacred, unutterable, blessedness, when, lying in thought at his bleeding feet, they water them, as it were, with genuine, grateful tears, from their pierced and broken hearts.

THE EMACIATION

VERSE 17—*I can count all my bones.*

THE more we consider the character of our Lord and Savior, the more does this conclusion force itself upon our minds, that his life must have been one entire suffering. A holy being in a sinful world, must have felt as a creature would out of its native element. A wonder as he himself was to men, they must have seemed more strange to him. That they could eat their food—exert their strength—enjoy their pleasures—bask in the sunshine—converse and smile, inhaling the fragrance of their eastern perfumes, and not love, with heart and soul, the God who gave them all, must have appeared to him, as it really is, unnatural and monstrous. To find men intelligent and reasonable; prudent and amiable; diligent and industrious; kind and grateful; on all occasions except one, towards all persons except one; and that occasion, the highest and noblest that could occupy their faculties, and that One the Being who made them by his hand at first, and by a constant exercise of his power, imparted life in every breath they drew, must have made him conclude that he was resident, either in a world of most daring rebels, or in a vast asylum of monomaniacs.[10] With too much truth, it may be said, he was in both. Man possesses noble and generous powers, but he will not render to God the tribute of them all. This willfulness renders him a rebel—and the universality of its exhibition on this *one* point, constitutes him a monomaniac. Moralists and physicians, viewing man from different points, and in various lights, have come to the same melancholy conclusion. The maxims of the world prudently coincide here with the

---

[10] A term for a psychological condition denoting an inordinate or obsessive interest or zeal confined to a single idea.

doctrines of divines; and that no man should trust his brother where self-interest is concerned, is a proverbial adage of undisputed wisdom. Self is the blind and blinding idol. It is the household god, in every man's heart, to which he pays a daily homage. Where, however, self is not brought into action, man can understand clearly, feel tenderly, and act in a noble and generous manner. He seems for once to have come to himself; but soon he relapses, and God, and his fellow creatures, are again excluded from the charmed circle of his selfish heart.

When Christ beheld the world he wept over it. He loved and pitied the sinners whom he saw, but that love and pity came back to his own heart with a fatal recoil. He did not look only upon the face, but into the heart of men, and knew them better than they knew themselves. If the very best of human beings perceive much in themselves to lament, how much more quickly could Christ detect it, in them, and in a more holy way abhor it? Therefore he must have been always sorrowful, and that sorrow preyed upon his frame. When only about thirty years of age, he looked as if he were almost twenty years older. "You art not yet fifty years old," was the observation of the Jews; which shows their idea of his age, taken from his face and figure. The prophet foretold this, "Just as many were astonished at you, so His visage was marred more than any man, and His form more than the sons of men... He has no form or comeliness; and when we see Him, there is no beauty that we should desire Him" (Isa. 52:14; 53:2). Such was the blessed Savior's personal appearance. He fasted often. He spent whole nights in prayer to God. He wandered about on his own blessed feet. He rested himself for very weariness on the side of a well, and asked for water to drink. He twice fed thousands, but never performed a miracle for self-supply. For several days immediately preceding his crucifixion, he obtained little or no rest. He walked to Jerusalem almost every morning, and returned to Bethany every evening. The day was spent in warning the crowded city; the night was passed in solitude, with prayer to God. Of himself at this time we may regard him as speaking in the words of the Psalmist, "I am gone like a shadow when it lengthens; I am shaken off like a locust. My knees are weak through fasting, and my flesh is feeble from lack of fatness" (Psa. 109:23, 24). "For my days are consumed like smoke, and my bones are burned like a hearth. My heart is stricken and withered like grass, so that I forget to eat my bread. Because of the sound of my groaning my bones cling to my skin" (Psa. 102:3-5).

On that ever-memorable night in which he was betrayed, no couch welcomed him to rest on. He left the upper room of the last supper for the garden of Gethsemane. There the wearied disciples slept while Jesus knelt upon his last bed. But that kneeling was not in rest; it was in unutterable anguish. His very flesh, too, as if equally willing with his groaning spirit, wept forth its blood in sympathy at every pore. In body and soul, Jesus appears to have been quite spent. To strengthen his humanity an angel was sent from heaven. Scarcely had this relief arrived when the traitor came. Instantly surrounded by the armed band, and violently seized, he was hurried back into the city. From one judgment-seat to another, he was carried, with little or no intermission, during the whole of the night. From Annas he was led to Caiaphas; from Caiaphas he was sent to Pilate; from Pilate to Herod; and from Herod back to Pilate again. The night, too, was cold. Even the hardy soldiers needed a fire to warm themselves. Peter, too, could welcome its heat, while perhaps his Lord was trembling with the chill of that large hall. As if the victim of human and satanic malice were not yet sufficiently diminished, they had to beat out his small remaining strength. Man scourged that back on which his sins were laid; and Christ allowed the stripes to fall without a murmur, that by them his people might be healed. From the fifth judgment-seat, he was at last led forth to Calvary and to crucifixion. Like other prisoners, it was necessary that he should carry his own cross. The burden was laid upon his blessed shoulder. His exhausted and emaciated frame could scarcely support its own weight. They observed his feeble tottering step;

they marked his sunken eye, his ghastly visage, his bending, trembling, figure. Sad sight! Even the Romans pitied it. Those ruthless soldier's who mocked his dying agonies, commiserated his burdened weakness, dragging his steps along. They stopped the procession. It was the centurion that issued the humane command. They removed the wood, and laying hold on Simon the Cyrenian, compelled him to bear it after Jesus. This is the only act of kindness which his enemies performed for him. And great indeed must have been the Savior's weakness when he could not bear even this weight; for as the large upright beam was generally left on Golgotha, it was only the cross piece that was usually laid upon the condemned. Somewhat relieved by this exchange, the progress to the mount of crucifixion was easier and speedier. There for the last time did the Savior of our souls lie down. The hard wood was his bed, a cross without a covering. The soldiers stretched his limbs and nailed them fast upon it, completely outstretched, as it lay upon the ground. Immediately as they raised it his emaciated frame was exposed to view. It is worn to skin and bone. He looks down on it. He surveys his wasted body. He exclaims, "I can count all my bones." So plainly did the stretching on the cross bring them all to view, that he was able, as it were, to count their number, and tell them one by one. "The skin and flesh were so distended by the posture of the body on the cross, that the bones, as through a thin veil, became visible, and might be counted; and the holy Jesus, forsaken and stripped, naked and bleeding, was a spectacle to heaven and earth."—*Bishop Horne on the Psalms.*

Learn, professing disciple, a never-to-be-forgotten lesson, from your Lord's emaciated frame. "Zeal for God's house consumed him, it had even eaten him up" (Psa. 69:9); the flesh was worn off his bones. With love to souls, and earnest desires for the glory of God, he spent his life. As it was a holy, so it was a whole burnt-offering, which he presented to his Father. In mercy to you, the Father accepted it. In mercy to you, the Savior substituted his body for yours, and his soul in your soul's place. In mercy to you, the Holy

Spirit exhibits to you this crucified Savior in the glass of the word, and offers all the benefits of his bitter sufferings to your acceptance. "I beseech you, therefore, brethren, by the mercies of God, that you present YOUR bodies a living sacrifice, holy, acceptable unto God, which is your reasonable service" (Rom. 12:1). Let the love of Christ constrain you to live no longer unto yourselves, but unto him that died for you, and rose again (2 Cor. 5:14, 15). Gratitude demands; let gratitude compel. The Lord loves a cheerful giver. Do not indulge the flesh, but the spirit. Keep your body in subjection. Dwelling in your celled houses, and enjoying the abundance of all things which the Lord sends, without a famine, on this favored land, see that your soul hungers and thirsts after righteousness. Alas for professing Christians! Luxury stints their spiritual growth! Sleeping, dressing, and eating, occupy the greater part of those hours which remain from the cares and business of life! Though Jesus had nowhere to lay his head, yet he would not take your downy pillow from you, but would have you to choose for your soul, the portion of the beloved disciple, to lie in the bosom of his love. And can heavenly desires arise within the loaded, pampered, flesh? Can that mind find communion with God, which grovels after earthly gratifications? Are indolence, and worldliness, and self-pleasing, the means of amassing spiritual and eternal riches? Are you a soldier of Christ, and do you never fight? Is there a race set before you, and have you no desire to win? Have you a cross to bear, and do you never attempt to bear its weight? Look here at your dying Lord. He has worn himself to a shadow in your service! "He went about continually doing good." Are you a follower of Christ? Are your feet treading in his steps? His were up-hill. His whole life was one laborious ascent. Do you press after him? The propensity to descend is natural, and like the power of gravitation, secret, constant, and powerful. Do you bear up against it? Is there vigor, earnestness, determination in your spirit? Are you fully awake? Is Christ's life stirring within you, enabling you to spend and to be spent in the best of services? Are you able to say, "With my soul I have desired You in the night, yes, by my spirit within me I will seek You early?" (Isa. 26:9). Are your prayers cold, formal, heartless, collections of words? Or are they earnest, fervent, persevering, accompanied with sighs and tears in secret, and often presented in petitions, desires, and waiting expectations? Your Savior loves *heart* work. He abhors mere *appearance*. Therefore when he sets for you the example, it is reality: and when he calls you, even to the most severe tasks, for the subjugation of those fleshly lusts which war against the soul, he bids you to anoint your head, and wash your face so that you *do not appear* to men to be fasting, but to your Father who is in secret, who will reward you openly.

THE INSULTING GAZE

VERSE 17—*They look and stare at Me.*

SENSITIVELY conscious of his condition upon the cross, the delicate feelings of the holy Savior were deeply pained by the gaze of the multitude. With impudent face they looked upon him. At their ease they surveyed him. To view him better, they halted as they walked. With deliberate insolence they collected in groups, and made their remarks to each other on his conduct and appearance. Mocking his quivering, emaciated body, they looked and stared at him.

How revolting is it to our feelings, to be made the subject of remark, the object of a stare! Pure and innocent minds are the most acutely wounded. The face of guilt is not so easily abashed. Jesus as a man was innocence itself. That lovely modesty, which is a sure ingredient in real worth, was fully possessed by Christ. In the account given of him by Isaiah 53:3 (margin), it is said, "And he hid as it were his face from us." Like the individual who must pass through a place where he is heckled and despised, he turns away his face, and seeks to escape from observation. Nor is such conduct prompted either by cowardice or self-accusation. It is a duty to his own feelings, to save them from such severe and painful trials. So was it with Christ: he shrunk back from the contemptuous gaze of the multitude. When he encountered it in their crowded cities, he hid his face against the wall, and hurried out of their streets. But here on the cross, everywhere he looked their eyes met his. Every one was staring with open eye-lid. His emaciated frame—his convulsive shudders—his spasmodic movements—his naked body—were the subjects of their ridicule, the objects of their insulting gaze.

There is something in the human eye which gives it peculiar power. It is, at times, as if a spirit, from another world, were looking through it. A glance arrests the attention; a look overawes the mind. We seem to be fascinated. No sooner do we turn our eyes away, than the hated object is again looked at. It is the peculiar prerogative of the wicked to stare down the good. This may seem but a light affliction, yet it is specifically recorded by the Spirit of God, as one of the painful experiences if him, who was tempted in all points as we are.

To be exposed to the gaze of the soldiers, the judges, the noble citizens, and the vulgar multitude, was a peculiar, and almost daily, trial of the early Christians. Indeed, in every age, those who live as strangers and pilgrims must be objects of remark. As a foreigner in his native costume is annoyed in our streets by the rude gaze of the people; so the Christian is a foreigner; his speech betrays him to be a man of "another country," and as he passes along the walk of life, he is looked at with inquiring astonishment, "Who can this be that differs from us? What is he that presumes to think and act on principles opposed to ours?" He is therefore stared at, first as a wonder, and next as an object of contempt. And the humble, modest Christian, who desires to slip through the world unnoticed, finds himself set forth as a gazing stock (Heb. 10:35). The bitterness of his wounded feelings obtains no relief, until the Spirit the Comforter brings to his remembrance what his Lord endured, and enables him to count it a privilege to be in this way admitted to the fellowship of his Master's sufferings.

Meditate frequently, O Christian, on the various trials which your Master was put through. Contemplate them with minute attention. Select first one, and then another, of his peculiar sorrows, till each of them successively obtains full consideration. A little sharp experience in yourself will forward progress substantially in this learning. When you are brought to say, "My heart is wounded within me,"—"my soul is exceedingly filled with scorning and contempt,"—"The proud have had me in great derision," you shall be able to enter more fully into communion with a despised and derided Master. Regard, then, your most severe trials as important lessons. Count it a high privilege to be admitted into the sacred sanctuary of the Savior's sympathy. Be there often. Sit in the silence of heart-felt grief at the feet of "The Man of Sorrows." Set his wounds and your own sins fully before you. Meditate on all you learn by the Scriptures he endured for you. Let your imagination picture, as vividly as it may, the "unknown sorrows and sufferings felt by him, but not distinctly known by you," until with increased gratitude, and inflamed affections you "feel the strong attractive power lifting your soul above," and you are able to say from the heart:

> JESUS, I my cross have taken,
>   All to leave and follow thee;
> Naked, poor, despised, forsaken,
>   Thou from hence my all shalt be:
>   Perish ev'ry fond ambition,
> All I've sought, or hop'd, or known;
>   Yet how rich is my condition,
> God and heaven are still my own.
>
> Let the world despise and leave me;
>   They have left my Savior too;
> Human hearts and looks deceive me;
>   Thou art not, like them, untrue;
> And whilst thou shalt smile upon me,
>   God of wisdom, love and might,
> Foes may hate, and friends may scorn me,
>   Show thy face, and all is bright.
>
> Go then, earthly fame and treasure,
>   Come disaster, scorn, and pain,
> In thy service, pain is pleasure,
>   With thy favor, loss is gain.
> I have called thee Abba, Father;
>   I have set my heart on thee;

Storms may howl, and clouds may gather,
All must work for good to me.

Man may trouble and distress me,
'Twill but drive me to thy breast:
Life with trials hard may press me,
Heav'n will bring me sweeter rest.
Oh! 'tis not in grief to harm me,
While thy love is left to me;
Oh! 'twere not in joy to charm me,
Were that joy unmix'd with thee.

Soul, then, know thy full salvation;
Rise o'er sin, and fear, and care;
Joy to find in ev'ry station
Something still to do, or bear.
Think what Spirit dwells within thee,
Think what Father's smiles are thine,
Think that *Jesus* died to save thee,
Child of heaven, canst thou repine?

Haste thee on from grace to glory,
Arm'd by faith, and wing'd by prayer,
Heaven's eternal day's before thee,
God's own hand shall guide thee there
Soon shall close thy earthly mission,
Soon shall pass thy pilgrim days,
Hope shall change to glad fruition,
Faith to sight, and prayer to praise.[11]

---

[11] Litany of the Greek Church.

THE PARTITION OF THE GARMENTS

AND CASTING OF THE LOT

VERSE 18—*They divide My garments among them,
and for My clothing they cast lots.*

THE exact, and minute, fulfillment of the words of Scripture, prove them to have been written by none other than the hand of God. Not one word falls to the ground. Turning to the Gospel of John, chapter 19, how literally is the prophecy of this verse fulfilled! With what emphasis does the apostle add, "*Therefore*, the soldiers did these things!" "Then the soldiers, when they had crucified Jesus, took His garments and made four parts, to each soldier a part, and also the tunic. Now the tunic was without seam, woven from the top in one piece. They said therefore among themselves, "Let us not tear it, but cast lots for it, whose it shall be," that the Scripture might be fulfilled which says: "They divided My garments among them, and for My clothing they cast lots." Therefore the soldiers did these things" (John 19:23, 24).

The clothing with which our blessed Lord was clothed, and the coat, rather the tunic, the garment worn next the skin, corresponding to the shirt of the present times, were seized. He was stripped of everything. The cruel mockers exposed him naked to his enemies. All crucified persons were treated in this humiliating manner. And we may readily conclude that not a single indignity would be spared that could cast contempt and shame, on him who was regarded as worse than the most vile of malefactors.

These words of John narrate the occupation of the soldiers. When the three crosses were firmly erected in their sockets, the active duty of the executioners was finished, and "sitting down they kept watch over him there." Each now was eager to obtain the usual benefit of office, the clothing of the condemned. The miserable thieves perhaps had little to leave. Nothing is said regarding them. But our blessed Lord had been apprehended in his usual apparel. The soldiers now seize upon it. He allows them to do so. There are four soldiers. They make four parts, and divide to every soldier a part. The tunic is not included in this division. It is kept by itself, for, "the tunic was without seam, woven from the top in one piece." This is recorded as if it were not a very common garment. Nor was it. The soldiers therefore envied its possession. They each desired to obtain it. This covetous disposition was overruled by Providence. That God who causes even the wrath of man to praise him, is able to make all his other passions to serve his high purposes as well. This apparently insignificant action, becomes a strong argument for the truth of Scripture to the end of time.

That nicely made attire was doubtless an acceptable garment to the Lord. He would not have it torn. Its seamless unity had wrapped his spotless body. It was well suited to One who, like itself, was a perfect whole. It was not of many colors like that of Joseph—a gaudy assemblage of many shades and patches. It hung upon our Lord, as the church ever should, a seamless thing of one uniform shade. Perhaps it was the cherished gift of some pious disciple. Tradition says it was his mother's present. Such works were peculiar to women in those times. Their book then was the loom: their pencil the needle. Christianity raises woman in the scale of being, and invites her to sit at the Master's feet equally with man. And woman's heart is grateful. The house of God witnesses to her piety, more frequently than to that of man. The associations of benevolence prosper through her instrumentality. She both occupies, and adorns, that position to which the religion of Jesus has called her. Gratefully attached as we behold her to the cause of Christ, now that he is in heaven, woman was equally so to his person when on earth. This seamless tunic had been made by some fair and skillful hand. The receiver of a robe of righteousness, might well return the present of a seamless garment! Fit emblem of grace and gratitude!

What a picture of a sinner's surety did Jesus on the cross of Calvary present! Not a shade, not a stroke was lacking! It was a perfect picture—a complete personification of the curse! The crown of thorns was around his brow; it formed his emblematic title, "KING OF THE CURSE!" His blessed body was exposed to view. Our first parents hid their nakedness amongst the trees of the garden; but Jesus hung exposed upon a tree, and suffered the SHAME OF THE CURSE. His hands and feet were nailed to the wood, he was transfixed immovably by the POWER OF THE CURSE. Scornful taunts and dreadful curses were heaped upon his head; he tasted the BITTERNESS OF THE CURSE. The light of his Father's countenance was withdrawn from him, and he endured the HORRORS OF THE CURSE. Behold this double picture—the transparent representation of the *Curse* and the *Redemption!* Gaze upon it with awe and love, with gratitude and reverence! Christ is dying under your curse, and yet scattering blessings around him! O take them! Receive the gracious exchange! Exclaim with the apostle, "Christ has redeemed us from the curse of the law, having become a curse for us" (Gal. 3:13); and gratefully exult with the prophet, and say, "I will greatly rejoice in the LORD, my soul shall be joyful in my God; for He has clothed me with the garments of salvation, He has covered me with the robe of righteousness" (Isa. 61:10).

The apparently trifling act, of casting the lot for the clothing of our Lord, is most significant. It contains a double lesson. It teaches us how greatly that seamless shirt was valued; how little valued he to whom it had belonged. It seemed to say, "This garment is more valuable than its owner." As it was said of the thirty pieces of silver, "that princely price they set on me;" so may we say regarding the casting of the lot, "How cheaply Christ was held!" The casting of the lot is at all times a solemn matter. It is man's appeal to something above and beyond his own judgment and his own will;

he postpones the decision of reason; he suspends the determination of his own judgment; he divests himself, for a time, of that which constitutes him a rational and intelligent being; he ceases to act as a man, and stands forth as a creature of perplexity, that looks to some other power, or being, to decide for him. Who is that being? What is that power? Those who use the lot alone can tell. The pious Jews of old who had recourse to it by Divine command, answer, "It is the Lord." "The lot is cast into the lap, but its every decision is from the LORD" (Prov. 16:33). Therefore Saul said to the Lord God of Israel, "Give a perfect lot," and Saul and Jonathan were taken, but the people escaped (1 Sam. 14:41). The holy apostles of the ascended Savior answer, "It is the Lord." "And they prayed and said, "You, O Lord, who know the hearts of all, show which of these two You have chosen to take part in this ministry and apostleship from which Judas by transgression fell, that he might go to his own place." And they cast their lots, and the lot fell on Matthias. And he was numbered with the eleven apostles" (Acts 1:24-26). The perplexed Christian answers, "It is the Lord." "I pray earnestly for his direction, and I abide satisfied with his decision." But the worldly man, when using the lot, positively refuses to give this reply. On important occasions, where his interests are at stake, he prudently repudiates the lot; but where matters are nearly on a balance, or where trifles, or amusements only, are concerned, he feels no hesitation to cast the lot, because the results are unimportant. Ask that man, "What is it that decides? What intelligence acts when you lay aside your own?" Whatever reply he may make in an affirmative form, this we may expect to hear in the negative, "It is not the Lord; I had no reference whatever to the Supreme Being when doing this." So decided are multitudes in this opinion, that they deem it a profanity to entertain the idea that God can be concerned in such a matter. But at the same time they admit that there must be something which settles the point; some power, or some non-entity of power, which conducts the uncertainty to certainty. To this they give the name of CHANCE. Of all words in human language that mean nothing, this is the most significant—the most emphatically *nothing*. The Scriptures repudiate it; moralists, philosophers, all thinking men, disown it. Chance is not counted a material thing, and if it belongs to the spiritual world, in which class is it to be ranked? Judgment has been already given, that it is not the Lord; therefore, neither can it be any of the angelic powers, for they are all his servants, and engage in no work but at his bidding. It must, therefore, be counted amongst the spirits of evil, and consequently to be dreaded rather than courted. Chance is, indeed, but another name for Satan: and it makes one shudder to think, that in the casting of their lots, the throwing of their dice, and the shuffling of their cards, men abandon their own reason, and submit to be guided from uncertainty, to certainty, from the unknown commencement of their game to its definite conclusion, by the great enemy of their souls. Therefore, let all Christians abominate these practices; let them cast the evil instruments of such games out of their houses. If they are so ignorant as not to know how to spend their time to better purposes, let them occupy their hands in works of charity, or read the writings of wisdom, or engage each other in edifying conversation. They bear sad testimony against themselves, when they reply that if they leave off these amusements, they shall fall into something worse. Unhappy inhabitants of the earth! Is necessity laid on you to pass only from one evil to another? Are you doomed to no other motion than that which is descending?

God's order is that of progress and advancement; his word charges us to rise from one degree of usefulness to another. It is our privilege, as it is our duty, to abound in good works; to redeem the time because the days are evil; and "whether you eat or drink, or whatever you do, do all to the glory of God" (1 Cor. 10:31). The whole universe of obedient beings, are going forward with their glorious Head. The path of eternity opens before them with new objects, and renewed powers, of light, beneficence, and love. The descending scale is trodden only by the disobedient.

They sink deeper and deeper into everlasting darkness; and the moral distance between them and the children of light is eternally increasing. Covet, then, earnestly the best, the most useful life. Let a heavenly ambition animate your heart. Seek for glory and honor, as well as immortality, Rom. 2:7. Refuse the fleeting pleasure of an hour, the favor of a worldly company, for the joys that never fade, and the approval of the King of heaven.

Though the lot is in this way abused in heathen and Christian countries, yet we must remember that its right and proper use has obtained the sanction of the God of truth. When, therefore, it is employed by the true Christian in a spirit of faith, and when circumstances absolutely require it, he may assure his conscience that he is not out of the path of duty. But he must also bear in mind, how difficult it is to determine the times and seasons. We are all apt to be misled by secret motives and partialities. Instead of a choice entirely free, there is too generally a leaning towards one side. The majority of Christians, therefore, will find the use of the lot, rather a snare, than a help to them, in their progress through life. Almost unconsciously to ourselves, we may be desiring to resort to the lot only to escape our proper responsibility. This is a dangerous state of mind. It directly tests the Most High. He discerns the lurking thought, and will not sanction it with his blessing. He has given us Reason as a monitor, the Word of Truth as a lamp, and has promised the Holy Spirit to be our teacher and guide. Why, then, should we close our ear to unerring instruction? It may be permitted to those who are "strong in faith," and perplexed in extremity of contradicting circumstanced, to resort with a humble and earnest prayer to the lot, as their only remaining door of deliverance from difficulty and dilemma; but Scripture furnishes a safer, and a better, rule; and accompanies it with a gracious promise from the Lord, when it gives this injunction, "In all your ways acknowledge Him, and He shall direct your paths" (Prov. 3:6).

THE IMPORTUNITY

VERSES 19-21—*But You, O LORD, do not be far from Me;*
O My Strength, hasten to help Me! Deliver Me from the sword,
My precious life from the power of the dog.
Save Me from the lion's mouth and from the horns of the wild oxen!

THE intensity of the Savior's anguish, and earnestness of his spirit, in the garden of Gethsemane, are as strikingly denoted by his actions as by his words. A strong and overpowering agitation is evident in *every* movement. He came and went between God and his disciples; his prayers were intensely brief; they were offered at intervals; they were three times repeated; he besought his chosen friends, saying, "Watch with me;" he retired; he prayed; he rose from his knees in the unutterable fullness of his sorrow; he came to his sleeping disciples; he exclaimed, "What? Could you not watch with Me one hour?" (Matt. 26:40); he returned again to the throne of grace; he cast himself upon the ground; his burdened, almost bursting heart, could only say the same words as before—grief had dried up the streams of thought, the flow of words, into only one channel; but even that he did not continue to use. His spirit was disquieted; he had no rest; again he rose from prayer; again he returned to his disciples—still no sympathy, they were all asleep; to them also he spoke in nearly the same terms; they did not know what to say—silence was the only answer he obtained from God and men. "So He left them, went away again, and prayed the third time, saying the same words" (Matt. 26:44). His agony increased; a bloody sweat burst from every pore; great drops fell to the ground. He prayed more earnestly, yet still used the same words; probably he now repeated some of them more than once, and accompanied each burdened word with intervals of heavy groaning, many tears, and strong cries (Heb. 5:7). His perseverance and importunity[12] prevailed; an angel from heaven appeared to him; he felt strengthened with an assurance that his petition was heard; he rose from prayer calm and self-possessed; the agitation was gone; he could now approach his disciples, and compassionately say, "Sleep on now, and take your rest."

While hanging on the cross on Calvary, our Lord obtained deliverance, in like manner, by the power of prayer. Though forsaken, he did not cease to claim assurance with an absent Father; though all was dark and silent, yet he still cried, and prayed, and interceded. As he bowed submissively in the garden, so did he justify God upon the cross; "You turn from me; you are silent, but you are holy," was his immediate acknowledgment. When painfully beset by spiritual foes, when his attention was, as it were, distracted by the malice of men, he returned instantly again to supplication. When obliged to listen to their taunts, when cut to the heart by their reproach, that God would not acknowledge him, he became only more earnest in his appeal, more determined in his grasp of faith, and said, "But You *are* my God from my mother's womb." When exquisitely tormented by the aching, quivering, pierced, flesh, he turned away from the wicked instruments, and recognized the hand of his Father in it all, saying, "YOU have brought me to the dust of death." Yet this, instead of driving him further in heart *from* God, made him press more intensely in spirit *towards* him. As it were, with a holy violence of importunity, that would take no denial, he cried as in these verses, "O LORD, do not be far from Me; O My Strength, hasten to help Me! Deliver Me from the sword, My precious life from the power of the dog. Save Me from the lion's mouth and from the horns of the wild oxen!"

In this powerful and importunate appeal to his Father, it is remarkable to observe in what new forms our Lord presents his

---

[12] Importunity refers to urgent and persistent pleading in prayer.

former petitions. Necessity invents arguments, and renders the mute eloquent. "Though we cannot answer God's logic, yet, with the woman of Samaria, we hope to prevail with the rhetoric of importunity."[13] Our blessed Savior still earnestly desired that same blessing of his Father's presence, for which he had been pleading from the commencement of this psalm. His heart was fully set in him to seek after this; therefore, he never wearied or grew faint. He is at no loss for words, designations, or arguments. In the compass of three short verses, he not only repeats the substance of all that he had said before, in reference to himself, his enemies, and his Father, but he redoubles his designations to each, and interjects forcefully convincing and powerful appeals for deliverance. He addresses his Father by two new names, "O Lord," and "O my strength;" he prays for himself under two new terms, "my soul," and "my precious life." His enemies, whom he had before compared to the bull, the dog, and the lion, he now further sets forth under two new images, "the sword," and "the horns of the wild oxen." At the same time, he throws the whole earnestness of his soul into the four accompanying brief, but rapid, urgent, and vehement entreaties: "Be not far from me—hasten to help me—deliver my soul—save me." This is the strong crying by which our Lord, as it were, lays hold of, and casts himself upon, the heart of his Father, He calls him "Lord," or Jehovah, the self-existent being, who is what he is, in and of himself, altogether independent of the created universe (Exod. 3:14). It is as if he would say, "I am changed as a man; my circumstances, my feelings, are different to what they ever were before; I am dying; but you are the living Lord, the same yesterday, today, and forever. I will, therefore, forget myself and my sad circumstances in thinking of you, O unchangeable Jehovah." Having stated what his Father is in himself, he next

---

[13] Bacon's Christian Paradoxes.

fastens his faith on an appropriate point in that relationship which subsisted between them, and calls him "My strength." Christ possessed almighty power in his own person, but for our sakes he refused to use it. He did not live upon himself, but upon his God. His own resources he would not use, but rather those of his Father, so that to him all the glory may return. His own power he exhibited in prayer, but his Father's power in performance. At his apprehension, when comforting the hearts of his disciples, he might with truth have said, "Do you not think that I cannot now command the angels to destroy this multitude?" But Jesus never sought his own glory; therefore his words were, "Or do you think that I cannot now *pray to My Father, and He will provide Me* with more than twelve legions of angels?" Here, likewise, in his last importunate cry, our Lord appeals to his Father as *his strength;* as one without whom he could and would do nothing; as one who must do all for him, or he must remain as he is.

Secondly, Our Lord's description of himself is twofold, and in nearly synonymous terms, "my soul," and "my life" ("my darling," margin). This latter term is employed also in another psalm to denote the soul, "Rescue [my soul] from their destructions, my precious life from the lions" (Psa. 35:17). Restoration of the soul to spiritual life and joy in the favor and presence of God, and not the life of the body, or its preservation from suffering and death, is the great subject of our Lord's petitions. He teaches us to set our hearts only on that which is of chief importance. He shows us where importunity shall neither be unwarranted nor unavailing. The soul is the great object of concern; it is the darling; the pearl of inestimable worth. If this is lost, all is lost. Therefore Christ, by the hand of faith, deposits his most precious human soul in his Father's care. He is here speaking as the firstborn of that "flock," of which he declares that no man can pluck one out of his Father's hand (John 10:29). He places his soul, his darling, his united one, that immaterial and indestructible part of the human nature which he had taken into union with himself, in the care of his Father's omnipotence; and earnestly appeals to him to deliver it.

Thirdly, The images used to represent our Lord's enemies are "the sword," and "the horns of the wild oxen." Each of these new figures denotes the *piercing* nature of those sufferings, which he was now enduring. The "sword," may be understood of the "wicked," which are "God's sword" (Psa. 17:13). But we may also consider it as denoting "the curse." The powerful word of the Almighty is represented in Scripture under the figure of a "sword" (see Eph. 6:17; Matt. 10:34; Rev. 1:16). The sword of the curse, denounced against every disobedience of the law, had, as it were, been kept in abeyance, and had never fallen on the head of sinful man. That sword had not been drawn from its scabbard. It had slept for four thousand years; but now the Surety of sinners was come; he, on whom the curse should fall, was hanging on the tree; therefore, the rousing call is made, "Awake, O sword, against My Shepherd, against the Man who is My Companion," says the LORD of hosts. "Strike the Shepherd, and the sheep will be scattered" (Zech. 13:7). Christ, the good Shepherd, had now been struck. "He gave his life for the sheep;" but while he resigned his body to death, he deprecated the piercing, separating power of the *"sword"* of the curse upon his soul. The *"horns of the wild oxen."* This figure denotes indomitable power and energy; and such is the characteristic of the wild oxen, or horned rhinoceros. The terms here used, depicts the greatest extremity of danger. Like a man who already felt the horn of the savage animal, who was actually being pierced, who was even now pierced by its sharp and tearing point, Christ prays for deliverance from the terrible power and nearness of his enemies.

The other designations given to his persecutors are the "dog," and the "lion." The latter is a well known scriptural emblem of Satan, the great enemy and destroyer of the soul. The occurrence of this figure, throughout this and other psalms, shows that the roaring lion, against whom we must watch, was prowling around the cross of Christ, seeking to devour and destroy one who thus far had effectually resisted him, steadfast in the faith (1 Pet. 5:8, 9).

The brief but expressive petitions which our Lord employs are extremely importunate. He first reveals the uppermost desire of his soul, "Do not be far from me." God's presence constitutes the deliverance which he desires: this is the only species of relief and comfort which he will accept; therefore, he urges that it may be no longer delayed, "Hasten to help me." He urges his Father with earnestness; he feels that the time is come for the dismissal of his spirit; he cannot bear the thought of breathing it out under desertion—in darkness and distress; he therefore cries, "deliver my soul;" and to express still further the extremity of misery, and, as it were, danger in which he was placed, he represents the jaws of the devourer, as already opened for his instant destruction, and cries, "Save me from the lion's mouth."

Having considered the importunity of our great High Priest, when he "offered up prayers and supplications with vehement cries and tears" (Heb. 5:7), let us improve the subject, Christian readers, to our own practical and spiritual benefit. Let us inquire, first, whether; secondly, on what grounds; and thirdly, to what extent, guilty creatures like us may use urgency in prayer before the great God.

First, *Is it allowable?* To this we must answer in the affirmative. Sinful and fallen as we are, the word of God fully warrants us to speak to him in prayer, not only in the most unreserved, but also in the most importunate, manner. For it is commanded, our Savior encourages it, Scripture furnishes examples, and its absence is complained of.

First, it is commanded. "You who make mention of the LORD, do not keep silent, And give Him no rest…" (Isa. 62:6, 7). "Put Me in remembrance; let us contend together; state your case, that you may be acquitted" (Isa. 43:26). "Come now, and let us reason together, says the Lord" (Isa. 1:18). "Let us therefore come boldly to the throne of grace" (Heb. 4:16).

Secondly, our Savior encouraged it. "The kingdom of heaven suffers violence, and the violent take it by force" (Matt. 11:12). "Strive, (agonize) to enter through the narrow gate" (Luke 13:24). "Ask, and seek, and knock" (Matt. 7:7). He spoke a parable to this end, that men always ought to pray, and not lose heart; that parable was concerning a widow, who by continual coming wearied an unjust judge to decide her cause (Luke 18:1). And on another occasion, when expressly teaching his disciples to pray, he used the picture of one friend begging a loan of bread from another at the unseasonable hour of midnight, and argues in this way, "I say to you, though he will not rise and give to him because he is his friend, yet because of his persistence (importunity) he will rise and give him as many as he needs;" and then practically applying it to the subject of his instruction, he added, "So I say to you, ask, and it will be given to you; seek, and you will find; knock, and it will be opened to you" (Luke 11:1-13). All exhortations to importunity are accompanied by most gracious encouragements. "Let us reason together; your sins shall be as white as snow" (Isa. 1:18). "I am he who blots out your transgressions: put me in remembrance; let us plead together" (Isa. 43:25, 26). Even the saddest of all announcements, "Your iniquities have separated you from your God; and your sins have hidden His face from you, so that He will not hear," is immediately preceded by a most seasonable and encouraging statement, "Behold, the LORD's hand is not shortened, that it cannot save; nor His ear heavy, that it cannot hear;" and even though the sins and the evil condition of the people are fully stated in the chapter, yet it is added that "the Lord wondered that there was no intercessor" (Isa 59:1, 2, 16).

Thirdly, Scripture furnishes examples. James assures us that "the effective, fervent prayer of a righteous man avails much;" and yet at the same time informs us that "the righteous man" whom he makes reference to, "was a man with a nature like ours." "Elijah prayed earnestly that it would not rain; and it did not rain on the land for three years and six months. And he prayed again, and the heaven gave rain" (James 5:16-18). The patriarchs were remarkable for their power and fervency in prayer. Abraham entreated the Lord for Sodom, until he trembled at his own importunity. Had he only persevered in his intercession to the very last, the cities might have been spared for a little longer; for the Lord patiently heard, granted every petition as it was offered, and did not departed until Abraham indicated that he would ask no more (Gen. 18:32, 33).

Jacob was honored by God with the new and honorable name of Israel, because he wrestled in prayer, until he prevailed. Though the angel said, "Let me go," in the vehemence of his spirit he replied, "I will not let You go, unless You bless me" (Gen. 32:26).

Moses interceded with great urgency, for the children of Israel. He was alone on the mountain with God, and beheld the divine wrath, ready to break forth. Though commanded to go down; though a promise was given to make of him a greater and mightier nation: he continued pleading with such earnestness and importunity, that the Lord said, "Let me alone, that I may destroy them" (Exod. 32:10; Deut. 9:14).

Daniel increased in importunity, as he proceeded in his beautiful and instructive prayer. He obtained an immediate answer when his petitions became vehement and pressing, "O Lord, hear! O Lord, forgive! O Lord, listen and act! Do not delay for Your own sake, my God" (Dan. 9:19).

In the gospels we read how the Syro-Phoenician woman prevailed with our Lord by the power of her importunity, and obtained that blessing for her daughter which otherwise she would not have enjoyed. She earnestly besought him, but he answered her not a word. She fell at his feet, but he turned away and passed on. His own disciples entreated him on her behalf, because she cried out after them; but he informed them that his commission was only to the lost sheep of the house of Israel. Still the woman came and worshipped him, saying, "Lord, help me." But he answered, "It is not good to take the children's bread, and throw it to the little dogs." With an earnestness which nothing could abate, and a faith which no objection could stagger, she at once admitted the truth of what he said, and converted it into an argument in her own favor, "Yes, Lord, yet even the little dogs under the table eat from the children's crumbs." Then Jesus exclaimed, "O woman, great is your faith! Let it be to you as you desire" (Matt. 15:22-28; Mark 7:25-30).

Fourthly, The absence of importunity is criticized. When the prophet confesses the great wickedness of the people, that all were as an unclean thing, that even all their righteousness is as filthy rags, and that God had hidden his face from them, and consumed them because of their iniquities, even then he finds fault saying, "And there is no one who calls on Your name, who stirs himself up to take hold of You;" and immediately sets himself with great earnestness to intercessory prayer (Isa. 64).

In various other parts of Scripture the same complaint is expressed or implied, "But you have not called upon Me, O Jacob; and you have been weary of Me, O Israel... Put Me in remembrance; let us contend together" (Isa. 43:22, 26). "I sought for a man among them who would make a wall, and stand in the gap before Me on behalf of the land, that I should not destroy it; but I found no one" (Ezek. 22:30). "He saw that there was no man, and wondered that there was no intercessor" (Isa. 59:16; see also Isa. 9:13; 31:1; Jer. 10:21, 25; Zeph. 1:6; Isa. 41:28).

It is recorded against Asa that in his disease he did not seek the Lord, but the physicians (2 Chron. 16:12); and it is assigned as the reason of Rehoboam's doing evil, "because he did not prepare (or fix) his heart to seek the Lord" (2 Chron. 12:14).

Hosea testifies that the wickedness of the people was highly aggravated by refusing to pray in their afflictions. "They did not cry out to Me with their heart when they wailed upon their beds" (7:14; also verses 7 and 10). With the same earnestness and vehemence, with which they cried out their distresses, so they ought to have called upon their God. But because they refused to do so, the Most High determined, "I will return again to my place, till they acknowledge their offence. Then they will seek my face; in their affliction they will earnestly seek me" (chap. 5:15).

Amos also specifies this as a peculiar feature of the prevailing depravity. He enumerates the various judgments by which God had visited the nation; and five times successively adds, to each of them, "Yet you have not returned to me, says the Lord" (chaps., 4, 6, 8, 9, 10, 11). He complains also that there is no one to raise up the fallen virgin of Israel; yet affectionately entreats them still to seek the Lord, and twice encourages them with the assurance that, if they do so, they shall live (chap. 5:2, 4, 6).

Were we to enter more into God's feelings as a father, and think of his eye resting on this broad earth, where so many millions of his creatures are too impassioned and busy to remember him, we would be better able to understand his complaint of the restraining of prayer, and his delight in those who acknowledge him. Oh how little is God accustomed to hear the voice of earnest, heart-felt, persevering prayer! How continually does the Lord witness our anxieties and exertions spent in vain attempts to extricate ourselves, and bring about that deliverance which he is able in a moment to grant in answer to prayer. Men may be brought to their wit's end, and never think of calling upon God; yet if, even then, they cry to the Lord, he will bring them out of their distresses (Psa. 107:27, 28). In every circumstance and trial of life—whether in the extremity of homeless wandering, of poverty and hunger (vs. 5); in prison and cruel bondage (vs. 10, 14); in disease, languishing sickness, and when at the point of death (vs. 18); on the stormy ocean and in the threatening storm (vs. 25); or when crops fail, and famine feeds on once fruitful fields (vs. 34, 38); let men but then turn to the Lord with strong crying and tears in all these calamities, and they shall find that he is very pitiful and of tender mercy (James 5:11). Whoever is wise, and will observe the various turns of this changeful life, shall learn from them all, the loving-kindness of the Lord (Psa. 107:43). Hezekiah's prayer was answered when he wept bitterly (Isa. 38:3, 5). Even the wicked Ahab was pitied, when he humbled himself before the Lord (1 Kings 21:27-29). And the idolatrous Ninevites were accepted, when they cried mightily unto God (Jonah 3:8-10). Do not let, then, the greatest of your earthly trials, or even the remembrance of your foulest sins, close up your heart in despondency, or prevent you from confessing your guilt, bewailing your condition, and fervently, and perseveringly, imploring mercy from the Father of mercies.

Secondly, if it is a commanded duty, for sinners to approach the God of heaven in prayer, with importunate petitions, we must next inquire, *On what grounds?* First, we answer, it must *not* be on the ground of any claim which we possess to mercy, or of any merit which our tears, or prayers, or remorse over sin, can furnish. Full consciousness of unworthiness produces a sorrow which, however great, can never be more than just. We must be entirely driven out of that all confidence in ourselves; be brought to see that we deserve only ruin and condemnation; and so be taught to cast ourselves simply on the mercy and goodness of Jehovah. Instead of extenuating our guilt, and using mild and softening terms, we will honestly confess all its aggravations, and cast the multitude of our sins upon the immeasurable mercies of the Most High; we will use this extraordinary, but prevailing argument, "Pardon my iniquity, for it is great" (Psa. 25:11). Secondly, it must be solely on the ground of God's mere mercy and goodness. Leaving ourselves wholly to his disposal; acknowledging that though the severest judgments come forth against us, they are only what we deserve; we must cast our care on the heart of a Father, saying with David, "I am in great distress. Please let me fall into the hand of the LORD, for His mercies are very great" (1 Chron. 21:13). This is what the Ninevites did. And never was an appeal made to the heart of God, without success.

But, thirdly, the Divine mercy has been revealed only in Christ Jesus. That sacrifice which satisfied the justice, has fully exhibited the goodness, of God. The Lord has come forth to man, in a full, but peculiar measure, of mercy. He who would approach his Creator, overlooking the atonement and propitiation by the blood of Jesus, is guilty of despising that very way which he professes to seek. "There is no other name under heaven given among men by we must be saved," but the name of Jesus Christ (Acts 4:12). It was therefore with earnest care that our Lord instructed his disciples to present all their prayers to God, "in his name" (John 16:23, 24). This expression signifies for his sake, and on his authority. Too commonly it is limited to the former sense. But our gracious Redeemer means that we should apply to the treasury of heaven, as beggars would at a bank, in the name of an individual whose credit is unlimited. Having taken the bankrupt name, he gives us his own instead. Therefore the apostle exhorts us to "do all in the name of the Lord Jesus" (Col. 3:17). "To give thanks always for all things to God the Father in the name of our Lord Jesus Christ" (Eph. 5:20). And our Lord assures us, "Whatever you ask the Father in my name, he will give you" (John 16:23).

It is, then, on the ground of our Surety's merits, that we must present all our petitions. The very fact of the existence of a surety, a freely provided surety, proves the goodness of the great Creditor, in a manner which even the immediate discharge of the debt could not have demonstrated. We might have supposed, that he had easily pardoned that, by which he was no loser. But the providing of an atonement, shows that a great loss had been suffered by sin; and the sacrificing of His own Son to accomplish that atonement, exhibits God as a double loser, in effecting the salvation of man. The goodness of God, therefore, stands out to view in magnificent prominence. We hear it uttered by the loud voice from Calvary, with an emphasis that should rouse the attention of the dead, and impart eternal stability to the faith of the living. The goodness of the Divine Father, exhibited in the sacrifice of his own Son, is that alone to which the Eternal Spirit directs our thoughts; on this he fixes our hopes; here he bids us to cast, without the shadow of a misgiving or a fear, all our cares and anxieties. Therefore the apostle demands, "Do you despise the riches of his goodness?" Do you not know that, "the goodness of God" is designed to lead you "to repentance?" (Rom. 2:4). Since God, then, has exhibited such love, take heed that you "continue in his goodness" (Rom. 11:22). Never allow dark and despairing thoughts to take possession of your heart. "The goodness of God endures continually" (Psa. 52:1). Let your confidence in, and your engagements with, that goodness, be therefore continually exercised. When Moses prayed, "Show me your *glory*;" the Lord answered, "I will make all my *goodness* pass before you" (Exodus 33:19). The glory of God is his goodness. When the seraphim praise the high and lofty One, they say, "The whole earth is full of his *glory*" (Isa. 6:3). And when the psalmist praises him, he exclaims, "The earth is full of his *goodness*" (Psa. 33:5). When Paul looks forward to the inheritance above, he names it, "An exceeding and eternal weight of *glory*" (2 Cor. 4:17). And when David expatiates on the same enlivening theme, he cries, "Oh, how great is Your *goodness*, which You have laid up for those who fear You" (Psa. 31:19).

"In the divine nature," says a profound writer,[14] "both religion and philosophy have acknowledged goodness in perfection; wisdom or providence comprehending all things; and absolute sovereignty or kingdom. In aspiring to the throne of *power*, angels transgressed and fell. In presuming to come within the oracle of *knowledge*, man transgressed and fell. But in pursuit towards the likeness of God's *goodness*, or love, neither man, nor spirit, has ever transgressed, or shall transgress. The Devil being an angel of light, affected power. Man being endowed with power, affected light or knowledge. Intruding into God's secrets or mysteries, he was rewarded with a further removing or estranging from God's presence. But as to God's

---

[14] Bacon.

goodness there is no danger in contending for, or advancing towards, a likeness thereof. In that point we can commit no excess."

This leads us, Thirdly, to inquire *to what extent may a sinner, being allowed on these good grounds, proceed in importunity of prayer?* We answer, he can commit no excess. The further he proceeds, the greater will the goodness of the Most High appear to him; the more he entrusts himself to it, the more will it uphold him. Importunity in prayer, is a pressing into the goodness of God. Instead of regarding him as either unwilling or unable to help, it exhibits him as ready as he is all-powerful. "Those who honor me, I will honor." The highest honor we can pay to God is to honor him with our confidence. Apart from this, mere outward services are destitute of their only acceptable ingredient, the homage of the heart. Confidence, then, in the goodness of God, if it exists at all, ought to exist in proportion to the amount of his goodness. There can be evidently no limit to the measure of our trust, except that which is furnished by that on which we trust. If that is small, our confidence must be small. If that is unlimited, our confidence in it ought to be unlimited. See how fully the patriarch Job understood the grounds of his confidence, and the unlimited extent to which he might, as it were, trespass on the goodness of the Lord. "Oh, that I knew where I might find Him, that I might come to His seat! I would present my case before Him, and fill my mouth with arguments. I would know the words which He would answer me, and understand what He would say to me. Would He contend with me in His great power? No! But He would take note of me. There the upright could reason with Him, and I would be delivered forever from my Judge" (Job 23:3-7). The "righteous" are those who present themselves before God in the imputed righteousness of Christ. All their reasons and arguments are based on the merits of their Surety. They wrestle in his name against their sins, their doubts, and fears. In his strength they fight against all the temptations and evil suggestions of the enemy of their souls; and even when afflicted with desertion and darkness, when the light of God's countenance is withdrawn, they still anchor themselves on a withdrawing God, and presume upon that great goodness which, as it gave Christ, will also with him freely give all things (Rom. 8:32). Like the psalmist, he humbly argues with the Lord, "What profit is there in my blood, when I go down to the pit? Will the dust praise You? Will it declare Your truth?" (Psa. 30:9). With the prophet also he adds, "Righteous are You, O LORD, when I plead with You; yet let me talk," or reason the case, "with You about Your judgments" (Jer. 12:1).

It is then only on the ground of the Savior's atoning sacrifice, that we can either offer the smallest petition, or rise to any degree of confidence in presenting it. In using the Savior's name, however, we shall do him great dishonor, if we do not place the fullest confidence in his acceptance with his Father. Were we invoking the name of a saint or an angel, there would be great cause for fear and hesitation. But not so when we employ the name of God's own and beloved Son. All that God has belongs to him; every thing that God can give, is open to his use; and it proves that we have little confidence either in God the Father, or in Christ the Son, when we address the one in the name of the other, and yet doubt whether a blessing will be given. You may object and say, "I do not doubt either God's willingness, or Christ's merits, but I doubt my own worthiness to partake of the benefits of his righteousness." We reply, You have no right to doubt your own worthiness. You ought to be as positively certain of your unworthiness, as you are of your own existence. Your worthiness, or unworthiness, is not a matter of opinion. It is a revealed truth that you are altogether unworthy. The very fact of a provided surety-righteousness implies it. And it is with the full consciousness of your own unworthiness, that we would press you to cast yourselves directly upon the surety-righteousness, as an all-sufficient and all-prevailing argument with God. Again it may be objected, "I neither doubt the goodness of God, nor my own unworthiness; but I do not know if what I pray for is agreeable to the will of God; how, then, can I be importunate?" This is an important matter. We shall consider the things which may be asked in prayer, under three heads—First, those in which the will of God is eternally and immutably the same. Second, those concerning which he has revealed his will particularly and expressly in the Holy Scriptures. And third, those which are circumstantial and personal. In regard to the first things, there should not exist any doubt in our minds, when we pray to God for them. The will of God must unchangeably and eternally be fixed on holiness. Whatever then is connected with honoring God's name as holy, or the sanctification of your own heart, should be the object of your fervent faith, your most ardent prayers. The hand of the diligent makes rich; holiness is the gold of heaven; and in proportion to your diligence, perseverance, and earnestness, in prayer, so will be your increase in eternal wealth. Secondly, those things which God has revealed: as for instance, that his kingdom shall come, and that the knowledge of the Lord shall cover the earth; being, with other truths, positively revealed, there is as little room to doubt regarding their ultimate fulfillment, as there is great room to pray for their speedy accomplishment. The Lord himself has appointed prayer to be the preceding means, "I will also let the house of Israel inquire of Me to do this for them" (Ezek. 36:37). To encourage this inquiry, the Lord condescends to say, "Ask Me of things to come concerning My sons; and concerning the work of My hands, you command Me" (Isa. 45:11). And our Lord teaches us to pray, "Your kingdom come. Your will be done on earth as it is in heaven" (Matt. 6:10).

In reference, therefore, to these two great divisions of things that may be prayed for, there ought to exist in the mind, the fullest assurance that they shall be granted; not because we pray for them, but because they are agreeable to the will of God; and because we know them to be so, we pray that his will in all things may be done, through Jesus Christ our Savior. Importunity here, therefore, may be to any extent, and can commit no excess.

In regard to the third division, namely, those petitions which are suggested by our own personal and peculiar circumstances; since we do not know the will of God, we can pray in faith, and with importunity, only when the desire itself is holy, and when we submit resignedly to the unknown will, whatever it may be. Our Lord in Gethsemane exhibited the fullest resignation, in harmony with the most earnest importunity. In the same way, it is necessary to our submission, as to our fervency, that we believe God's will to be good—"good-will towards men." In mentioning, therefore, any material matter in prayer, we must leave it entirely and confidently to the good will of God. We must also settle it in our minds, whether it is indispensable to our salvation. It may be good for us that we should never obtain it. In distresses and difficulties, (for it grieves the heart of our Father to witness the distress of his creatures) we may spread our case with great freedom before the Lord; casting ourselves upon his goodness in Christ, we may use great importunity in appealing for deliverance. But as we do not know what is best for ourselves, even in such cases, we seek out our own happiness, as well as discharge a necessary duty, when we renounce our own wishes, saying, "not my will, but yours be done." In regard, however, to spiritual blessings, in which we positively know that God is glorified, as well as our own sanctification promoted, we do not need to use a reserving clause. To say in such prayers for spiritual blessings, "not my will but yours be done," is to imply that our desire is to attain holy graces, but that God's will is to deprive us of them. When we say spiritual blessings, we do not allude to the *gifts,* but to the *graces* of the Spirit. The former are given variously to every man as the Lord the Spirit sees fit to minister. But in regard to the graces—love, joy, gentleness, self-control, etc., against which there is no law human or divine, there is no limit to the bounty of God, and there should be no limit to our requests. When we pray for these, we should not entertain any doubts as to their being given to us. In proportion to the value we attach to them, and the fullness of our desire for their possession, so will be our earnestness and importunity in prayer to obtain them. To this, however, we are brought only by the Spirit of grace and of supplications (Zech.

12:10). "Likewise the Spirit also helps in our weaknesses. For we do not know what we should pray for as we ought, but the Spirit Himself makes intercession for us with groaning's which cannot be uttered. Now He who searches the hearts knows what the mind of the Spirit is, because He makes intercession for the saints according to the will of God," Rom. 8:26, 27.

The greatest of all spiritual and eternal blessings, is the presence of God. On this our heart's strongest desires ought to be fixed. This is the subject which warrants and rewards the most vehement importunity. Even in the greatest darkness of soul, even while the countenance of God is withdrawn, nothing can honor God more as a Creator, or gratify his heart more as a Parent, than that we should make the light of his countenance, the first and last object of our desires, and be restless and unhappy so long as it is turned away from us. Indeed, not to be importunate after this, proves that we are destitute of the feelings of a child, and shows that we possess little or no love to our heavenly Father. It was this that nearly burst the filial heart of Christ, in the garden, and on the cross. His whole soul desired to enjoy the smile of his Father's countenance. He knew the goodness of his Father, and he knew that the further he pressed into it, the more of it he would obtain.

In regard, then, Christian reader, to the extent to which you may use importunity in prayer, here is the greatest of all spiritual and eternal blessings open to you. "The LORD God is a sun and shield; the LORD will give grace and glory; no good thing will He withhold from those who walk uprightly" (Psa. 84:11). The Lord will bestow HIMSELF. Ask largely, and you shall obtain largely; pray earnestly, and you shall receive immediately. God is not willing to hide his face forever from you. His intention is this, "I will return again to My place till they acknowledge their offense. Then they will seek My face" (Hosea 5:15). "Seek the Lord," then, "and his strength; seek his face evermore" (Psa. 105:4). Strive to be able to say, "When You said, "Seek My face," my heart said to You, "Your face, LORD, I will seek" (Psa. 27:8). Though enveloped in thick darkness, remember that "The Lord is able to do for you exceeding abundantly above all that you can ask or think" (Eph. 3:20). If, then, like your great High Priest, you are in darkness and deserted, continue to pray for the return of God's presence to your soul; there is no petition can you present that is more agreeable to his ear, or more conducive to your own salvation. Be encouraged, then, to imitate this example, by considering that he who left it is now interceding at the right hand of the Majesty on high. Come, therefore, boldly to the throne of grace (Heb. 4:16); and do not cast away your confidence, which has great reward (Heb. 10:35), "for we have become partakers of Christ, if we hold the beginning of our confidence steadfast to the end" (Heb. 3:14).

Keep close, then, under the sheltering wing of Jesus; "in whom we have boldness and access with confidence through faith in him" (Eph. 3:12). Begin, continue, and end all your hopes in Him; place the fullest confidence in his acceptance with his Father; draw out all your arguments from the treasury of his righteousness; present them without doubting; urge them without hesitation. "The Lord is well pleased for his righteousness' sake." Bring this forth, then, as your strong reason; and with ceaseless importunity, as you value your own salvation, plead it before God. Will he plead against you with his great power? No. He will put strength in you to persevere, until, like your Lord, you are able to exclaim, "You have answered me."

CHRIST ON THE CROSS IN LIGHT

THE DELIVERANCE

VERSE 21—*You have answered me.*[15]

IMPORTUNITY prevails with God. He that will not be satisfied without the blessing, shall be satisfied with it. Ask, and you shall have; seek, and you shall find; knock, and you shall gain admittance. Christ spoke a parable to this end, that men ought always to pray and not to lose heart. He here proves the truth of his own teaching. During this whole morning of persecution, his mind was stayed on God. Throughout the period of desertion, his soul earnestly sought the comforting presence of his Father. In the heaviest gloom of the darkness, he did not yield, but still pressed forward in spirit to the light. Now the light has come—the true light of a Father's love—a Father's countenance of gracious approval. God withstands his pleading no longer. Though he does not grant it to him because he is a friend—a son—yet because of his importunity, he gives him whatever he needs. All that the holy Christ needs, or desires, is centered in God himself, "You are my life, my light, my peace, my bliss, my all; your smile is my sunshine; your approval my

---

[15] For the transposition here adopted, see Bishop Horsley. Ainsworth, in his Annotations, says, "You have answered me;" a speech of faith inserted in his prayers, therefore next follows thanksgiving. "*Answering*" is here used for *safe delivering upon prayer*, as the Chaldee translates, "*have accepted my prayer.*"

The psalm is thus divided into two parts. The first in darkness, and the second in light. The one all sorrow, the other all gladness; the one descriptive of the sufferings of Christ, the other of the glory that should follow (1 Pet. 1:11); the one expressing Christ's endurance of the cross, the other the joy that was set before him (Heb. 12:2).

prosperity; your love my reward; your glory my crown; without you I am poor; and with you rich, take what you will away." Now all this has come. The tide of eternal love flows in full current into the heart of Christ. The stream of his love had never ceased; as a river to the sea, it had still sent its waters to their source. Christ had come forth from the bosom of the Father; throughout life he enjoyed uninterrupted communion with him—conscious possession of a home in his heart. On the cross, however, nothing but a dark thick cloud could be discerned. His affections rose up as before, but there was no return as formerly—no response. The arrow of prayer seemed to be lost in the depths of that cloud, yet he believed that his own Father lived beyond; he still felt persuaded that Father loved him; he still believed that the door of his Father's house would not always be shut against him. Now his faith is victorious. God, as it were, addresses him, as he himself did the Syro-Phoenician woman, "O Son, great is your faith! Let it be to you as you desire." Christ's importunity had said, as it were, "I will have light;" and the Hearer of prayer answered, "You shall have light." Christ's strong love could not, and would not, bear being turned away; it indirectly said, "I will never rest until I enjoy communion with you again." The Father replied, "You shall be admitted to the fullness of joy in my presence." And here the pleading Savior exclaims with gratitude and exultation of heart, "You have answered me."

What a relieving view this presents of the dark hour of the crucifixion! It removes the painful doubt; it shows us that the Son of God did not depart out of this life under the hidings of his Father's countenance. Disquietude and anguish of spirit were dispelled; every troubled feeling was hushed to repose; the lowering clouds of evening were dissipated, and the Sun of Righteousness set in the calm effulgence of pure and glorious light.

What an example of the power of fervent, persevering prayer is here set before us! The advocate had urged every plea, had addressed God by every name and character, had set forth the necessities of his case In the most urgent manner, had returned again and again with protest, and appeal, and argument, and entreaty, and at last had set himself as an importunate petitioner that would take no further denial. This prevails. God grants his request to the very utmost. "The kingdom of heaven suffers violence, and the violent take it by force" (Matt. 11:12). Like Jacob of old, the Savior said, "I will not let You go, unless You bless me" (Gen. 32:26). And he was blessed; all his petitions were granted; the whole tone of feeling and of desire is altered. Who can express what the Savior must have felt? The psalm changes from sorrow to joy. "You have answered me," is the first cry of victory. It is not, "I have prevailed; I have conquered;" but it is, "You have heard me." The honor is all given to God. He that sits on the throne is true and faithful. To Him be all the glory!

Let the desponding Christian take courage. Deliverance shall be sent. Light must soon arise. "In due season you shall reap if you do not lose heart." Beware of timid thoughts and anxious fears. Lay hold on God's strength; "He never said to any of the seed of Jacob, 'Seek me in vain'" (Isa. 45:19). God is the hearer of prayer. He will in no way cast out those who come to him in his Son. Let this successful example of that Son be ever before your mind. Like him, be unwearied in supplication. As he is your best pattern, so let him be your only ground of confidence, in prayer. Let the word, or doctrine, of his surety-ship and righteousness abide in you. His word will purify your desires. Longings after things that are holy, just, and good, will be kindled by the Spirit of holiness within your heart. The earnestness of your petitions will be expended on heavenly realities; and if his word in this way abides in you, you shall ask WHAT YOU WILL, and it shall be done for you (John 15:7).

How powerful is the *will*, for good or evil! The sinner *will not* abandon his pleasures, he refuses to receive correction; he will go on, though it be to destruction; and he shall go. The true Christian, however, is one who is *made willing* by the Spirit of God, to do the very reverse. He is willing to abandon sin; he hates it; he *will* seek to be pure, he *will* strive to be holy, he *will* "follow hard after God;" and he shall find him; and he shall be sanctified.

The promise made by the Father to the Son is, "[Your] people shall be *willing* in the day of thy power" (Psa. 110:3). Until God's Power, even his Holy Spirit, come into the heart, man is willing to walk only in the way of that heart. His will goes forth spontaneously, to the things that please him. It does so naturally, and without an effort. When therefore the Quickener enters, in the day of his power, he first works in the man to will, and then to do, for God's good pleasure (Phil. 2:13). This is a rational mode. It is exactly according to the manner in which we influence our fellow men. Our own will being directed towards an object, in which we wish their assistance, we first set ourselves to gain their will, their consent, then their co-operation. To this end we show them how good, desirable, and advantageous, the object is. We remove their prejudices. We succeed in turning the full tide of their inclination towards that, which they at first, perhaps, regarded with aversion. Our end is gained. They become one with us in spirit. So is it with the work of the Spirit of God. He finds the *will* of every man turned away from the Creator—fixed on self and worldly objects. He seeks to change that will, and therefore shows how good God is, how advantageous his service, how dangerous the course we are pursuing. He desires us to turn to God, and he shows God turned towards us. He commands us to love our heavenly Father, and he proves how much he loves us. He enjoins us to serve God, and he reveals him serving our cause, and securing our best interests, in the person of his own Son. Apart from Jesus, the Spirit of God does nothing. From him, all the lessons of heavenly wisdom are derived. The sufferings and death of Christ in our stead form the grand arguments by which the Spirit of God influences the human will.

Nor is the mode of this operation of the Lord the Spirit, either mysterious or extravagant. He deals with our souls in a distinct and intelligible manner. He influences our mind by the truths contained in the Holy Scriptures. When we open these treasures of wisdom, he opens our hearts to believe that there is reality in what we read. He teaches our consciences to give every word its own pointed meaning, and a personal application to our own hearts and lives. For instance, when we read of the love of Christ, he enables us to say, "It is true; therefore he loved me and gave himself for me." When we read, "Be holy in all your conduct," he inclines us to add, "It is right; therefore I will seek to be altogether holy." How different this to the listless manner in which we before traced the sacred page! This is life: it is reality; it is intelligence; it is just what ought to be. It is not the formal perusal of one chapter after another; promises, threats, commandments, sounding in our ears in one unbroken and unmeaning monotony. It is the spirit of the reader catching (rather caught by) the Spirit of the Author, and entering into each varied sentiment, with all the zest and animation of an understanding intellect, an approving conscience, and an obedient heart. This makes man a new creature towards God. This is his being born again, born of the Spirit, "begotten by the truth." As says James, "Of his own will He brought us forth by the word of truth." As Peter also, "Since you have purified your souls in obeying the truth... having been born again, not of corruptible seed, but incorruptible, through the word of God..." Our blessed Savior likewise in his intercession for the infant church prays in this way; "Sanctify them by Your truth. Your word is truth." And it appears to be in answer to this solemn prayer, that in the first council held at Jerusalem, the Hebrew testified regarding the Gentile converts saying, "God made no distinction between us and them, purifying their hearts by faith."

What a deliverance is this! The man is passed from darkness into light. The end is gained. He has become one in spirit with the great Spirit. He now wills to do what God would have him. He wills to be holy, to be like God. Through every trial of prosperity and adversity he still desires the same thing. Though providential dispensations change, and sun and storms alternate, he keeps on his way, following hard in spirit after the source of light and love. His will, in believing prayer, prevails with God, because it is in agreement with the will of God. And, like the Savior, he issues forth from the darkest cloud, exclaiming, "You have answered me."

The natural man, in his unconverted state, is thus made a conscious example of the power of the Divine Will. He is changed into a new creature. He experiences a spiritual resurrection. He passes from death to life. As in this change, we witness an exemplification of the power of the will of the Holy Spirit, on unbelieving man; so we are permitted to witness, in the development and progress of this new spiritual life, instances of the power of the believer's will, on a humbly accommodating and prayer-hearing God. The simplest prayer is a sublime mystery. The feeble voice of a child, influences the great God. A burdened, conscience-stricken, offender, who strikes his chest, and says, "God be merciful to me a sinner," moves the heart of his Creator, and changes his dealings towards him. "Prayer moves the arm that moves the world." From where does this come? The secret of the mystery consists in this, that prayer is a spiritual act. It is the operation of the Spirit of God. No heavenly desires, no confessions of sin, no breathings after God, can rise in any human heart, without the direct and immediate agency of the Holy Ghost. He works in every man. His visits are witnessed in every conscience. Without him we are not only asleep, we are dead in soul. If, then, the Spirit is the author of prayer, it necessarily follows that all his suggestions therein will be according to the will of God (Rom. 8:27). It is obvious that he cannot, and will not, inspire any desire but what is in full accordance with the Holy Mind. Our will, then, in prayer, is the will of the Spirit of God; the object to which our desires are drawn, is the object which God desires; the strength of our affection towards it, is the power of the Spirit working in us; the earnest importunity which we exercise in prayer, is the expression of the intensity of the Holy Spirit's desire for the accomplishment of the object. The success which attends believing and fervent prayer, is the crowning act of Him who begins, continues, and ends, all good works in us. The mystery, then, is explained. Prayer prevails, because God inspires it. He works in us to ask, because he purposes to perform. The prayer that precedes, is as much his work, as the blessing which follows is his gift. Prayer is itself part of the blessing. But someone may object, "It is presumptuous to say, or imagine, that all our prayers are inspired by the Holy Ghost." But remember, we now speak only of true, spiritual prayer. Alas, the great majority of our prayers are but collections of words. To read over a page or two of devotional expressions, is not prayer; to pour forth an extemporaneous address to God, is not prayer; these may bear the appearance, but we now speak of the reality of prayer. True prayer is the utterance of the heart—the soul's meeting with its God. The sacred term of *prayer* ought never to be applied to any thing besides. When, then, we state the scriptural position, that the heart is dead towards God, and not only cannot utter, but has nothing within it to utter before him, we must arrive at the conclusion, that wherever, in the universal family of man, there is a conscience partially, or fully, enlightened, a heart faintly stirring towards God, or earnestly inquiring after him, that conscience, and that heart, derive their light, and their desires, only and entirely from the Spirit of light and life, of grace and of supplications. Presumption, then, lies not in saying, "You, Lord, have also done all our works in us;" but in imagining that we possess the good in ourselves. The deepest humiliation leads us to say, "I cannot think a right thought of myself." The presumption consists in saying, "I do not need the Spirit of God to assist me to pray." (See Jude 20; Eph. 6:18).

Reader, this is a solemn heart-searching truth. O how it condemns our cold, formal, heartless, prayers. These never reach the ear of the Lord God of Sabaoth. If you would prevail in prayer, your whole heart must be engaged in your petitions. Be in earnest; let your application to the true Physician be as much a reality, as is your consultation with him who relieves your bodily diseases. Under a sense of pain and agony, your heart is not listless, nor your words unmeaning. Realize to yourself that the Lord is a living, acting, being. If you can rest quiet under trouble, without casting it upon God; if you can lie under the hidings of his face, and not feel the most overpowering anxiety to be restored to favor; it is only natural and proper that you should remain burdened and uncomforted. To relieve you from sorrow, while in such a state of mind, would prove your ruin. If the rod does not bring the child to a right mind, its removal is more fraught with danger than its continuance. The wise parent perseveres with the chastisement, until it accomplishes the desired end; his severity is the fruit of judicious love; he is more eager to withdraw the infliction, than to administer it; he would not continue it one moment longer than is absolutely necessary.

If, then, O Christian, you are now lying under the hidings of your heavenly Father's countenance, do not desist from prayer. Again, and again, and again, return; seek opportunities of pouring out your heart—your whole heart; do not let one thought, or feeling, or desire, remain withheld. Seek also public means of grace; let your confessions and supplications be intermingled with those of the worshipping assembly; at all times, and in all places, however your hands may be occupied, let your heart be engaged with God. Unknown to all around you, let quick, successive, earnest, petitions, carry your spirit in silence, from the presence of men, to the presence-chamber of the great King. Remember, there is ONE standing there, ready to present your petition; put it into his hand, he can fully sympathize in the most delicate feeling, the most pressing need, the most unutterable anguish. Give many petitions, and furnish many arguments, that he may have many to present in your name; be importunate with him, that he may be able to carry forward your importunity to his Father. Remember, that he intercedes in your name, when you pray in his; those petitions alone, rise to heaven, which are presented in his name; no blessings descend to us, but those to which the great High Priest attaches our names. Meditate much on this point; it will give you clear views in reference to prayer; it will strengthen you to be humbly bold, and earnest, and importunate. Christ gives you his name to use, and you must give him yours to present; Christ gives you his righteousness as your plea and argument, and you must return it to your Advocate as the only plea to be urged on your behalf; Christ gives you his Holy Spirit, and you must give him your whole spirit; for the worshippers whom he regards, are those who pray in spirit and in truth. Remember, that you are permitted to draw upon the Eternal Bank only in the name of your Surety; and that to benefit you, he also must draw expressly in your name. You must therefore pray, not in general and indefinite terms, but in special and particular requests. You must state your case, its name and nature, with its every modification of circumstance; you must confess your utter inability to help yourself, and your great unworthiness that he should do any thing for you: you must specify the particular *blessing* you wish, the *amount* of it that is necessary, and the *time* by which it must be received. According to your urgency of petition and strength of faith, so shall it be done to you. The great and gracious Surety has placed his own interest at the treasury of heaven to your use; with the most tender consideration he has put a letter of unlimited credit into your hands, signed and sealed with his own blood; he has said, "If my words abide in you, you will ask what you desire, and it shall be done for you" (John 15:7). Here is the ground and warrant of your request. It is sufficient for your case, even though it were ten times more sad, sinful, and insupportable. On this ground it is impossible to use too great a boldness of petition, too vehement an urgency of prayer. It is only, if the words of Christ are kept in remembrance, so as to regulate our wills and desires, that we have any right to expect a blessing, or even to ask for its bestowal. The carnal mind thinks itself entitled, from a partial view of this passage, to ask for the gratification of its desires, for whatever things it desires; and when these are withheld, the father of lies tempts it to turn infidel, and to discard the Bible, as a book of deceptive promises. But the regenerate heart seeks to have its desires sanctified, and fixed only on the things which God approves, and then it knows it cannot covet too large a portion of spiritual blessings. This is what the Savior means when he says, "If my words abide in you." His "words" contain a declaration of the name of him to whom we are to approach; that name is THE FATHER; his "words" inform us that the Father's favor is life, and that the Father's presence is salvation; his "words" direct us to make God the sum and center of our desires, teach us that seeking after him is our first duty, and declare that apart from his blessing, nothing can be really desirable or beneficial.

If, then, these words abide in your heart, they will actuate and govern all its desires; your will shall be subdued to the will of God; your deliberate and principal desire will be to enjoy his love, to be purified for his communion, and to be wholly and completely his, in soul and body, in time and eternity. Having in this way your whole mind directed to one object, namely, the Divine will: you may ask what you will in reference to its accomplishment, and it shall be done for you. The more petitions you present in this way, the more answers shall be bestowed. The greater urgency you use, the sooner shall you be relieved. The more pressing and importunate you are on this ground, for immediate audience, and instant deliverance, the more certain, and prompt, will be your success. This was how Jesus prayed, who is the High Priest of our profession. What is the subject of his prayer? What is the ever recurring petition which he presents? Is it to be taken from the cross, to be removed from under the affliction? Is it to have the pains of his body mitigated—his revilers blasted—or his own death prevented? By no means. On none of these is the filial heart of Jesus set. The full current of his thoughts flows towards one object—the favor of God, and the return of conscious enjoyment of that favor. Was it not this which extracted the bitter cry, "My God, My God, why have You forsaken me?" Is it not his twice repeated entreaty? "Be not far from me." Does he not press himself, as it were, upon his Father's attention, as one that belonged to him, and for whom it was his duty to care, saying, "I was cast upon You from birth?" And when the light returns, and peace dispels the sorrow, what is the argument by which he seeks to influence his Church's gratitude, and excite her praises of his Father? Is it not because he had "not hid his face from him?" This was the pearl of price for which the God-man cast aside every other consideration. Pains, sorrows, grief's, enemies, tortures, and death itself, were all as nothing in his estimation, when compared with the light of his Father's countenance. This was worthy of Christ: his filial heart fastened its affections on a Father's love. He felt death in every thing else. He never would, he never could, rest contented until he enjoyed it again. Alas! It is our sin and shame, that this is not the first and highest object of our desires. Not to be importunate after *this,* is a spiritual crime of a grievous nature. If a justly offended earthly father, turned from us, until we confessed our offence, and implored reconciliation, is it not adding sin to sin, if we delay our acknowledgment, and feel indifferent to his friendship? Does it not prove that we are fast sinking in the moral scale, becoming hardened and insensible to every finer feeling of our nature, if we can contentedly pass year after year without caring for a Father's love, or imploring his Fatherly pronouncement of blessings over us? How much more guilty, and lost in depravity of feeling, is it to continue our impenitence and disregard, in the face of daily proofs of that Father's love and kindness? Should he prevent our painful confession and acknowledgment, by overtures of friendship; should he himself anticipate our request, by entreating us to be reconciled; and should he try to effect our reformation and secure our love, by a frank and generous declaration of his forgiveness, how hard, stubborn, and seared must the heart be that rejects him! Yet this is what we do against God. He is our Father; he is the Parent we have offended, yet it is he that begins the reconciliation (2 Cor. 5:19, 20). It is his bounty that supplies us every moment, and his heart that is wounded by our indifference and unconcern. See then what necessity there is for your instantaneous repentance, and immediate confession and supplication. Learn what enormity it is, not to be anxious and importunate to enjoy the light of the Father's countenance. O man! Gather here all your thoughts—here center your affections—on this fix your most intense desires. Immortal being! Love and seek Him who gave you being and immortality with a breath! Say with David, "As the deer pants for the water brooks, so pants my soul for You, O God. My soul thirsts for God, for the living God" (Psa. 42:1, 2). And again, "My heart and my flesh cry out for the living God" (Psa. 84:2). If the heavy affliction under which you lie, prevents your rising to such a full, ardent, and undivided, desire after God, do not let the strong current of your affections be lost in other channels. Call home your thoughts, summon your utmost resolution, look to the Holy Spirit for strength; and give yourself to fervent, unceasing, and importunate prayer. See how earnest and importunate the psalmist is under a similar affliction, which again sets him forth into view as a type of the Man of Sorrows. Hear how he pleads and prays, how he pleads and entreats, "Save me, O God! For the waters have come up to my neck. O God, in the multitude of Your mercy, hear me in the truth of Your salvation. Deliver me out of the mire—let me not sink—let not the floodwater overflow me —let not the deep swallow me up. Hear me, O Lord, turn to me—do not hide Your face from Your servant, for I am in trouble—hear me speedily—draw near to my soul—redeem it—deliver me" (Psa. 69). Imitate this example; do not set any bounds to your prayer, no limit, no termination, but success. Pray until you are heard. Pray until you obtain admission to his favor again. You shall not need to use such importunity long. "In due season you shall reap if you do not lose heart." Like David, you shall be enabled to add, "I will praise the name of God with a song, and will magnify him with thanksgiving" (ver. 30). Or like your Lord, your darkness shall be turned into light, and while you are yet speaking, God will answer, and cause you, by the blessed nearness of his presence, to exclaim, "You have answered me."

THE GRATITUDE

VERSE 22—*I will declare Your name to my brethren;
in the midst of the assembly I will praise You.*

HAVING obtained relief from the oppressive darkness, and regained conscious possession of the joy and light of his Father's countenance, the Redeemer's thoughts and desires now flow into their accustomed channel. What is that channel? The glory of God in the salvation of his Church. These were the two objects for which he had lived more than thirty years. He never had a thought or wish that was not intimately connected with the one or the other. But we must not call them two, as though they were entirely distinct. In the heart of Christ these two were one. It was not only God's glory for which he lived; it was not only man's salvation for which he died; it was for both; it was the one in the other. It was to glorify God in saving man, and to save man in glorifying God, that Christ lived and died. God was glorified in the declaration of his name; man was saved by means of that declaration, Christ's thoughts therefore ran instantly to their grand, their twofold, object. He bursts forth with an acclamation of praise; he utters aloud his Father's goodness, and his own gratitude; he expresses anew his determination and delight to do the duty he had undertaken, "I will declare Your name to my brethren: in the midst of the assembly I will praise You."

How amiable, how lovely, does the Lord appear, to the Christian's apprehension, when he speaks in this way! He is still the same kind friend that he was before our sins pierced him; he uses the same gracious term as formerly; he has not forgotten us; his spiritual resurrection is accomplished; the first name he utters is, "my brethren." After his literal resurrection, he did the same.

When Mary met him near the tomb, he said, "Go to my brethren and say to them, I am ascending to my Father, and your Father; and to my God and your God" (John 20:17).

Gracious Savior, how full of love you are! What humility is in your nature! What tenderness in your words! You unite us so perfectly with God; our timid hearts are comforted, our consciences quieted. What we could not venture to hope, you teach us to believe. We know your Sonship, but we doubt our own; yet in one breath you call God your Father, and ours also, as if you would prove, beyond all doubt, that in you, he is ours, and that through you, we are his. Of a truth it is so. We behold God in you, and are glad; God beholds our nature in you, and is satisfied. Glorious Reconciler, in your single person accepting manhood and bestowing Godhead! More blessed in your giving than in your receiving. You have condescended to take our form, and we will aspire to be conformed to your image, that you may be the first-born among many brethren (Rom. 8:29). Blessed are you, infinitely more blessed, in giving the name of brethren, than in receiving that of brother! We hesitate to call you so, because it seems to do you a dishonor; yet you are not ashamed to call us brethren, as if it were your glory (Heb. 2:11). Well may you ask, "Who are my brothers?" For whoever does the will of your Father in heaven, is your brother (Matt. 12:48, 50). O help us then to live as the brethren of the Holy One ought to live; let this be a name of power within us; let it kindle in us all brotherly affections and kindred desires; let it influence us to live worthy of your name; may we who have already laid enough of sin on your devoted head, from here forward cast it from us and from you! Like the brethren of Joseph, may we live on the fullness, and rejoice in the brotherhood, of Him whom we stripped and sold! This will delight your heart; you shall see the travail of your soul, and shall be satisfied; you will glorify your Father; you will magnify his name with thanksgivings; in the midst of the congregation you will praise him. Teach us to learn, help us to *sing*, your song. Send the Spirit of love and harmony into our hearts, that we may learn the strains of the angelic choirs. That Spirit animates the redeemed before the throne, and inspires the redeemed before the footstool; the song is one; the leader Christ; the singers brethren; discord is for ever fled:

> "Then jointly all the harpers round,
> In mind unite, with solemn sound,
> And strokes upon the highest string,
> Make all the heavenly arches ring.
> Ring loud with hallelujahs high,
> To him that sent his Son to die,
> And to the worthy Lamb of God,
> That loved and washed them in his blood."

The "assembly" spoken of in this verse is explained by the apostle in his Epistle to the Hebrews. He quotes this passage, and applies it to the Church, "For both he who sanctifies, and those who are being sanctified, are all of one; for which reason he is not ashamed to call them brethren, saying: I will declare Your name to My brethren, in the midst of the assembly I will sing praise to You" (Heb. 2:11, 12).

What a view does this present to our minds! Christ looks from the cross to the Church. The gratitude of his heart is to be uttered in the assembly of his saints. "For where two or three are gathered together in My name, I am there in the midst of them" (Matt. 18:20). He puts his own Spirit within them, so that they may participate in his sentiments. As he entered bodily into the room, where his disciples were assembled, so is he spiritually, but really, present, in every company of his faithful people. He meets with them; he blesses them while they are blessing God. When they pray for his Spirit, he hears them, and while they are yet speaking, he sends him into their hearts. The petitions which they offer, he presents to his Father in his own name. He has a full right to do so, for he makes one in the midst of their assembly. As the elder brother of every sincere worshipper, all the prayers and praises ascend in his name. Christ came to glorify the Father, the Spirit comes to glorify the Son, and the sanctification of the

Church is the glory of the Spirit. The three Persons of the Godhead obtain the triple honor of creation, redemption, and sanctification. The Church is the object of threefold love, and care, and power. It is to the Church that Christ declares the name of the Father. He reveals it by the instrumentality of his written word, and of his faithful ministers. He gathered his disciples one by one around him; he instructed them how to regard God, and how to address him as a Father. He had but small companies of twelve, and seventy, and one hundred and twenty, who steadfastly attended his personal ministry. To them he declared this name of God, and told them to proclaim it to others. For this purpose he endued them with power from on high, and immediately three thousand souls were added to the number of his professed worshippers. From that time, the churches walking in the fear of the Lord, and in the comfort of the Holy Ghost, were multiplied (Acts 9:31). At the present day they are found in every quarter of the earth. The promise that was made to the first small company, shall not fail to sustain and comfort the last, "Lo, I am with you always, even to the end of the age." Time shall fail, but not Christ's promises. The end of the world, but not of his word, shall arrive. He will be better than his word, he will be with them also throughout eternity. "Rejoicing in the habitable parts of the earth," Christ rejoices more in the habitable hearts. He seeks to dwell in men by his Spirit. We are individually "temples;" collectively, "a temple." Jesus is our High Priest. He prays in us, he prays with us, he prays for us, he prays by us. His praises ascend with ours; he inspires us with his own gratitude, and expresses by our lips, his heartfelt thanksgivings. The self-containing and mysterious name, "I am that I am." he explains to mean, "God is love." Having cleansed the temple of our hearts from fear and selfishness, by this explanation written in his own blood, he sits in the midst of our concentrated affections, and praises God with us in our closet. When congregations assemble, he condescends to meet with them. Where his members are, there their Head is present. Though unseen by them, he is in their midst. His Spirit animates their hearts; in their psalms, and hymns, and spiritual songs, he praises the great Deliverer—his Father and their Father, his God and their God!

Gratitude is a noble and generous sentiment! It elevates man above the beasts that perish; unites him to the superior intelligence; and, as it were, repays the benefactor with an acceptable interest. Gratitude is one of the fairest plants in the garden of the heart. It is the sunflower of the soul. Roused by the first gift of light, it follows the whole course of the solar orbit. With drooping head it mourns his absence, and with eyes upraised gratitude welcomes his return. Let this be the emblem of our souls. The Christian's heart should blossom with perpetual gratitude. Looking unto Jesus with glowing feelings, we should mark his course, and follow it with thankfulness. Shall he declare to us the paternal name by which we may address Jehovah, and shall we not cry Abba, Father, with all the love and gratitude of which our hearts are capable?

But this verse sets before us a far higher gratitude than that of the Church; it testifies that of Christ the Head. "I will declare Your name. In the midst of the assembly I will praise You." Oh how we wonder with great admiration at the gratitude of Christ! He is God over all; "I and my Father are one." "Without Him nothing was made that was made." Yet he gives thanks for all things, and gratefully acknowledges that bounty and goodness which supplies himself and others. "He took the seven loaves and gave thanks" (Mark 8:6). He stood at the grave of Lazarus, and said, "Father, I thank You that You have heard Me" (John 11:41). When the seventy disciples returned to him, "Jesus rejoiced in spirit and said, I thank You, Father, Lord of heaven and earth" (Luke 10:21). Likewise after supper, when he instituted the memorial of his dying love, he gave thanks before them all. Jesus had a grateful heart. Gratitude is an ingredient in perfect love. We are grateful for being loved. Christ taught us the NAME he loved, that we might love it also. God's various names declare what he is in himself, and what he is to us. It is of great importance by what name we most usually think of God. Those who commonly speak of him only as the Almighty, are generally destitute of near, lively, and realizing views of his love in Christ, and of his paternal character. Of all the scriptural names of God, that of *"Father"* is the most precious. Christ taught his disciples, saying, "When you pray, say, *Our Father.*" "I find an indescribable delight in using these words, '*Our Father,*' and, in praising, confessing, and praying for myself, as one of his large family, I generally begin with the thanks due to God for having made himself known as our Father."[16]

All the other titles and attributes of God seem to meet in this name, as in a center, and to emanate from it with illustrious rays. It is a most simple, yet all-comprehensive name. There is also another which we would notice, because it is not peculiar to one, but applicable to all the Persons in the sacred Trinity. That name is JEHOVAH.

"When the Lord speaks of himself with regard to his creatures, and especially his people, he calls himself 'Jehovah—I am that I am' (Ex. 3:14). We should understand this of God the Father, and of God the Son, and of God the Holy Ghost, One God. He does not say, I am their light, their life, their tower, their strength, but only *I am.* He sets his hand, as it were to a blank, that his people may write under it what they please, that is for their good. As if he should say, 'Are they weak? *I am* strength. Are they sick? *I am* health. Are they in trouble? *I am* comfort. Are they poor? *I am* riches. Are they dying? *I am* life. Have they nothing? *I am* all things. *I am* justice and mercy. *I am* grace and goodness. *I am* glory, beauty, holiness, eminency, supremacy, perfection, all-sufficiency, eternity, JEHOVAH. I AM whatsoever is suitable to their nature, or convenient for them in their several conditions. I AM whatsoever is amiable in itself, or desirable to their souls. Whatever is pure and holy—whatever is great and pleasant—

---

[16] Memoir of Miss Jane Graham.

whatever is good, and needful to make them happy, that I AM.' So that, in short, God here represents himself unto us as one universal good; and leaves us to make the application to ourselves, according to our several needs, capacities, and desires; he saying only in the general—I Am."[17] Well, therefore, may the Psalmist exclaim, "Let the righteous be glad; let them rejoice before God; yes, let them rejoice exceedingly. Sing to God, sing praises to his name: extol him who rides on the clouds, by his name Yah, (or Jehovah,) and rejoice before him" (Psa. 68:3, 4).

---

[17] Bishop Beveridge.

THE INVITATION

VERSE 23—*You who fear the LORD, praise Him!*
All you descendants of Jacob, glorify Him,
and fear Him, all you offspring of Israel!

HAVING expressed his own grateful determination; having given utterance to the fullness of that submissive love which occupied his own heart; the Redeemer next calls on others to join in blessing the Father of all mercies. How natural this is! The true lover longs to hear others praising the object of his affections. Who are these others? They are the members of his Church, that "assembly" in the midst of which he delights to dwell. They are divided into three companies. The fearers of the Lord, the seed of Jacob, and the seed of Israel. Appropriate parts in the great anthem of praise are assigned to each. The fearers of the Lord are invited to praise him. The seed of Jacob to glorify him; and the seed of Israel, to fear, that is, to reverence, the Lord.

These three companies are all one in Christ. They represent his people on earth, in three stages of advancement. In order that none may imagine themselves to be excluded, they are each particularly addressed, and individually invited to join the Savior's song of grateful adoration.

First, those who fear the Lord are addressed. This is a striking characteristic of all those who have experienced even the least degree of true faith. All disciples are not equally advanced, but all are distinguished from the world around them by this peculiarity. They fear the Lord; they know that he is everywhere present; they believe that he takes notice of all they think, and say, and do. They know him by these names, "The Almighty," "The great and terrible God." They generally speak in such terms as these, "The Divine Being, the Deity, the Supreme Ruler of the universe, the Judge of all;" or with this addition, "Our Creator, Our Merciful Preserver." Knowing so much of the Sacred Name, they stand in awe, sometimes their fear amounts almost to dread. Occasionally it is softened into a milder sentiment.

To fear the Lord, is a lesson with which every disciple must be familiar. It is the first in the school of Christ. All need not be learning it, but all must know it by heart. Advanced scholars go on to higher lessons, but they must never forget this first rudiment of spiritual knowledge. Where is it taught? Only in the school of Christ. There the true light is shining, and all without is darkness. When any man enters this school, his previous attainments are disregarded; he is set to learn the alphabet of his nature in the light of eternity. To his horror, he perceives that the entire alphabet is black, and all the letters different in size and form; he learns that his whole nature is corrupt, that almost all the actions of his life are curved and crooked, while even the straightest of them are black, dotted, or crossed. Unaccustomed to such instructions, he is slow to learn them, blots his textbook with his tears, and dreads every word and movement of his Teacher. God appears to him to be rigid and severe; he looks up to him only at intervals, and that with dread; he feels unable to approach him with filial confidence, but yet he is persuaded and determined to learn the lessons; he hears of the progress of others, and is encouraged to diligent application. Thus is it with many of the first class in the very earliest stage of their spiritual life. An appropriate duty is set before them. They are encouraged to praise their Teacher. Instead of regarding him with feelings of apprehension, and speaking of him as a severe master, they are told to praise him for all the trouble, care, and attention, he is bestowing upon them. O you trembling Christians, let all you know of God be turned into a matter of praise and you shall be strengthened in your hearts, and enlarged in your confidence towards him. Do not be cast down when your sense of proficiency is small, as if you never would learn; but make a right use of the little you have acquired, and you shall soon advance to higher lessons. All true Christians set apart special times for prayer. They would find it good also to have special seasons for praise. Adoration and thanksgiving do not, in general, bear an adequate proportion to the petitionary part of our worship.

This world has been compared to a music book, divided by empty spaces and black lines, yet on each of these there is a note, and he must sing who learns it. Praise God, then, as your Creator; praise him as your Preserver; praise him as the Almighty; praise him as the just and righteous Lord; praise him as the supreme Ruler and Governor of all things. If God appears to your apprehension only as great and terrible, yet praise him as such, and his terribleness shall not make you afraid. It is because you do not praise as you proceed, that your progress in heavenly knowledge is so slow. He who thanks God for what little he has learned, shall surely be taught more. A grateful heart makes us active and improving servants. He that does his will shall know concerning the doctrine (John 7:17); shall be instructed in all wisdom. You timid Christians, do not deprive the Lord of the honor due to his name. While you mourn over your sins, praise him who has taught you to hate them; be afraid of being lost, and praise him that you are not lost already; look upon yourself as nothing, and praise him who gave Christ to be your all in all. Think little of your own prayers and resolutions, and praise him who came to pray and intercede on your behalf. You who fear the Lord, praise him. If you cannot praise him for what you are, thank him for what you are not— that you are not blind, and deaf; and dead, both in soul and body; that you are not as careless and worldly-minded, and fond of sin, as you were before. Should fears and doubts, however, so harass your spirit, that you cannot praise God on your own account, rouse yourself to praise him for what he has done for others. Praise him for the deliverance vouchsafed to your Lord and Savior on the cross, and for that glorious work which he wrought in Christ when he raised him from the dead; praise him for all that he has done in the Church—his acts of grace in apostles, prophets, and martyrs of old time; and in sin-denying, holy-living, Christians in the world around you; praise him for the Scriptures of truth; the means of grace; the hope, however faint, of salvation. Let every fearer of the Lord in this way endeavor to occupy his thoughts with subjects of praise, and he shall soon advance to higher strains, even to the glorifying of God's great name.

Such are the seed of Jacob; these are scholars whom the law, as a schoolmaster, has brought to Christ; these are they who lay hold on the heel, the bruised heel, of their elder Brother. Jacob, strictly signifies, the heeler; that is, one who lays hold upon the heel, and gains an advantage by another's fall. Jacob did so when he was born; it was his first act, therefore he was named Jacob (Gen. 25:26). So is it with some Christians in their new spiritual birth; they are enabled by the Spirit of God to lay hold at once of the bruised heel of their elder Brother, and through his fall and humiliation, rise to hope and heaven. They have no consciousness of spiritual existence, but what is connected with the knowledge of a crucified Redeemer. They learn the first, in the second lesson; they feel a fear, and a love, of God, springing up in their hearts at one and the same moment. They cannot say that they have experienced all those fears and apprehensions of which others speak; but yet they have learned the name of God in Christ, and are satisfied. They are glad they praise the Lord, yes, they glorify him. Stirred up by a powerful gratitude, they seek to spend and to be spent in his service; they cannot think enough of his goodness; they cannot speak enough of his love; they cannot do enough in his service; they occupy their thoughts in heavenly meditations; they speak often one to another, and their hearts burn with holy love and gratitude to God. They regard that day as lost, which does not see some labor of love, some act of charity, for his name's sake.

Such are the seed of Jacob. We have described them when their "first love" (Rev. 2:4), is fresh and full; but yet, it may be, that after a while they shall experience the life of their father Jacob. They may have to wander far, and be exposed to trials, and before some of these they may fall, to show them their own weakness. Over other trials they may be carried harmless, to teach them the strength of him who bears them. But as they journey on, it will be their principal desire to glorify God. The main bent of their minds will be to honor his holy name. They will vow to be faithful servants unto death and the Lord shall be their God wherever they may be led. The gods of the people amongst whom they come shall not receive the homage of their hearts. Should Providence bring them into a lower capacity, so that their lot is to serve others, they will so strive to glorify God in all their conduct, that when about to depart, their superiors may have reason to desire them to remain, and to add, "For we have learned by experience that the Lord has blessed us for your sake" (Gen. 30:27). Again, through the kindness of the Most High, should they be blessed abundantly on every side, so that all that they have is multiplied, they will glorify the Lord in it all, and say, "We are not worthy of the least of all the mercies, and of all the truth, which You have showed to Your servants" (Gen. 32:10).

Thus, throughout their whole life, the true seed of Jacob will glorify the Lord. Here they are invited to do so, and they willingly comply. Is not our God worthy to be honored and extolled? Did he not give his own Son out of his bosom, to an ignominious and painful death, that they might never die? Will they not therefore glorify him? When that Son was dying on the cross, did he not hear his cry and answer his petition—accepting the Surety for the sinner? Will they not therefore glorify him? Hear how the Savior encouraged his followers to do so, "By this my is Father glorified, that you bear much fruit; so you will be my disciples" (John 15:8). Will the servant disobey the master? Surely he would not willingly offend. He will seek to abound in services of love; nor will he ever be content with himself, until he has testified of his inward gratitude by his outward obedience. The true seed of Jacob is not one that is satisfied with the religion of the head, or of the lip. He seeks to possess that of the heart, and of the life. His is not a sentimental, but a practical, piety. It evaporates not in warm emotions, or flowing words, but proves its vitality by act and deed. He has learned that without holiness no man shall see the Lord; and the first desire of his heart is to be holy in all manner of conduct. He knows that he cannot prove his love to God, but by his love to man, and therefore is ready both to do, and to give, for the benefit of his neighbor. In this way he proves himself to be the true disciple of him, who glorified God, by going about continually doing good. Nor does he secretly revel in his own goodness, or build on his own righteousness. He knows that before a perfect God, no work of an imperfect being can merit acceptance; and that, by the perfect law, it must be condemned. Therefore, having no right in himself to the inheritance, like one of the true seed of Jacob, he takes hold of his Elder Brother; he lays his hand on that bruised heel, the humanity of Christ crucified (Gen. 3:15). Nor will he let go his hold. It is his life. He takes all his righteousness from him. He obtains the blessing, the inheritance, from that elder brother, not an Esau who curses, but a Jesus who blesses.

How shall we further describe the true Christian? Is not his private life spent in prayer? His public life, is it not one of conformity to the pattern of Christ? His eye is more strict to watch the movements of his own heart, than to scrutinize the motives of the hearts of others. He knows his own shortcomings are many, and does not enlarge on the failings of his neighbors. Yet to their *sins*, he is not blind, as to his own he is not partial. Words of love and faithfulness are not so unaccustomed to his tongue, as are those of flattery and praise. He loves his friends, and therefore desires to see them free from every fault. While others are talking at a neighbor's back, he is admonishing him face to face. He silences the scandalous, by refusing to take up their report; or confounds their faces, by demanding their authority for its truth.

His maxim is not to please himself, but to glorify his God. When surrounded by trials, when placed in circumstances of painful perplexity, when apparently about to lose all that is most dear to him in life, he does not trust in his own prudence, or lean on his own strength, but after having done all, and while doing all, that man can do, he trusts only in the unerring wisdom, the sustaining power, and unfailing resources, of a covenant God, on whose love in Christ he casts his burden. If his petitions do not immediately succeed, he does not faint, he cries again and again. The closet of prayer is his field of spiritual combat. He wrestles on in earnestness of supplication (Hosea 12:3-6). He follows the Lord with importunity of spirit, and because it is the glory of God which he desires, he will not allow himself to be denied. He brings forth strong arguments, and like his father of old exclaims, "I will not let you go, unless you bless me." So he prevails with God, and obtains a new name, becoming hereafter one of the seed of Israel. "Your name shall no longer be called Jacob, but Israel; for you have struggled with God and with men, and have prevailed" (Gen. 32:28).

The seed of Israel are called upon to "fear," that is, to reverence the Lord. The word rendered "fear" in the first part of the verse, is not the same as that which is so translated in this last clause. The former means to be afraid; it denotes timidity, anxiety of apprehension, dread. The latter signifies to reverence, to regard with respect, to hold in veneration and esteem. It is used to denote that sentiment, with which an inferior should regard a superior. The word *reverence* is the most appropriate in this place. The original term is likewise used to express a high degree of fear or terror, but generally when arising from a sense of superior force, power, or greatness. As applied here to the seed of Israel, it is remarkably appropriate. Let all the seed ponder the responsibility which it commands, for the evil against which it guards them is of an insidious nature. Reverence God: "Do not be high-minded, but fear." Do not boast—you do not bear the root, but the root you. "Work out your own salvation with fear and trembling, for it is God who works in you." These New Testament warnings are similar to that of the text. They are addressed to those who are supposed to know by experience, the power of believing prayer. They have prevailed with God, let them not presume. They have obtained a new name, let them guard against spiritual pride. When Jacob had wrestled and prevailed with the angel of the covenant, he might have felt tempted to think highly of himself. This great condescension of God towards him, might produce, through the suggestions of Satan, low thoughts of heavenly power, and lofty ideas of his own. That holy awe and reverence, which ought to characterize every creature, when thinking and speaking, of the God of heaven, might be destroyed. That lowliness, that abasement of spirit, that renunciation of our own will in prayer, which Christ himself exhibited, might be displaced by sentiments of an opposite nature. Jacob might have conceived that it was his own power that prevailed, rather than the intentional and amazing condescension of God that yielded. On subsequent occasions, he might approach the throne of grace, more as a prince, than as a supplicant. His prayer might partake more of the nature of a demand, than of a request. And, with an irreverent familiarity, he might now address that great and glorious Being, for whom before he entertained a holy awe. To this surnamed Israel we would say, "Shrink back." To all his seed, Christ here says, "*Reverence God*,"— mildly couching his command under the form of an invitation to join his thankful song. The Lord Jesus is our Israel, of whom Jacob was the type. He, too, has prevailed with God; but he did not diminish by one iota, that holy reverence with which he regarded his Father. The saints in heaven have all more or less prevailed (Heb. 11:33, 34); yet there, they cast their crowns in humble abasement at his feet.

Let all the seed of Israel, then, revere their God. As they must not overlook the Godhead of Christ, in his manhood, so let them not forget the condescension of the Hearer of prayer, in their own victories by prayer. How grievous is it, that men should address their heavenly Father in terms of earthly friendship and familiarity; should mistake the cries of over-wrought feeling, for the wrestlings of true faith; and substitute a long and loud supplication, for a child-like waiting upon God! Alas, that any disciples of Christ should act like the priests of Baal! Unhappy men! They leap and cry aloud after their manner! Their god is meditating, or busy, or on a journey, or perhaps he is sleeping, and must be awakened. But our God is the living God, the all-present King: emphatically designated *"The Hearer of prayer,"* in contrast to the deaf and mute gods of the heathen nations. Why then, should professing Christians act towards their Lord as if he were no better than these? Why should they shout, as though God were unable or unwilling to hear, "fatiguing Heaven with the prodigious clamor of their outrageous entreaty?" Let it not be so with the seed of Israel. Well meaning, but mistaken Christians, have fallen into this snare in every age. A caution, therefore, on this point, is highly necessary at all times, and to all classes of persons. Of all these three classes of professing Christians, none require to be more on their guard than the last. To live in the fear of God, or to be self-denying and diligent in glorifying his name, are not the paths in which mere professors, or deceitful hypocrites, love to walk. Men seldom put on any appearance, but that which is most attractive. A false profession, a mouth that shows much love, and a frequent use of peculiar words and phrases, high-sounding names and titles, are the things they lay hold of in religion. They have enlisted to wear the uniform, but not to fight the battles, of the soldiers of the cross. They call themselves the seed of Israel, princes among common Christians, and favorites of Heaven. But it is not he who commends himself that is approved, but whom the Lord commends (2 Cor. 10:18). The Israelite indeed is a man without deceit (John 1:47). He does not seek the approbation of men, but strives to commend himself in all things to God. He has fully, and experimentally, learned the various lessons of the school of Christ. He fears the Lord in his inmost heart. He glorifies the Lord in his outward conduct. He reverences the Lord with the most sacred sentiments of his soul. The first petition in his prayer invariably is, *"Hallowed be Your name."* When an answer is granted to his entreaties, his language is not, "I have prevailed," but simply and humbly, "You have answered me." If, naturally of an ardent spirit, he strives to keep it in check. He remembers that so long as he is in the body, he must be most upon his guard, when most conscious of the love and approbation of his Lord. Peter had no sooner obtained a blessing, than he brought himself under a rebuke. Let us, with John, even though leaning on our Lord's bosom, always address him with REVERENTIAL LOVE. This is the highest, and most blessed, state of feeling to which we can attain. It is that of the Redeemed above; it is that of Christ upon the cross; it is that to which he here invites us; it is that which we shall possess in the eternal world of glory—LOVE, bounded by no sentiment, but that of reverence;—REVERENCE, adorned and actuated by a love as boundless as it shall be everlasting.

THE TESTIMONY

VERSE 24—*For He has not despised nor abhorred the affliction of the afflicted;*
nor has He hidden His face from Him;
but when He cried to Him, He heard.

WHEN the Scriptures call to the performance of duty, they present us at the same time with a suitable and adequate reason. Here is an instance. The three classes of the Master's scholars had been invited to join him in praising God, and a powerful reason is added, drawn from his experience of God's faithfulness. He bears his testimony on the Lord's behalf, He seems to place himself in the position of the Psalmist, when he says, "Come and hear, all you who fear God, and I will declare what He has done for my soul" (Psa. 66:16). Christ had cried, "Why have You forsaken me?" He had protested to his Father that his distress was unnoticed, that his cries were unheard. But he testifies of his goodness; records his clemency, his mercy, and his love; and stimulates his Church's gratitude and praise by this encouraging reason, for God "has not despised nor abhorred the affliction of the afflicted; nor has He hidden His face from Him, but when He cried to him, He heard."

What a direct refutation does this give to all the taunts and accusations of his crucifiers! They had insinuated that God would not have him, that he had no delight in him. But here Christ testifies, "God has not despised nor abhorred the affliction of the afflicted." They had said that God would not listen to his prayers, but here Christ declares, "When I cried to Him, He heard." And lest his own cry of God's desertion, and forsaking, should afflict the minds of his disciples, he further decidedly asserts, "God has not hid His face from me." What comforting assurance! Christ did not descend into the tomb under the hiding of his Father's face. The darkness was over all the land only "until the ninth hour." Then the light returned; and, with the material, came also the spiritual light.

The one relieved the face of nature, the other relieved the heart of Christ. It relieves our hearts also. It comforts us to know that the ever-blessed Redeemer died in a calm of soul, and that before he left this life he was able to declare that his Father's face was turned to him in love. Forsaking was strictly a judicial act. It was the act of a just and righteous Judge. But there was no change in the heart of the Father, towards his well-beloved Son. The heart of love still yearned towards him, though the countenance of love was turned away. Why was it averted? Because the eye met sin; that thing which God cannot look upon without abhorrence, was laid on Christ. That is why the countenance of the Father was withdrawn. For this reason, and this reason only, was the Holy One forsaken. With all the emphasis of which language is capable, let it be declared that there was no abhorrence of the Bearer, but only of the burden. Let this distinction be fully borne in mind. Let it be ever before our thoughts, bright with the light of eternal truth—God could not but abhor the one; God could not abhor the other. This was all purity, all righteousness. That was all vile, all repulsive. Had a mere man borne the sins of the world, both burden and bearer must have been objects of the Divine wrath. But in the case of Christ, it could be the burden only. Yet because he took it up, and was in the eye of the law covered with imputed sin, the light of God's countenance was for a time turned away. Under this judicial desertion, Christ fixed his faith and hope, not on the countenance of the Judge, but on the heart of the Father. Had that been turned away, there could be nothing to trust in. This is, therefore, an important distinction, both as regards Christ our Master and ourselves. It teaches us, in the darkest trial, to know where our strength lies. It furnishes us with food of an imperishable faith. It shows how Christ prayed, and how, as the great Advocate, he prevailed. It admits us within the veil, and unfolds how the anchor is both sure and steadfast. It presents Christ himself, safely passed through an awful storm by its unyielding hold. That anchor is the *loving-kindness* of Jehovah, which takes sure hold by the promise on the one side, and the oath of God on the other. Thus, our Lord on the cross, and all who have fled to it for refuge, found strong consolation by these two immutable things, in which it is impossible for God to lie (Heb. 6:17-20). Let it therefore be deeply impressed upon your hearts, that God is love; while he does not love your sin, yet be fully persuaded that he loves your soul. Keep this distinction plainly before your mind. The apostle exhorts you to do so. He says, do not, "be discouraged when you are rebuked by Him; for whom the LORD loves He chastens" (Heb. 12:5). Let your adversities, therefore, teach you a better lesson than your prosperities can possibly render. Let them be tokens to you of the love that dwells in the heart of God. Though you can perceive nothing but the uplifted rod, yet believe that the hand that wields it is your Father's, and that his heart towards you is love. Thus shall you be comforted in trouble, strengthened in weakness, and rendered victorious over every temptation. Thus shall you be like your Lord. Thus shall you be able, in time and in eternity, to bear your feeble, but unfaltering, testimony, to the faithfulness of Jehovah, and to call on all around you to join your hymn of thanksgiving; saying, for God "has not despised nor abhorred the affliction of the afflicted; nor has he hid his face from him, but when he cried to him, he heard."

The intention of even the most severe trials is to glorify God. During their continuance they are indeed grievous. One hour of pain appears longer than a day, and a whole day of joy passes like an hour. This shows how erroneous all judgment founded on appearances must be. In providential dispensations, God often *appears* to be rather an enemy than a friend. At such seasons, then, remember that it is said in the Proverbs, "Faithful are the wounds of a friend, but the kisses of an enemy are deceitful" (Pr. 27:6). Let these very wounds, under which you hurt, be proofs to you that God *is* a friend, and not an enemy. Do not seek then to exchange your gifts for deceitful gratifications. The more severe the trial is, the greater is the opportunity afforded you to glorify God. The worst of all sorrows, deprivation of his comforting presence, puts you in a situation to prove that you love the Lord for himself alone, and not for a selfish end: this honors God, and confounds Satan (Job 1:9). Still confide, then, in God's power and willingness to grant desired relief. Faith in the love and willingness of a heavenly Father, is the stay of the oppressed heart; it imparts strength to prayer, and life to intercession. Therefore, to unsettle our minds in regard to the love of God, is the great aim of the adversary of the soul. It is a fundamental doctrine of holy Scripture that God afflicts in love; we are told to receive his chastisements as a means intended for our good. All afflictions are certainly rods of wrath, but it is wrath springing from love. To those who are "new creatures" in Christ Jesus, these afflictions are, moreover, proofs of *paternal* affection, showing that "God deals with them as with sons." But in reference to human beings, still out of torment, or who are not judicially abandoned by the Spirit of grace, all afflictions are intended either for their temporal or eternal good; and can only fail by their resistance to the grace of God. The last pang which dying nature feels is the infliction of a God, whose longsuffering mercy has come to an end, or whose work of grace in the furnace is completed.

Throughout the whole of life, by daily preservation, the bounties of nature, and constant occasions of gladness, there is unceasing testimony given to men of the love and goodness of their Creator. The things that are seen—the flowing rivers, the boundless ocean, the spangled heavens, the verdant landscape, the majestic mountains, the animal creation, wild and tame, testify to his eternal power and Godhead, his beneficence and love. Thus man is without excuse. And though there is a thorn with every rose, it is love still, goodness still. The flower is uppermost, nearest, most inviting; its fragrance ascends upwards, and diffuses itself around; the sweet voice of its breathing teaches man's heart to rise with thankfulness to God. But if the ungrateful mortal grovels still with downward eye and hand, it is kind to prick him for his earthliness. Were the thorn placed where the rose is; were it as large and many-edged as are its petals; were it as tempting in color, inviting in fragrance, and still as sharp and piercing in itself, we might well imagine with the heathen, that the earth was made by an evil spirit, who delights in the misfortunes and miseries of his creatures. But it is not so. The book of nature teaches by every leaf that, "God is love." The Word of God twice declares in a single chapter "God is love; God is love" (1 John 4:8, 16).

Many are the proofs of this truth, which Nature, Scripture, and our own experience furnish. The answering of prayer is not the least of the believer's testimonies that God is love. When, like the Psalmist, we have approached the throne of grace in sorrow of heart and depression of spirit, how often have we risen from our knees with relieved and grateful feelings! The gracious Friend of sinners has exchanged his yoke with us for ours. Weary and heavy-laden, we go to him and find rest. How easy is his yoke to the neck, how light his burden to the shoulder! (Matt. 11:28, 30). It is a yoke of love, a burden of joy! Prayer puts our burden upon Christ, and ourselves under his yoke. "This poor man cried out, and the Lord heard him, and saved him out of all his troubles" (Psa. 34:6). "I love the Lord, because he has heard my voice and my supplications. Because he has inclined his ear to me, therefore will I call upon him as long as I live" (Psa. 116:1, 2). "Come and hear, all you who fear God, and I will declare what He has done for my soul. I cried to Him with my mouth, and He was extolled with my tongue. If I regard iniquity in my heart, the Lord will not hear. But certainly God has heard me; He has attended to the voice of my prayer. Blessed be God, who has not turned away my prayer, nor His mercy from me!" (Psa. 66:16-20).

Is the Christian, then, surrounded by trial? Is he overwhelmed? Does he seem to be cast out of God's sight, and feel as though far off from his presence? Prayer will bring him near. Prayer will effect his complete deliverance. But it must be true prayer. It must be an earnest appeal of our hearts to the heart of God, through Jesus Christ. "You shall seek Me and find Me, when you search for Me with all your heart. And I will be found by you, says the Lord" (Jer. 29:13, 14). Is the Christian, then, under the dark cloud of temporal or spiritual trial? Has the nearest and dearest object of his heart been removed out of his sight by the relentless hand of death? Do lingering sickness and disease detain him in yearly endurance? Or has poverty, and its attendant evils, come upon him with its iron grasp? Prayer will bring the Comforter, the Physician, the Omnipotent, to his aid; for, whatever are his circumstances, this is the scriptural exhortation, "Trust in him at ALL TIMES; you people, pour out your heart before him; God is a refuge for us" (Psa. 62:8). Let him therefore say, "Lord, I am oppressed; undertake for me" (Isa. 38:14). "Hear my cry, O God; attend unto my prayer. From the end of the earth I will cry to You, when my heart is overwhelmed; lead me to the rock that is higher than I" (Psa. 61:1, 2). The Lord will not despise his supplication. It is positively declared in reference to prayer, the Lord, "gives to all liberally and without reproach" (James 1:5). Persuasion of the Lord's willingness to hear, and tenderness of consideration, enlarges our hearts in prayer before him. The psalmist knew this, and said, "O you who hear prayer, to You all flesh will come" (Psa. 65:2). Yes, "whoever calls on the name of the Lord shall be saved" (Rom. 10:13). God never said to any of the seed of Jacob, "seek Me in vain" (Isa. 45:19). "The Lord is very compassionate and merciful" (James 5:11). Men are often brought low by their own iniquity, nevertheless God regards their affliction, when he hears their cry (Psa. 106:44). "A broken and a contrite heart—these O God, You will not despise" (Psa. 51:17). The heart of our blessed Lord was broken on the cross, but there also it was healed. Though his Father had not for a time attended to his prayer, he had never *despised* it; though he abhorred the burden which Jesus had taken upon him, he had never *abhorred* the *affliction* of its afflicted Bearer. Though he hid his *face* from him as a Judge, he did not shut his *heart* against him as a Father, but when he cried to him he heard. We may therefore apply to Jesus on the cross, what is spoken by the prophet, in the name of the Lord, to the afflicted Church, "For a mere moment have I forsaken you, but with great mercies I will gather you. With a little wrath I hid My face from you for a moment; but with everlasting kindness I will have mercy on you" (Isa. 54:7, 8).

THE VOW

VERSE 25—*My praise shall be of You in the great assembly;*
I will pay my vows before those who fear him.

THE joy and gratitude of our adorable Lord rise to such a height at this great deliverance—his heart so overflows with fresh and blessed consciousness of his heavenly Father's nearness, that he again pours forth the expression of his praise. By its repetition, he teaches us that this is not a temporary burst of gratitude, but an abiding determination, a full and settled resolution. He puts it, like the preceding twenty-second verse, into the form of a vow, but carries forward his thoughts to a higher and eternal object, "My praise shall be of You in the great assembly."

The "great assembly" is a phrase taken from the assembling of the tribes, from all parts of the land of Israel (1 Kings 8:65). At such seasons, our blessed Lord was ever ready to fulfill his high commission. In the synagogues of the different places to which he came, and in the Temple when he arrived, our Savior proclaimed to the assembled multitudes the acceptable year of the Lord. We may fully apply to him the words of the Psalmist, "I have proclaimed the good news of righteousness in the great assembly; indeed, I do not restrain my lips, O LORD, You Yourself know. I have not hidden Your righteousness within my heart; I have declared Your faithfulness and Your salvation; I have not concealed Your loving-kindness and Your truth from the great assembly" (Psa. 40:9, 10). In the gospel of St. John our adorable Redeemer is exhibited before our eyes, as in a moral picture, in the very act which the Psalmist here foretells, "On the last day, that great day of the feast, Jesus stood and cried out, saying, "If anyone thirsts, let him come to Me and drink. He who believes in Me, as the Scripture has said, out of his heart will flow rivers of living water. But this He spoke concerning the Spirit, whom those believing in Him would receive;

for the Holy Spirit was not yet given, because Jesus was not yet glorified" (John 7:37-39).

The earthly Jerusalem and Temple were typical of heaven, and its worshipping hosts (Heb. 9:9). The apostle explains it in this way and says, "the Jerusalem which is above is free, which is the mother of us all" (Gal. 4:26). In the Epistle to the Hebrews, he represents the once crucified, but ever exalted, Savior, as having entered into the holy place of a greater and more perfect temple—standing there as a mediator, and presenting the blood of sprinkling in fulfillment of his vow. The twenty-second verse of this psalm informed us, that in the midst of the Church, while it continues militant on earth, Christ will praise his Father: and here we are assured that in heaven itself, in the general assembly and Church of the first-born, in the city of the living God, the heavenly Jerusalem, his praises shall be heard, and his vows be performed. (Heb. 9:24; 12:22-24).

No sooner was this promise made, than it was accomplished. In a few seconds after the period at which we conceive that our Lord inwardly repeated this verse, he performed his vow, and breathed out his spirit into the hands of his Father. Then the soul of Jesus entered into the world of spirits; there in the presence of the redeemed, and of all the listening angels, he presented his praises to his Father and their Father, to his God and their God. Shortly after, also, the soul of the penitent malefactor appeared in Paradise, to add his joyful praises to their grateful notes.

The faithful Redeemer is still fulfilling his vows in the experience of every believer. He carries on his intercession in heaven, and he sends down his Spirit on earth. The good Shepherd still cares for his sheep, and assures our hearts of his love, by declaring to us his duty, "As the Father gave me commandment, so I do" (John 12:49; 14:31). And he is still "doing" at the court of heaven all that is needful for his Church. The souls of the redeemed, are now beholding how faithfully he there discharges his "commanded duty," as High Priest and Advocate, on behalf of their brethren who are still on the earth.

The "great congregation" in which our Lord vows to offer high praises to Jehovah, signifies, in its fullest sense, that assembly in which the whole company of the redeemed shall meet, and be united forever. A great congregation, indeed, shall then assemble, from Abel, the first soul that was saved, to the last man of God's elect, who shall be snatched from off this burning world. Then, and there, will Christ pay his vows. These vows are that he would fulfill all the Father's will, and that he would lose none of those whom the Father should give to him. These vows are, that he, as the head, and that the redeemed, as the members of his body, should give praise and glory to God, in place of all that shame and dishonor which the first Adam and his posterity had wrought. With all the glorious company of his redeemed, shall the once despised Jesus of Nazareth stand forth, the admiration of angels, and give utterance to those praises which the brief period of time shall supply to awaken the echoes of eternity!

He will pay his vows before them that "fear him." As this term includes *all* his people, so it assures those timid, but sincere Christians, who, though not ashamed to confess his name, are yet afraid to appropriate his promises, that they shall not be left out. None shall be lost. Christ as their head, as the Father of the everlasting age (Isa. 9:6), shall present himself, and all who have truly loved him, before the throne, and say, "Here am I, and the children you have given me" (Heb. 2:13).

Such we may conceive to be, in part, the fulfillment of the Savior's vows, at the period of his everlasting glory. To place beyond all doubt the integrity of his purpose he has not left one unfulfilled in the progress of his earthly humiliation. To the most minute particular of his Father's will, our Lord attended with scrupulous exactness. And it might be, just at this moment, in harmony with this verse, that our dying Lord said, "I thirst." Some may consider this to have been uttered in connection rather with the fifteenth verse, as a proof of the exhaustion of his frame. This may appear to be more natural, but we rather incline to regard it as spoken at this time, in token of his willingness to fulfill all that was required of him. The statement of the evangelist leads us to conclude that these two words, "I thirst," were uttered out of a sense of duty, and with the express intention to fulfill all that was written of him. "After this, Jesus, knowing that all things were now accomplished, that the Scripture might be fulfilled, said, "I thirst!" (John 19:28). Therefore, so that not one thing might be left undone, unsuffered, or unfulfilled, he said it. He was faithful in all things. His vows were fully performed. To the very last mite, the Surety paid our debt; he drank to the very dregs that cup of suffering which had been prepared for him. Therefore, in imitation of your example, we your unworthy disciples shall say, with the strongest and most grateful determination, with our living voice, our dying breath, with our song of time, our hymn of eternity, "Our praise shall be of You in the great assembly; we will pay our vows before those who fear You."

Bring home this lesson, Christian reader, to your heart. Christ made no vow, which he did not perform. How many have you uttered, which you have never fulfilled? On the bed of sickness, and in the prospect of death; on the stormy deep, in expectation of shipwreck; at the couch of a beloved relative, under fear of bereavement; in the hour of need, distress, and perplexity; how many vows have been sent up to the registry of heaven? When the Father heard your cry, and granted deliverance, how long has he been made to wait for the performance of your promise? Perhaps he is waiting till now. Remember, God is not to be mocked. When you make a vow to God, do not delay to pay it; for he has no pleasure in fools (Eccles. 5:4) who cry out speedily in distress, and laugh when the danger is over. Go back, then, in your history. Recall the scenes and stages of life, through which you have passed. Do not let your memory be treacherous. Do not let your conscience be partial. Deal honestly with yourself. There is no unfaithfulness in the Lord, who will surely require of you your vows (Deut. 23:21). "Better not to vow than to vow and not pay. Do not let your mouth cause your flesh to sin, nor say before the messenger of God that it was an error. Why should God be angry at your excuse and destroy the work of your hands?" (Eccles. 5:5 6). Therefore, "Do not be rash with your mouth, and let not your heart utter anything hastily before God. For God is in heaven, and you on earth; therefore let your words be few" (vs. 2).

It is a solemn fact, proved in the experience of ministers, that on an average, only two or three persons out of thousands, perform those vows in health, which, with so much earnestness, they had made on the bed of sickness. This is an appalling truth, and casts a dark shade over death-bed repentance. We would discourage none, even at the eleventh hour, from fleeing to Christ, who will in no way cast out any who truly turn to him. But the heart is so deceitful, no human being can pronounce an opinion on the truth even of his own repentance, when it is not tested by contact with the world, and its temptations. While on this side of the grave, we must warn all, not to trust on an uncertain basis. Beyond the end destination of life, we follow no man. Human judgment is suspended, when a creature passes into the court of that Judge, who knows the secret state of every heart, and who never pronounces a sentence, in the justice of which the conscience of the criminal himself does not fully agree! If, then, dear reader, you are putting off your repentance to another day, be entreated now while it is called today. "Behold, now is the accepted time; behold, now is the day of salvation" (2 Cor. 6:2). Tomorrow may be too late. There may not be a tomorrow in your mortal history. If there are vows, O Christian, still unfulfilled, standing against you, confess your sin immediately; cry to the Holy Spirit for strength and integrity of determination; give yourself no rest, till you have discharged the solemn obligations, under which you lie, to glorify God, by fully and daily performing your vows (Psa. 61:8) and press forward to a cheerful compliance with the exhortation of the apostle, "Therefore by Him let us continually offer the sacrifice of praise to God, that is, the fruit of our lips, giving thanks to His name" (Heb. 13:15).

THE SATISFACTION OF THE MEEK

VERSE 26—*The meek*[18] *shall eat and be satisfied.*

THE narrative of the gospel informs us that when our Lord had fulfilled the last prophecy of Scripture relating to his mortal life, and had cried, "I thirst," that one, standing by, held a sponge with vinegar to his mouth. And here we picture in our minds the Savior, as if feeling the raging thirst more intensely by this partial relief, turned at once, and for ever, from all earthly supports, as empty and insufficient, and solaced his mind with meditation on the river of God's pleasure again opened to him, and on that refreshing, satisfying, and unfailing water of life, which he would give to his people, with the living bread. So abundant does his own prepared gospel feast appear in contrast with this unsatisfying sip, which he had just received, that he declares, "The meek shall eat and be satisfied."

In these words our Lord describes the character of his disciples, their privilege, and their condition. First, their character is "the meek." The disciple should resemble the Master. The characteristic feature of our blessed Lord was that of meekness. He desires his people to be like-minded. "Learn from me," he says, "for I am [meek] and lowly in heart, and you will find rest for your souls" (Matt. 11:29). The wisdom of the schools had never taught this lesson. When "the Teacher" came, his doctrine was despised as tame and base. How true is it, "the natural man does not receive the things of the Spirit of God, for they are foolishness to him!" (1 Cor.

---

[18] While NKJV reads "poor" instead of "meek," we have retained the King James reading of the verse for ease of understanding throughout the chapter. Meekness is the theme and therefore verses containing the word meekness have been retained in the KJV. –Ed.

2:14). And how true also is the converse, "the wisdom of this world is foolishness with God!" (1 Cor. 3:19). To possess a high and noble spirit, to be able to maintain our dignity, to resent all affronts with effect, and bend before the power of no man, is a matter of much importance in the estimation of the world. It is deemed wisdom, strength, and greatness. Some, however, of the ancient philosophers could spurn even this as beneath them. They aspired to the dignity of a perpetual calm, which no wickedness could ruffle, no evils disturb. Their stoical serenity, was an artificial compound of selfishness, pride, and apathy. No such ingredients enter into Christian meekness. It is the meekness of wisdom (James 3:13); of a wisdom based on a knowledge of self, that humbles; a knowledge of God, that softens; a knowledge of the vanity of time, and the importance of eternity, that abases the soul. This meekness, too, is one of the fruits of the Spirit (Gal. 5:23). It is not a native production of the human heart in this fallen state. There is a mildness and softness, natural to some men, which have much of the appearance, but may not possess the qualities, of genuine meekness. This shows itself towards all men (Titus 3:2). It is not gentle before superiors, and tyrannical to inferiors. It walks with "all lowliness;" does not force its opinion upon others or itself before them (Eph. 4:2). Instead of contending with those that oppose them, it sets itself rather to instruct them for their good (2 Tim. 2:25). And rather than retain even a just displeasure at offenders, is anxious for their amendment, and willing to restore them to favor (Gal. 6:1). True meekness has a constant regard to God, yields every thing to his guidance, and does not murmur at the severest of his providential dealings. A full and perfect example of this virtue was never, but once, exhibited on earth. That example was our Lord. He was invariably meek. Even Moses, the meekest of men, failed in respect of it, and was excluded from Canaan. Even still he was pre-eminent for it above all men that dwelt on the earth (Num. 12:3). But so fully, so perfectly, did this virtue exist in Jesus, that when the apostle would exhort the Corinthians to peace and amity with each other, he beseeches them by the meekness and, gentleness of

Christ (2 Cor. 10:1). Meekness is a lovely and useful virtue. It adorns humanity, and renders life pleasant. It is most acceptable to God: "the ornament of a meek and quiet spirit… is in His sight of great price" (1 Pet. 3:4).

Our Lord, therefore, pronounces his benediction on all who are such, "Blessed are the meek, for they shall inherit the earth" (Matt. 5:5). They seem now to be outcasts, and others lord it in possession. But the time is at hand when Jehovah "will decide with equity for the meek of the earth" (Isa. 11:4), and give them the kingdom in possession.

The meek are the beloved pupils of the great Teacher. "The meek will he guide in judgment, and the meek will he teach his way" (Psa. 25:9). This is part of the peculiar office to which the Spirit of the Lord anointed him. "The Spirit of the Lord God is upon me, because the Lord has anointed me to preach good tidings to the meek" (Isa. 61:1). Let us therefore comply with the exhortation of the prophet Zephaniah, that we may exhibit his character before God and men, and enjoy the blessedness connected with it. "Seek the LORD, all you meek of the earth, who have upheld His justice. Seek righteousness, seek humility. It may be that you will be hidden in the day of the LORD's anger" (Zeph. 2:3).

Secondly, their privilege is set before us, "The meek shall eat." This implies, first, that a supply has been provided for them; secondly, that they are welcome: and thirdly, that they are willing to partake.

First, a supply is provided for them. The Scriptures fully declare this. In various places it is described under the figure of an earthly feast. Our Lord himself uses this parable, "The kingdom of heaven is like a certain king who arranged a marriage for his son, and sent out his servants to call those who were invited to the wedding; and they were not willing to come. Again, he sent out other servants, saying, 'Tell those who are invited, "See, I have prepared my dinner; my oxen and fatted cattle are killed, and all things are ready. Come to the marriage"'" (Matt. 22:2-4). The prophets looked forward to it: "in this mountain The LORD of hosts will make for all people a feast of choice pieces, a feast of wines on the lees, of fat things full of marrow, of well-refined wines on the lees" (Isa. 25:6). Therefore, also, they cried aloud with a universal invitation, "Ho! Everyone who thirsts, come to the waters; and you who have no money, come, buy and eat. Yes, come, buy wine and milk without money and without price. Why do you spend money for what is not bread, and your wages for what does not satisfy? Listen carefully to Me, and eat what is good, and let your soul delight itself in abundance" (Isa. 55:1, 2).

Such is the scriptural representation of the gospel of Christ. God first declares, by these figurative terms, the necessity and appropriateness, the sufficiency and freeness, of provided spiritual blessings in Christ; and then invites, and commands, man to come and take whatever he requires. How different is true Christianity in this respect, from all the false religions of the heathen world! How contrary to that perversion of scriptural religion, which is made by every natural heart! Man imagines that he has a great work to perform, before he can draw near to God, and obtain all that is needed for his soul in time and in eternity. He cannot conceive, and will not be persuaded, that God has already made a full supply for him, and that all that he has to do is to receive and eat. It appears to him, that the first advance must be made on his own side. He knows and feels that he is the inferior, indeed, the offender. He regards God in the same manner in which he would an earthly sovereign, and concludes that it is both right and just, that he should confess his faults, beg for pardon, and plead for a reconciliation. It is indeed just and right that he should do so. But what if the Great King does not wait on our slow return? What if he awaits us with an overflowing kindness? And comes, and stands, and calls, "Incline your ear, and come to Me. Hear, and your soul shall live... Let the wicked forsake his way, and the unrighteous man his thoughts; let him return to the LORD, and He will have mercy on him; and to our God, for He will abundantly pardon. For My thoughts are not your thoughts, nor are your ways My ways," says the LORD" (Isa. 55). What shall we say in this case? How shall we act? Surely if it was right that we should turn to the Lord before, it is much more incumbent now, when he so lovingly invites us!

This is exactly what God has done in the gospel. He prepares the feast; he sends the good news of a full and free salvation, and adds, "All things are ready, come to the wedding" (Matt. 22:4). He shows us that we are welcome to partake of its blessings—pardon, peace, righteousness, strength, wisdom, sanctification, and everlasting redemption. But man replies, "Though the feast be ready, I am not yet ready to receive it." He is too proud to go as he is—too disobedient to go at once—too suspicious to go without asking questions—too doubtful as to the terms and sincerity of the invitation to be convinced that it is really intended for himself. And so many who have some desire to partake of these blessings, are as effectually deprived of them, by these willful hindrances, as the others are by their farms, and purchases, and quiet domestic comforts. Where God places no difficulty, they do. They say to themselves, "Since the Savior has done so much, we must do something." They therefore enter upon a religious course of life. They put aside bad habits, leave off certain sins, and practice the opposite virtues. They attend the means of grace, read the Scriptures, observe regularly all their acts of devotion, private and public. It may be, also, that they use self-denial, weep over their failings, fast, give alms, and follow rigid and harsh practices. But all this, notwithstanding, is spoiled by their inward motive. To obtain reconciliation with God, and to recommend themselves to his mercy, is their great, their avowed object. They think that they must entreat God to be reconciled to them, and will not believe that He is beseeching them to be reconciled to Him (2 Cor. 5:21). In their view it seems absolutely indispensable, that they should first lead a religious life, for at least some period of time; continue in the daily and hourly practice of Christian virtues; and so recommend themselves to God's approval; and they will not be persuaded that God demonstrates his love toward them, in that while they were still sinners, Christ died for them (Rom. 5:8). They imagine that the bestowment of blessings in this free manner, before the religious services are rendered, is the very way to prevent their performance. Now, let it be remarked, that the argument, here, lies not against the services, but against the *motive* from which they spring; and, we may add, that such an objection proceeds on a total misconception of the *object* which God has in view. It is not the mere performance of service that God looks at. Were this what he desires, then the principle of natural men would be correct, their practice wise, and their success certain. But God's heart seeks first, not a religion of service, but a religion of love. He wishes to see, before and around him, not a variety of servants who work for reward, but an assemblage of children, who are actuated by gratitude for what he has already bestowed. We may appeal to their own feelings. Imagine two congregations. The one meets to pray and praise, in order to commend themselves to God, as religious and devout worshippers. The preacher exhorts them to avoid sin, to love righteousness, to practice love in order that they may be able to look back on a well-spent life, and so obtain commendation at the last, from their merciful God and Savior. He concludes; the people return to their houses, satisfied that they have discharged a binding duty. The other congregation meets to pray and praise, in order to testify their gratitude to God for sending his Son to die as their surety, and to obtain a greater likeness to his holy image. The preacher exhorts them to avoid sin, to love righteousness, to practice love, out of love and gratitude to that Savior, who bought them with his blood. He tells them that the only well-spent life which God acknowledges, is that of Jesus of Nazareth; that, therefore, they must look back only upon that; and enjoins them to place all their hope of mercy at the last, only on the merit of his righteousness. He concludes; the people return to their houses, saying, "Our best services are unworthy of His acceptance, who so loved us. Let us be more diligent to serve

Him, and never cease to praise His name, who bought us with his blood."

Now, we ask, as the services are similar, which motive is noble, generous, and praiseworthy? Who would prefer that their children should be actuated by the former, instead of the latter? Which of these two motives, brings most honor to God? Which of them humbles man? Which of them ensures the most loving obedience? Beyond all doubt, the latter. This, then, is the *object* which God has in view. To implant this motive of love in our hearts, Christ died. To inform us of his death, the Gospel is sent. The feast is furnished; and proofs of God's love towards us are exhibited so that we may be incited to enter cordially into all the services of worship, and may perform all our acts of love, out of love and gratitude to him. But though men believe, as an article of their creed that, "Jesus Christ suffered under Pontius Pilate," yet their knowledge of his death has little or no influence on their affections. Why? Because they do not believe in the *motive* that prompted it. They do not think that God really feels a cordial love towards them. They imagine that as we love only what is good or attractive in its own nature, and cannot entertain any affection towards a repulsive object, so God cannot love them, till they shall have done something to please and serve him, and to prove that they are not undeserving of his favor. Thus they begin from themselves. The reconciliation, they imagine, must commence on their part. The love is to flow upwards, from their hearts, towards the heart of God, and so gain his love. Though the Scriptures plainly declare, "In this is love, not that we loved God, but that God loved us" (1 John 4:10); and again, "We love him, because he first loved us" (vs. 19); they still will not be persuaded that their principle is unsound. Why? Because it is too agreeable and flattering, to be let go of quickly. God's principle is one that maintains his own glory, and lowers man. It puts God first, man last. It makes God the generous giver, and man only the receiver, the beggar. But

238 | CHRIST ON THE CROSS IN LIGHT

man's principle is quite the reverse. It exalts man, and dishonors God. It sets man first, God second. It allows man to approach God, not as a mere beggar, but with something in his hand to give; and it represents God as withholding his love, and his blessing, till man can produce the price. No wonder, then, that man naturally contends earnestly for a principle, which is so friendly to his own self-complacency! It is difficult to convince him contrary to his own dignity, and in opposition to the principles of his fallen nature! Difficult! It is impossible! Why? Because man is not naturally what this verse describes: he is not meek; his pride makes him spurn the Gospel. Therefore the apostle calls on us all to "receive with meekness the implanted word, which is able to save your souls" (James 1:21). Of ourselves, we cannot do this. The Spirit of God alone can produce this good fruit in our hearts. We must, therefore, pray to Him to bring this about in us. We must pray to Him to cast down all imaginations, and every high thing in us, that exalts itself against the knowledge of God, and to bring into captivity every thought to the obedience of Christ (2 Cor. 10:5). When the Holy Spirit has thus rendered the heart meek, to receive the words of the gospel, we find that it contains indeed a rich and full supply of spiritual nourishment. The prophet experienced it to be so. "Your words were found, and I ate them, and Your word was to me the joy and rejoicing of my heart" (Jer. 15:16). Our Lord says, "The meek shall eat;" the prophet says, "I did eat." As in eating, we make personal use of the food that is set before us, so it is signified here, that we must make a personal application of the gospel. When it invites, we are to accept; when it commands, we are to obey; when it threatens, we are to fear; when it promises, we are to believe; when it encourages, we are to take comfort; and when it examines, we are to say, "Search me, O God, and know my heart... and see if there is any wicked way in me" (Psa. 139:23-24). This is the personal application of gospel truths, which is intended by this metaphor. It is not a carnal eating, like that of the Israelites (Deut. 16:11, 14), but spiritual, on the true sacrifice of the Lamb of God. As our Lord when alluding to leaven, did not meant that of bread, but of "doctrine" (Matt. 16:12), so when he says, "I am the bread of life" (John 6:48), he means, that he is the doctrine of life; his doctrine is the bread of the soul. When also he says, "My flesh is food indeed, and my blood is drink indeed," he means, "The doctrine of my taking your nature, is a substantial proof of my love to you, on which your soul may meditate, to gain strength for eternity, as your body feeds on food, to gain strength for time. And the doctrine of my blood-shedding to remove your guilt, is an ever-living truth, to which your conscience may have recourse in its thirst for forgiveness, as your parched flesh drinks of a flowing fountain for refreshment." This is the doctrine which the Spirit of God must enable us to receive with meekness, that it may save our souls.

"The meek shall eat:" they do eat. They apply it to their own hearts and consciences every day. This is the food which the world does not know of. Their food is to do the will of God. His will is, first, that they should believe the doctrine of his love; secondly, that they should love him in return; and thirdly, that from love to him, they should love all men, and go about continually doing good. His will, therefore, they daily study to fulfill. It is their delight. It is their strength, their nourishment, their life. The more they are enabled to fulfill it, the more easy does its performance become, and the higher does their own peace and happiness rise. The more they partake of this heavenly food, the more they desire that others should enjoy it, and therefore they thus invite all, "O taste and see that the Lord is good; blessed is the man who trusts in Him" (Psa. 34:8).

In the third place, this verse describes their condition. It is that of satisfaction, "The meek shall eat and be satisfied." The supply that is provided is not only ready, it is full, it is abundant. There is enough, and to spare, for all. Nor is there only a full supply. It is also rich. The quantity does not exceed the quality. The smallest portion is a satisfying portion. It does not disappoint the expectation. It imparts a full and most contented feeling to the soul. No one needs to say, "I must seek something else." How unlike to the portions of this world! They do not satisfy. Their abundance clogs, their richness nauseates, their variety sickens, their quality dissatisfies. We hasten from one to another, and still seek for only another, which may perhaps afford full satisfaction. This is the universal experience of men, "There are many that say, Who will show us any good?" (Psa. 4:6). In contrast to these, the meek are taught to say, "Lord, lift up the light of Your countenance upon us" (Psa. 4:6). This was the satisfying portion which our Lord so earnestly sought when on the cross. This was what he found. This is what he now enjoys. In God's favor is life; at His right hand there are pleasures forevermore. The meek find the fullest satisfaction in that favor now. They shall enjoy it hereafter. It is not only a full and rich, but also an increasing satisfaction, "The meek shall increase their joy in the Lord" (Isa. 29:19). It is not the satisfaction of an hour, or a day, or a year, but of a life. The relish for it continues, by reason of a constant increase. It does not decrease by use. It does not evaporate in enjoyment. It is the satisfaction, which the long benighted traveller feels, who perceives the dawn of a light that shall increase to perfect day. His satisfaction rises as the sun ascends. Christ is a sun of righteousness to the meek. The first dawn of his light imparts satisfaction to their souls, and every increase of his light gives an addition to their happiness. But not only is it full, and rich, and unmixed, and increasing, it is eternal. The satisfaction of God himself, has become the satisfaction of the heart of man. Christ is its source. God is eternally well pleased with the perfect righteousness of his Son, and his people experience it to be an eternal satisfaction to their souls. They are abundantly satisfied with the fatness of God's house (Psa. 36:9; 63:56). Christ the Lord is their portion. He is unchangeable. Their portion therefore is unchanging, and inexhaustible, their satisfaction perpetual. It shall not cease; it cannot cease. Their satisfaction is that of the heart, eternally resting on the heart of Christ. They believe that he loves them; and though he declares that all he has is theirs, yet do they value his love, infinitely beyond all that he can bestow upon them. The Spirit of Christ has entered into their hearts, and has made them partakers of his joy. The joy of Christ must be eternal, their joy therefore shall be eternal. The satisfaction of Christ is everlasting; therefore their satisfaction must be everlasting. Christ prayed for it on the night on which he was betrayed, "These things I speak in the world, that they might have my joy fulfilled in themselves... Father, I desire that they also whom You gave me may be with Me where I am, that they may behold My glory which You have given me... I have declared to them Your name, and will declare it, that the love with which You loved me may be in them, and I in them" (John 17:13, 24, 26).

The meek are satisfied in poverty. Distress and trouble do not impair their peace. When trials overtake them, they are satisfied that God intends them all for good. When temptations assail them, they find a satisfaction in meditating on Christ, who was tempted in all points as they are, yet without sin. The doctrine of his living, and suffering, like themselves, in human flesh, for their benefit, is "food indeed" (John 6:55). When, mourning over their many sins, and daily shortcomings, they are made to thirst after a free and full forgiveness, they obtain complete satisfaction by meditating on the Lamb of God, whose blood cleanses from all sin. This doctrine of his atoning blood is "drink indeed." "They eat," and drink, "in plenty, and are satisfied, and praise the name of the Lord their God, Who has dealt wondrously with them" (Joel 2:26).

Being in this way taught by the Spirit to learn of Christ; being in this way made meek; being in this way enabled to receive the engrafted word; being in this way personal partakers of it, as by a spiritual eating; the meek are filled with a free, full, abundant, rich, sweetly exceeding, increasing, and eternal satisfaction. It is a satisfaction of conscience, of heart, of judgment; a satisfaction of love, and of enjoyment; a satisfaction in poverty and wealth, in health and sickness, in life and death, in time and throughout eternity.

THE SEEKERS OF THE LORD
PRAISING HIM

VERSE 26—*Those who seek Him will praise the Lord.*

THE mind of Christ on the cross appears to dwell with delight on the thought that his people shall experience what he himself enjoys. He had now tasted of his Father's goodness, and was satisfied; and it seems to be with gratification that he declares "the meek shall eat and be satisfied." He had also earnestly sought the favor of God, and had given thanks that he had found it; and now he turns from his own joy, to that of his disciples, as if his were not complete without theirs, and says, "Those who seek Him will praise the Lord."

It is declared by the Redeemer, "Seek, and you shall find" (Matt. 7:7). The command is imperative, the promise is faithful. The performance, therefore, ought to be sincere and persevering. "You shall seek Me and find Me, when you search for Me with all your heart" (Jer. 29:13). The true seeker of God shall become a finder of real joy. He may not now be able to rejoice, but in due time he shall praise the Lord. As it was with Jesus in the garden of Gethsemane, the seeker may be in anguish of spirit; he may have a most bitter cup to drink; his will may be strong against it, yet he will not faint. Again, and again, and again, will he seek the Lord; and though he may not be able to praise him with joyful lips, yet he will praise him with a submissive heart, and render the substantial praise of obedience. Or again, like Jesus on the cross, the seeker may be so enveloped in darkness, that he may be constrained to cry, "Why have You forsaken me?" yet he will continue to seek, and search, and seek again, with all his heart. He will cry, entreat, beseech, use every argument which wisdom, or necessity, can suggest, and follow up all, by an unceasing importunity of earnestness. Remember you are not alone; you have an all-prevailing Intercessor. Christ had no advocate on his side, yet he persevered till he prevailed. Having, therefore, such a High Priest, you may draw near with boldness. He is worthy of the fullest confidence. Like Christ, too, the seeker shall find, and shall praise the Lord. There is no doubt on this point. The promise is as express as the command. "I did not say to the seed of Jacob, 'Seek Me in vain'" (Isa. 45:19). The wrestler shall become a prevailer; Jacob shall be named Israel; the beggar shall become a bestower, he gets blessings, and he gives praises. This is how it shall be with every one that seeks the Lord, not only with all his heart, not only perseveringly, but also in the right time. The Scripture addresses every man and says, "Seek the Lord, while he may be found" (Isa. 55:6). There is a period approaching when it shall be too late. God has limited a certain day, saying in David, "TODAY, if you will hear his voice, do not harden your hearts." "Behold, now is the accepted time; behold, now is the day of salvation" (Heb. 4:7; 2 Cor. 6:2). Christ wept over Jerusalem, because she let slip the period allotted to her. God declares regarding many, "They shall seek me diligently, but they shall not find me" (Prov. 1:28). Let this warning rouse the slothful professor. Let it alarm the careless sinner. Should he inquire, "But how shall I seek the Lord?" we reply, first, by earnest, secret, prayer. This is a work which cannot be engaged in by any friend in your place. It is a personal seeking. If your own heart is not engaged in it, you can obtain no blessing. Let secret, earnest, private, prayer, be daily exercised by you; cause constant petitions to ascend, wherever you are, and however you are occupied. Remember, that prayer is the first and most needful part of your duty in seeking the Lord. But do not neglect other means. Seek God in his church, in the assembly of his people. Where his word is preached, and spiritual worship ascends, he is present to bless; do not fail to meet your Lord there so that you may obtain his blessing. Seek him also by diligent reading of the Holy Scriptures, which are as a lamp to guide you to his presence.

Seek the Lord by all the means of grace, and ordinances of his appointment, but do not rest in the mere use of means. Ask of the Spirit of God to make them helps, otherwise they shall prove to be hindrances. Above all, and along with all, seek the Lord by faith. Believe that he is willing to reveal himself to you; be persuaded that he is not far from you; that he notices your every inquiry. Believe that he is more willing to hear than you are to pray, more ready to give than you are to ask. Such faith honors God. It prevails. Those who place confidence in God shall never be confounded; "they shall praise the Lord that seek him." In the flesh you shall praise God. You shall find him to be a Father, a Preserver, a Friend, a Savior, a Comforter. With the fleshly body, all seeking shall be put off. Then the praises of the Lord, which commenced in time, shall increase, shall swell symphonious, and the arches of heaven shall resound with the music of eternal gratitude!

•

THE ETERNAL LIFE

VERSE 26—*Your heart shall live forever!*

HAVING regarded his people under two of what ought to be their most prominent characteristics, meekness, and seeking of the Lord; having solaced his mind with the consideration of their happiness and their gratitude; their satisfaction with his blessings, and their praises of his heavenly Father for them; our Lord next meditates on their imperishable condition. And to render that thought fruitful of peace, and grace, and strong consolation, to our souls, he graciously expresses it in the form of this affirmative assurance, "Your heart shall live for ever." He does not say, you shall live forever, but your *heart*. He knows that the great majority of his disciples must die, and be laid in the grave. Only an Enoch, in the antediluvian world, and an Elijah, in the time of the prophets, had passed from earth to heaven, without tasting death. A long period of intervening time must elapse, before any similar event should happen. And as, even then, the living saints, who shall be clothed with their house from heaven (2 Cor. 5:2, 4), shall be comparatively, a very small part of the whole redeemed family, our Lord in speaking of the eternal and blessed life, uses a term which comprehends them all, and says, "Your heart shall live for ever." We understand it to signify their everlasting spiritual condition. The heart, the new heart, the sanctified soul may be removed from one place to another, as at death, from earth to heaven; but still, its state, its condition, its desires, its feelings, its life, are the same.

"Your heart," that is, not your outward man, but the hidden man of the heart (Ezek. 36:26); the renewed spirit of the mind; the new man which is created after the image of God, in righteousness, and true holiness (Eph. 4:23, 24). "The heart," that is, the inward holy feelings and desires; the spirit of love to God and man; that state of mind which is, as it were, the heart of penitence, and prayer, and purity, "shall live for ever." The life which animates it, is the life of the Spirit of God. It is, therefore, a life of union with him, from whom that Spirit comes. It is the life of membership with the head, even Christ, from whom the whole body having nourishment ministered, shall increase with all the increase of God (Col. 2:19). Therefore Christ said, "Because I live, you will live also" (John 14:9). And the apostle, enlarging on the same blessed truth, declares, "Your life is hidden with Christ in God. When Christ who is our life appears, then you also will appear with him in glory" (Col. 3:2, 4). This eternal life, then, this living of the heart forever, is not a mere unending existence. It is not a far off thing, as too many consider it, which is only to be enjoyed in the future state of being. It is a present reality. It is a life begun on earth. It is an actual possession, not merely a future prospect. "He who believes in me HAS everlasting life" (John 6:47). "He who believes in me shall NEVER die" (John 11:26). "We know that we HAVE passed," says the apostle, "from death to life" (1 John 3:14). If these express statements of Holy Scripture are not sufficient to prove that this life has a present, actual, commencement in this state of being, as well as an unceasing continuance in that which is to come; and if any still inquire, What is eternal life? Let the Savior's testimony terminate every doubt, for he says, "This is eternal life, that they may know You, the only true God, and Jesus Christ whom You have sent" (John 17:3). However simple this statement appears to be, yet many are unable to attach a definite idea to the declaration, that eternal life consists in the *knowledge* of God. This arises from not keeping in view the scriptural, and therefore only true, meaning of death and life. Death is separation. Man is an intellectual and moral, as well as a material being. Separation from wisdom—*ignorance,*—is intellectual death. Separation from holiness—*sin,*—is moral death. Separation from spirit—*dissolution,*—is material death. How did this triple death come? By him who had the power of it (Heb. 2:14). Satan struck his deathblow on the proudest part of man. He induced him to seek after forbidden knowledge, and so effected his separation from the true wisdom. This was intellectual death; that is to say, man's powers of mind were now turned into another channel, and no longer thought, discerned, and judged, in concert with the mind of God. As the blind eye is dead to this material world, so a blind or perverted intellect is dead to the high wisdom of heaven. Man's nature is such that he can only love the things he sees; and now that his intellectual vision has become blind to spiritual realities, his affections are engrossed with the things of sense. Intellect may be called, the head of a spiritual being. To dazzle him with a thought too great for his capacity, may be the same in the spiritual world, as a stunning blow on the head is in this world of matter. The natural effect of a stun is *insensibility,* which may be analogous, among spirits, to death. If this analogy is correct, it enables us to understand the process of Adam's fall. His intellect was dazzled, his heart became insensible, and being thereby fallen from God, or dead in mind and heart, nothing remained but the passing of a just judgment to effect the separation of soul and body. Material and moral death are the double result of intellectual death. As then, death, through Satan, entered by means of stolen knowledge, so now, life, through Christ, enters by means of revealed knowledge.

"This is eternal life, that they might know You." "I have declared to them Your name, and will declare it, (in order) that the love with which You have loved me may be in them, and I in them" (John 17:26). The true declaration of God's character, or name, by Christ, brings love into the heart that believes it; just as the false declaration of God's character, by Satan, brought aversion and dread into the hearts of our first parents. Therefore, the apostle blesses the Christians in this way, "Grace and peace be multiplied to you, in the knowledge of God, and of Jesus our Lord" (2 Pet. 1:2). He reminds them, also, by what means they had escaped the pollutions of the world, "Through the knowledge of the Lord and Savior Jesus Christ" (2 Pet. 2:20). And therefore concludes his epistle with these words, "But grow in the grace and knowledge of our Lord and Savior Jesus Christ," (2 Pet. 3:18). Satan came to man as deception and falsehood; Christ comes as righteousness and truth As it was by belief of the lie that man fell, so it is by belief of the truth that man is saved. The lie received is death to the soul; the truth received is life. Adam ate of the fruit of the forbidden tree, and died; we eat of the bread-fruit of the tree of life, and live for ever (John 6:48, 51). "The words that I speak to you," says our Lord, "are spirit, and they are life" (John 6:63). They are so when received in the meaning, and to the purpose, which our Lord himself intends. All who so receive them, find them to be spirit and life. It was the command of God, that proved the word of life to creation; but now it is the Son of God, that is the word of life to the soul. Therefore he declares, "He who hears My word, and believes in Him who sent me, HAS everlasting life, and shall not come into judgment, but has PASSED from death into life" (John 5:24). Eternal life, therefore, is a present reality. We do not wait for its possession till a future period. "This is the testimony, that God HAS GIVEN us eternal life, and this life is in his Son. He who has the Son has life; he who does not have the Son of God does not have life. These things I have written to you who believe on the name of the Son of God, that you may know that you have eternal life" (1 John 5:11-13).

By this phrase—eternal life, something greater is meant than when we say, everlasting life. Eternity includes past, present, and future. Everlasting, refers only to the two latter. Eternal life, then, is that which never had a beginning. It is the life of God. When man was created to live, and move, and have his being in God, that eternal life which was in God, became an everlasting life in man. Since, however, it comes from, and is of, God, it is rightly called in Scripture eternal life. In itself it is eternal; but in reference to man, in whom it has a beginning, it is everlasting. Life's first entrance into man was by a word; so now its new entrance, its new birth is by "The Word." "In the beginning was the Word, and the Word was with God, and the Word was God.

He was in the beginning with God. All things were made through Him, and without Him nothing was made that was made. In him was life, and the life was the light of men. And the light shines in the darkness, and the darkness did not comprehend it" (John 1:1-5). This is a most remarkable, comprehensive, and important, passage, as beautiful as it is instructive. God is the Word—the Word is Life, the Life is Light, the Light shines in darkness, the darkness did not comprehend it. Being God, it is eternal; being Word, it is intellectual; being Life, it destroys death; and being Light, it dispels darkness; but being intellectual and moral light, the darkness of ignorance and sin does not comprehend it. This non-comprehension is willful. God the Word, the Light, the Life, was not far off, but had come near. The Word was made flesh, and dwelt among us. That flesh with human tones uttered forth the word from within; it said, "The words that I speak unto you, are spirit and they are life" (John 6:63). "They are part of myself; I take this form; I use these tones, to suit your state; what your ears now hear, believe. Receive my words into your hearts; hear, and your soul shall live—it shall live for ever."

God the Son being thus exhibited as the Word, the Word being embodied in the Scriptures, the Scriptures being addressed to the intellect and heart of man, and the entrance of the words or truths of these Scriptures, being the instrumental means of salvation, natural men are tempted to conceive that salvation is a mere intellectual process; they regard the words and doctrines of Scripture as so many problems and propositions, to which they must yield their assent. There they rest satisfied. But they overlook the fact, that the truth is moral, as well as intellectual; that it is life, as well as light; that it is addressed to the heart, as well as to the understanding, "With the heart, one believes unto righteousness" (Rom. 10:10). What does he believe? "The word of righteousness" (Heb. 5:13). "Christ," the Word, "is of God made unto us righteousness" (1 Cor. 1:30). Receiving Christ, then, into the heart, man receives righteousness; and he receives also whatsoever Christ is besides, wisdom, strength, sanctification, and redemption. The soul being thus united to Christ as its righteousness, becomes freed from guilt and condemnation; to Christ as wisdom, is delivered from ignorance; to Christ as strength, is restored from weakness; to Christ as sanctification, is saved from unholiness; to Christ as redemption, is rescued from eternal bondage. Being united to Christ the Light, darkness is dispelled; to Christ the Life, death is destroyed; to Christ the Word, all the treasures of wisdom and knowledge are laid open before it (Col. 2:3); to Christ the true God, finds again, in him, that God whom it had lost, and that eternal life which it had forfeited (1 John 5:20). This is the restoration, the resuscitation, of the soul. It is put in possession of everlasting life, because it is put in possession of Christ, who is eternal life; and it is concerning this revived, this renewed, soul, this newborn spirit of man, that this verse speaks, and declares, "Your heart shall live for ever."

In the present condition of the believer, however, this life is feeble and confined. His flesh not being a partaker of it always contends against it. The flesh recognizes, and understands, its own natural life, but this other life is strange and irksome to it. The flesh must therefore be destroyed, that the life, the true life, may be free. The shell must be thrown off, that the living creature may appear. The cocoon must be burst, that the new creature may fly to another and happier region. The death of the body, therefore, is emphatically the life of the spirit. The soul goes to God: but it must previously have been of God. It must have had the eternal life abiding in it; otherwise, at its separation from the body, it must pass into eternal death. If, however, the eternal life has entered into it, before it leaves the flesh, then assuredly, on its removal from the body, it enters into the eternal life.

What we have now considered is altogether above, and beyond, earthly existence. This is true LIFE; it is all happiness; pure enjoyment; bliss unutterable, and uninterrupted. This is indeed TO LIVE, in the noblest, purest, most exalted sense. This is the height of human and angelic happines. It is heaven. It is existence, possessing whatever is desirable, and freed from all that is undesirable. It is the entire satisfaction of every need, and feeling, and faculty of the soul's nature.

Reader, do you desire to possess this blessedness? Then *"lay hold on eternal life"* (1 Tim. 6:12, 19). It is the free gift of God through Jesus Christ our Lord (Rom. 6:23). Receive Christ now into your heart. "This is the testimony, that God has given us eternal life, and this life is in his Son" (1 John 5:11). It is in Christ, the second Adam, so that it may be secured to us forever. When life was lodged in the first Adam, he quickly lost it; and were it placed in any of us his children, we would lose it also. While, then, we bless God for this free gift, let us render unbounded, everlasting, praises and thanksgivings, that it is bestowed in such a manner, as to render loss on our part impossible, and the utmost efforts of the enemies of our souls futile and ineffectual.

THE CONVERSION OF THE WORLD

VERSE 27—*All the ends of the world shall remember, and turn to the Lord, and all the families of the nations shall worship before You.*

HAVING thus taken a view of the personal character, the peculiar privilege, and the everlasting condition of his disciples individually, our Lord directs his thoughts onward to the glorious subject of the whole world's conversion unto God. Even now, that he is at the right hand of the throne on high, he still looks forward to the same object which he contemplated from the cross on Calvary. If over even one sinner returning from the error of his ways, the angels of God rejoice, how much more will He who bought him with his blood? Who shall estimate the Savior's joy, the angels' gladness when multitudes of sinners, when all the sinners that stand upon the earth, shall remember themselves, and turn unto the Lord? What finite mind can conceive the glorious subject aright? It is foretold in prophecies—it is celebrated in psalms—it is announced in gospels—it is declared in epistles, it is unfolded in revelations, that "all the ends of the world shall remember, and turn to the Lord, and all the families of the nations shall worship before Him!"

These words unfold to us part of that joy which was set before the Lord, while on the cross, and on account of which he patiently endured its agonies, and despised its shame. His mind seems to turn to it with peculiar delight. He dwells on it with deepest interest. He enlarges on the amazing theme; has his thoughts so occupied with its various details, that he enlarges upon them in the remaining portion of the psalm; and is so fully satisfied with this prospective view of the fruit of the travail of his soul, that no other desire remains, and he concludes the psalm, and his mortal life together, saying, "It is all fulfilled."

It is declared in this verse, "All the ends of the world shall REMEMBER." This is a remarkable expression. It implies that man has forgotten God. It represents all the successive generations of the world as one. And then it exhibits that one generation, as if it had been in paradise, suddenly remembering the Lord whom it had known there, but had long forgotten. Imagine an individual to have lost a valuable jewel; that he can neither recollect its exact appearance, nor its full value, nor the place where it was lost; that he occupies himself in a continual search; often thinks he has found it, and mistakes other objects that partly resemble it—and that at last he gathers all the valuable things he can collect, and bestows on them the name, or names, of his favorite, deplored, and invaluable jewel. Imagine that after a time, he suddenly recollects the time when, and the place where, it was lost. The form, color, size, and value of his jewel, come vividly to his remembrance. He starts up with delight, casts aside his collected valuables, rushes to the spot, and darts his hand upon the lost treasure. Apply this picture spiritually, and it will represent the conduct of man in reference to God. Having lost sight of the Glorious Being who was seen in Eden, man looked for him in air, and earth, and sea. In his eager, but blind search, he took many things for God. He examined every good and valuable thing that met his observation. He converted every useful thing into a god. To supply that deficiency which he felt, he collected to himself gods many, and lords many. As years rolled on, he still added to the number; and that the object which he sought might somehow or somewhere be found, he deified himself, and every thing in nature. Every thing, too, not in nature, of which he heard, or could conceive, he did deify, lest that one thing which he did not worship, might possibly be God. Even all this did not satisfy. Man was not sure that he had found his object. His soul still craved after a Being, whom it did not know how to describe. Perplexed, and standing thoughtful in the wisest city of his idolatry, he bethought himself of an expedient, and hastily set himself with his children to erect an altar to "The Unknown God." St. Paul came amongst them after they had been so engaged. He reasoned earnestly with them: "Then Paul stood in the midst of the Areopagus and said, "Men of

Athens, I perceive that in all things you are very religious; for as I was passing through and considering the objects of your worship, I even found an altar with this inscription: TO THE UNKNOWN GOD. Therefore, the One whom you worship without knowing, Him I proclaim to you: God, who made the world and everything in it, since He is Lord of heaven and earth, does not dwell in temples made with hands. Nor is He worshiped with men's hands, as though He needed anything, since He gives to all life, breath, and all things. And He has made from one blood every nation of men to dwell on all the face of the earth, and has determined their pre-appointed times and the boundaries of their dwellings, so that they should seek the Lord, in the hope that they might grope for Him and find Him, though He is not far from each one of us; for in Him we live and move and have our being, as also some of your own poets have said, 'For we are also His offspring.' Therefore, since we are the offspring of God, we ought not to think that the Divine Nature is like gold or silver or stone, something shaped by art and man's devising" (Acts 27:22-29). What an appropriate address! How exquisitely adapted to their state of mind! Like men groping in the dark, they were "feeling after the lost Godhead." Yet so blind, and self-willed, were they, that they mocked this messenger of the true God, and despised his doctrine. The gospel is not always successfully declared. It has not, even now, obtained universal supremacy. The dark places of the earth are still crowded with human beings who are groping after light, and truth, and God. However eagerly they embrace their innumerable gods and goddesses, they are still seeking to increase their number. But it shall not be so, when the period spoken of in this verse arrives. Then the Glorious Being seen in Eden, shall be recognized "in the face of Jesus Christ" (2 Cor. 4:6). Those busy idolaters, who ransack the ends of the world, and crowd their houses, and fill their hands, with gods, and lords, and images, shall cast their idols to the moles and to the bats, and fall upon their knees in earnest supplication, and adoring reverence.

Such shall be the case. The fullness of the world shall be converted unto the Lord. Not a nation or kingdom shall be ignorant of his name. The Lord has sworn, and will not relent. In his own time he will show forth his glory, and all the ends of the earth shall see the salvation of our God. So plainly was this event exhibited before the psalmist in prophetic vision, that he speaks of it as if actually beholding its complete accomplishment; "The Lord HAS MADE KNOWN his salvation… All the ends of the earth HAVE SEEN the salvation of our God" (Psa. 98:2, 3).

The converted nations shall not only obtain remembrance of their past loss, but shall also be filled with the knowledge of present duty. "They shall turn to the Lord, and all the families of the nations shall worship before him." When the Lord takes unto him his great power, and reigns, though there will be fearful judgments and dreadful destructions, yet we ought not to forget that this great power is as much, if not more, of a moral than of a physical, nature. His might, which can make every knee of man to bow, and even make devils tremble, shall, at its proper moment, exercise a moral power to secure also the homage of the heart. His people shall be made willing in the day of his power to worship the Lord in the beauties of holiness (Psa. 110:3). The Scriptures fully assert this fact. "All nations whom You have made shall come and worship before You, O Lord, and shall glorify Your name" (Psa. 86:9). This is the fulfillment of the Father's promise, and of the Son's expectation. It is the joy that was set before him on the cross. It is the high reward which that bitter death obtained. Hear how the Father addressed the Son, "Indeed He says, 'It is too small a thing that You should be My Servant to raise up the tribes of Jacob, and to restore the preserved ones of Israel; I will also give You as a light to the Gentiles, that You should be My salvation to the ends of the earth.'" Thus says the LORD, the Redeemer of Israel, their Holy One, to Him whom man despises, to Him whom the nation abhors, to the Servant of rulers: "Kings shall see and arise, princes also shall worship, because of the LORD who is faithful, the Holy One of Israel; and He has chosen You." (Isa. 49:6-7). The same truth is stated by the apostle, as a necessary consequence of the Savior's obedience, "Therefore God also has highly exalted Him and given Him the name which is above every name, that at the name of Jesus every knee should bow, of those in heaven, and of those on earth, and of those under the earth, and that every tongue should confess that Jesus Christ is Lord, to the glory of God the Father" (Phil. 2:9-11). What a glorious prospect! He who was mocked by Pilate, Herod, and the Jews, shall be worshipped by all people. The inhabitants of the world, who now love sin, shall all then have learned righteousness; for "the earth shall be full of the knowledge of the Lord, as the waters cover the sea" (Isa. 11:9). Who would not desire that it may be hastened?

> "Waft, waft, ye winds, his story,
> And you, ye waters, roll,
> Till, like a sea of glory,
> It spread from pole to pole."

It is our high privilege to be called to join in the prayers of our Head. He is now in heaven supplicating on behalf of sinners, and his Church on earth ardently engages in the same intercession—

"O God, the Creator and Preserver of all mankind, we humbly beseech You for all sorts and conditions of men, that You would be pleased to make Your ways known unto them, Your saving health unto all nations."

"O merciful God, who has made all men, and hate nothing that You have made, nor desire the death of a sinner, but rather that he should be converted and live, have mercy upon all Jews, Turks, infidels, and heretics; and take from them all ignorance, hardness of heart, and contempt of Your word; and so fetch them home, blessed Lord, to Your flock, that they may be saved among the remnant of the true Israelites, and be made one fold under one Shepherd, Jesus Christ our Lord, who lives and reigns with You and the Holy Spirit, one God, world without end. Amen."

All the works of the Lord are carried on by prayer. He pours forth his Spirit upon his church, to ask for those things which he designs to accomplish. When he assures the scattered children of Abraham, that he will restore them again to their own land he declares, as a preparatory measure, "I will also let the house of Israel inquire of Me to do this for them..." (Ezek. 36:37). When the people are to look upon Him whom they have pierced and mourn, it is not till the "Spirit of grace and of supplication" has been poured upon them from on high (Zech. 12:10). Our Lord teaches us to pray, "Your kingdom come." The souls who compose the Church above cry day and night before God, "How long, O Lord?" (Rev. 6:10; Luke 18:7). The Church below thus presents herself at his footstool:—"Beseeching You, that it may please You, of Your gracious goodness, shortly to accomplish the number of Your ELECT, and to hasten Your kingdom; that we, with all those that are departed in the true faith of Your holy name, may have our perfect consummation and bliss, both in body and soul, in Your eternal and everlasting glory, through Jesus Christ our Lord. Amen." Let us not then despond. The increase of prayer at the present day, for this object, is a pledge and proof that it will surely, perhaps speedily, be accomplished. Though so many millions of human beings still exist in heathen darkness, let our faith be strong in the sure word of prophecy, and though the vision tarry, yet let not our hearts be discouraged. The Lord Jesus, the Head, and the members of his Church, by the same Spirit, unite in the same expectation, and in the same petitions. The psalmist rejoices in the prospect, and says, "O You who hear prayer, to You all flesh will come" (Psa. 65:2). And in the name of the whole Church he thus prays for the blessing of the Lord, and rejoices at the effect which it will produce in the whole earth. "God be merciful to us and bless us, and cause His face to shine upon us, that Your way may be known on earth, Your salvation among all nations. Let the peoples praise You, O God; let all the peoples praise You. Oh, let the nations be glad and sing for joy! For You shall judge the people righteously, and govern the nations on earth. Let the peoples praise You, O God; let all the peoples praise You. Then the earth shall yield her increase; God, our own God, shall bless us. God shall bless us, and all the ends of the earth shall fear Him." (Psa. 67).

THE ENTHRONEMENT

VERSE 28—*For the kingdom is the Lord's, and He rules over the nations.*

HERE is assigned the reason of that remarkable change in this idolatrous world which the previous verse had described. So great an event must have an adequate cause. That cause is that the Lord has taken to himself his great power and has reigned (Rev. 11:17).

Christ is not now reigning as king of the earth, but interceding as priest at the right hand of the throne on high. There he will continue to officiate on behalf of his Church, until it shall please him to offer up the fullness of that prayer which God the Father has entitled him to present, "Ask of Me, and I will give You the nations for Your inheritance, and the uttermost parts of the earth for Your possession" (Psa. 2:8). From this passage we may conclude, that the conversion of the heathen nations has been going forward on earth, according to the extent of petition which Christ presents in heaven. The extension of the gospel in our own day, is the immediate result of a special request on the part of our great High-priest. He asked for the islands of the south, and God the Father bestowed them. He asked for the villages of joy in one of the plains of India, and hundreds have acknowledged the name of Jesus, to the glory of God the Father. The last request which he shall present, will be for the uttermost parts in possession. At present they are his by right, by promise, and by expectation. But no sooner shall he prefer the petition, than they shall become his by possession. As he said before he was lifted up upon the cross, so will he pray before he is exalted to the throne, "Father, the hour is come; glorify Your Son, that Your Son may also glorify You." Daniel beheld this in the night visions, "And behold, one like the Son of Man, coming with the clouds of heaven! He came to the Ancient of days, and they brought Him near before Him" (Dan.

7:13). Then and there, it may be, he will say, "Give me the heathen for my inheritance, and the uttermost parts of the earth for my possession." "To Him was given dominion, and glory, and a kingdom, that all peoples, nations, and languages should serve him. His dominion is an everlasting dominion, which shall not pass away, and His kingdom the one which shall not be destroyed" (Dan. 7:14).

This is the kingdom which our Lord here contemplates from the cross. It forms part of the vision of joy that was set before him. Thus, in the fullness of time, the kingly throne shall be set for the Lord Jesus. The office of priest shall cease. The period of grace and salvation shall terminate. He will sit upon the throne of his glory. He shall be crowned King of kings and Lord of lords.

By the phrase "kingdom of God," which occurs so frequently in Scripture, we are to understand either his kingdom of grace, or his kingdom of glory, and sometimes both. But what is the kingdom of grace, and what the kingdom of glory? The kingdom of grace, is where God reigns in a gracious or merciful manner; the kingdom of glory, is where God reigns in a glorious or all-powerful manner. The kingdom of grace is now being established over our world. "God was in Christ, reconciling the world to Himself, not imputing their trespasses to them" (2 Cor. 5:19). He is now extending the scepter of mercy towards sinners. He rules and reigns over their hearts by his Spirit. He bears with those who reject his authority. He is affording them both time and opportunity, to turn from their rebellion, and to become his subjects and servants. *This is the kingdom of God's grace.* But the kingdom of God's *glory* shall be set up in its own time, and then he shall take to himself his great power and reign, from the one end of this earth to the other. Then the loud voice shall be heard in heaven, saying, "Now salvation, and strength, and the kingdom of our God, and the power of His Christ have come" (Rev. 12:10). Then the scepter of mercy shall give place to the throne of judgment. Sinners shall no longer be invited to salvation; there shall be no more space for repentance; and Christ himself shall say, "bring here those enemies of mine, who did not want me to reign over them, and slay them before me" (Luke 19:27). But to those who were subjects of his kingdom of grace, he shall say, "Come, you blessed of My Father, inherit the kingdom" (that is, the kingdom of glory) "prepared for you from the foundation of the world" (Matt. 25:34).

The kingdom of grace, then, is preparatory to the kingdom of glory; and this term, "kingdom of God," including both these, is to be defined as that sphere where God is acknowledged, and reigns as king; or where God *ought* to be acknowledged, and ought to reign as king. On this earth, God ought to reign supreme; but Scripture informs us that he does not reign universally, and is not acknowledged as king, save by a small part of its inhabitants. Satan is called *the prince* and *the god* of this world. In heaven itself, he first unfurled the black banner of rebellion. Driven from there he planted it on our earth, and with a serpent's hiss, summoned man to his standard. The king of the lower creation joined the enemies of his Maker. He stretched forth his right hand to the forbidden tree; and, as it were, registered an oath in nature, that no allegiance was hereafter due to the authority of God. Satan's triumph was now complete: he had lost a crown in heaven, but he had established a throne on earth. Man, attempting to be his own master, became the slave of Satan, and all he possessed his prey. Proud of his acquired dominions, he exercises a tyranny of darkness over them all. He keeps a vigilant watch on every part. When he presumed to present himself amongst the sons of God, and was interrogated, "From where do you come?" he instantly replied, "From going to and fro on the earth, and from walking back and forth on it" (Job 1:7). And when he attempted to prevail over our blessed Savior in the wilderness, the last temptation to which he had recourse, was to show him all the kingdoms of the world, and the glory of them, in a moment of time, with this proud and kingly speech, "All this authority I will give You, and their glory; for this has been delivered to me, and I give it to whomever I wish. Therefore, if You will worship before me, all will be Yours" (Luke 4:6, 7).

Thus we learn from the Scriptures, that the kingly power of God was denied from the beginning; and that Satan's power and kingdom are now extended over the whole earth. When, therefore, our Lord commands us to "seek first the kingdom of God" (Matt. 6:33), he means that it should be our earnest desire and endeavor, that the kingship of the earth may again be exercised by Him to whom it belongs, and that the dominion of Satan may be speedily deprived of all its power over ourselves, our neighbors, and the world at large.

To illustrate this truth, let us suppose that the Queen of these realms were banished from her throne by a wicked and powerful faction. Suppose that traitors were in possession of power, and that no friends of the exiled queen dared show themselves. Imagine that the dethroned sovereign sent an unknown messenger to comfort the hearts of her different friends with secret intelligence of her return with a mighty army. How should that messenger address them? Would he not say to one, "Do not be faint-hearted, the Queen shall soon be restored?" How would he warn another, not to be dazzled with the new order of things, for it will speedily be destroyed. Might he not address a young man in this way, "Do not be ambitious of their honors, but seek first the kingdom of the Queen and her restoration, and then you shall enjoy them all?" And would he not comfort and encourage every one of them under their losses and trials for the Queen's sake, with the assurance that she was near at hand with powerful armies, to take possession of her kingdom, and to restore joy and gladness amongst all her loyal, but now mourning and oppressed, subjects?

Such is the address of Christ in his first discourse, the Sermon on the Mount. *He* is the unknown messenger. He is the sovereign himself in disguise, cheering the hearts of his friends with suitable words. "Blessed," says he, "are those who mourn, for they shall be comforted. Blessed are those who are persecuted for righteousness' sake, for theirs is the kingdom of heaven. Blessed are you when they revile and persecute you, and say all manner of evil against you falsely, for my sake." Teaching them how to address their prayers to God, the second petition which he bids them offer is, "Your kingdom come." And, lest they should be tempted to seek comfort and quiet under the usurper of his throne, he solemnly exhorts them, "Seek first the kingdom of God." Be on the Lord's side, take part with your lawful sovereign; seek no rest, no honors for yourself under the tyranny of the usurper, but seek first the restoration of your royal Master. Let it be the principal object of your life to further the establishment and prosperity of his kingdom. Seek that his grace may reign in your hearts, and that no foreign power obtain an influence over you. Seek that that King who reigns in righteousness, may be the God of your families, the Ruler of your country, and the only Governor among the nations. Seek that Satan's kingdom may be overthrown, and that the kingdom of glory may be hastened; "that blessed time," foretold in prophecy, when "all the kingdoms of this world shall become the kingdoms of our Lord and of his Christ" (Rev. 11:15).

But, alas! This is a duty awfully neglected, because we shut our eyes to the real condition of things. We are unwilling to admit the Scripture truth, that "the whole world lies under the sway of the wicked one" (1 John 5:19).

Let us never forget that ours is a conquered world; that power now is in unlawful hands; but that full possession is being disputed with the rebels. This is why it is that we read in Scripture of wars and fights—of captains, leaders, and armies—of soldiers, weapons, and suits of armor. This is why it is that we are, as it were, enlisted into the service of the Captain of our salvation, by those beautiful, appropriate, and emphatic words, "In token that hereafter we shall not be ashamed to confess the faith of Christ crucified and manfully to fight under his banner against sin, the world, and the devil: and to continue as Christ's faithful soldiers and servants unto our life's end." It is a war of principles, of truth and error, of good and evil, of light and darkness, in which we are engaged.

The contest has been, and is, whether righteousness and truth shall keep possession of the earth; or whether iniquity and error shall prevail. The field of battle is the heart of man. "The weapons of our warfare," says the apostle, "are not carnal but mighty in God for pulling down strongholds, casting down arguments," (or reasoning's,) "and every high thing that exalts itself against the knowledge of God, and bringing every thought into captivity to the obedience of Christ" (2 Cor. 10:4, 5). What those weapons are by which such a noble victory is obtained, the same apostle informs us: "Put on the whole armor of God, that you may be able to stand against the wiles of the devil. For we do not wrestle against flesh and blood, but against principalities, against powers, against the rulers of the darkness of this age, against spiritual hosts of wickedness in the heavenly places. Therefore take up the whole armor of God, that you may be able to withstand in the evil day, and having done all, to stand. Stand therefore, having girded your waist with truth, having put on the breastplate of righteousness, and having shod your feet with the preparation of the gospel of peace; above all, taking the shield of faith with which you will be able to quench all the fiery darts of the wicked one. And take the helmet of salvation, and the sword of the Spirit, which is the word of God; praying always with all prayer and supplication in the Spirit, being watchful to this end with all perseverance and supplication for all the saints..." (Eph. 6:11-18).

Such is the armor which our God has provided for us. It is a spiritual armor, because it is a spiritual warfare. The battle is now waging in the heart of every one of us, and is being urged in the world around us. Christ endowed his Church with his own Spirit, under the name of "POWER from on high" (Luke 24:49); saying, as it were, to his widowed spouse, "Go in this might of yours." Under the dispensation of the Spirit, the Church ought to have obtained greater power and extension. But alas! She has been unfaithful to her Lord's parting command, "Go into all the world, and preach the Gospel to every creature" (Mark 16:15). She has been unfaithful to the Spirit, in whose power she was to fight all the battles of the Lord. She has been unfaithful to her own solemn engagements in the baptismal covenant. The sad result testifies against the Church of Christ. Twenty centuries have passed away, and the great majority of the earth's inhabitants are still in heathen darkness! Christ has been greatly disappointed of that fruit which he might well have expected to reap from the exertions of his Church. With the fullest justice we may suppose him to address her now, as he did the Church of Sardis, or of Laodicea, of old, "I have not found your works perfect before God..." "These things says the Amen, the Faithful and True Witness, the Beginning of the creation of God: I know your works, that you are neither cold nor hot. I could wish you were cold or hot... As many as I love, I rebuke and chasten. Therefore be zealous and repent." (Rev. 3:2, 14, 15, 19). Of late years, great exertions have been made to send the glad tidings of salvation to every quarter of the globe; but when compared to the amount of work to be overtaken, these exertions, valuable and extensive as they are, appear to be but as the contributions of a noble river to the mighty ocean. It may be that the Lord has been delaying from year to year, till his Church should more effectually discharge her duty: or rather in his longsuffering towards sinners, has been allowing them a protracted space for repentance. Time, however, is fast rolling on, and sooner or later, ONE on whose head are many crowns, and whose name is called the Word of God, shall come forth. The armies of heaven shall follow him, for he is King of kings, and Lord of lords (Rev. 19:16). "In that day shall there be one Lord, who shall be KING over all the earth"[19] (Zech. 14:9). Then shall it be said, "God has gone up with a shout, the LORD with the sound of a trumpet. Sing praises to God, sing praises! Sing praises to our King, sing praises! For God is the King of all the earth; sing praises with understanding. God reigns over the nations; God sits on His holy throne" (Psa. 47:5-8). That "shout" is an attendant sign of the Lord Jesus Christ himself (1 Thess. 4:16). That "trumpet" is the sounding of the last, the seventh angel, when the great voices in heaven shall be heard saying, "the kingdoms of this world have become the kingdoms of our Lord and of

---

[19] KJV retained.

His Christ, and He shall reign for ever and ever" (Rev. 11:15). Then shall be fulfilled the promise made to the Virgin Mary by the mouth of the announcing angel, "The Lord God will give Him the throne of His father David" (Luke 1:32).

This title of *"ruler"* or *"Governor"* in the text, is expressly applied to the Lord Jesus, in a passage which subjoins a most remarkable testimony to his Divinity. "But you, Bethlehem Ephrathah, though you are little among the thousands of Judah, yet out of you shall come forth to Me the One to be Ruler in Israel, whose goings forth are from of old, from everlasting" (Compare Matt. 2:6, and Micah 5:2). The children of Israel are now dispersed throughout the earth. Many days have they abode without a king, and without a prince; but when the Governor shall issue his mandate among the nations, and when he shall pour upon the children of Israel the Spirit of grace and of supplication, then they shall seek the Lord their God, and David their king (Zech. 12:10; Hos. 3:5). For "behold, the days are coming," says the LORD, "that I will raise to David a Branch of righteousness; a King shall reign and prosper, and execute judgment and righteousness in the earth. In His days Judah will be saved, and Israel will dwell safely; now this is His name by which He will be called: THE LORD OUR RIGHTEOUSNESS" (Jer. 23:5, 6). Then shall it be said among the nations, "The Lord reigns" (Psa. 96:10). The just God, even the Savior will say, "Look to Me, and be saved, all you ends of the earth! For I am God, and there is no other. I have sworn by Myself; the word has gone out of My mouth in righteousness, and shall not return, that to Me every knee shall bow, every tongue shall take an oath" (Isa. 45:22, 23). And it shall come to pass that all nations shall worship the king, the Lord of Hosts; and holiness to the Lord shall be inscribed on every earthly thing (Zech. 14:16, 20).

When we contemplate this glorious event, what language, what prayer, can express the feelings and desires of our hearts? Surely, every Christian will say for himself, "Even so, come, Lord Jesus, in your glory. Reign till your enemies are made your footstool: and remember me, Lord, when you come into your kingdom!"

THE UNIVERSAL WORSHIP

VERSE 29—*All the prosperous of the earth shall eat and worship;*
all those who go down to the dust shall bow before Him.

HAVING considered the vastness and glory of the prospect,
our Lord next contemplates the reality and minuteness of its
accomplishment. He sets before his mind individual cases, and
particular facts. He appears to look upon this picture of the
future, as we do on a grand historical painting of the past. It
seems natural to gaze with silent admiration on the picture as a
whole, then to fix the attention on particular groups, and testify
our sense of the general excellence, by enlarging upon the truth
and beauty of its several parts.

Our Lord here specifies a fact, which fully proves the
universality of that holy worship which shall pervade his
kingdom. "All the prosperous of the earth shall eat and
worship." The term in the original denotes the great and mighty
of this world. It is most frequently used in an unfavorable sense,
in reference to the wicked. We understand the passage,
therefore, to signify that even that class, who are now the most
self-satisfied, haughty, and proud because of their wealth, who,
possessing all their heart's desire, are too commonly at present
despisers of Christ and his gospel, shall then be found amongst
the crowd of humble worshippers.

To how many does the Scripture speak in this way? "You
say, I am rich, have become wealthy, and have need of
nothing" (Rev. 3:17). How often did our Lord turn away from
the great and rich men of his generation, who scorned his
doctrine, and solace his mind with this reflection, "To the poor
the gospel is preached." But when the kingdom shall be given
into the possession of our Messiah, even that class who now
despise, shall all then glorify him. "The kings of Tarshish and of

the isles will bring presents; the kings of Sheba and Seba will offer gifts. Yes, all kings shall fall down before Him; all nations shall serve Him... And He shall live; and the gold of Sheba will be given to Him; prayer also will be made for Him continually, and daily He shall be praised" (Psa. 72:10, 11, 15). It shall be even so. Christ's triumph shall be complete. His worship shall be universal; even the "prosperous" shall despise their former dainties, and shall "eat" with delight what Christ has prepared. They shall no longer refuse the bread of life, but will esteem it better than the honey or the honeycomb.

But there is another point to be specially noted in the great picture. So minutely and fully shall the word of God be fulfilled, so universally shall Christ be honored, that also "all those who go down to the dust shall worship before him." We do not understand this phrase to mean simply all those who die, but to refer to that class of whose death little more is generally noted, than that they go down to the grave. This is a delicate and appropriate phrase, when speaking with reference to those human beings who lead an unnoticed, animal existence; who pass away as though they had never been, and whose souls are not numbered with the redeemed. It is sufficiently expressive. It is remarkably descriptive. It comprehends all that we feel disposed to say regarding them, "They go down to the dust." God's people lie down to sleep—the others descend to the dust. Though it is true that the bodies of both classes alike decompose in the tomb, yet the mind naturally describes them by that particular which is most characteristic of each.

We understand, then, the whole verse to speak of the two great classes, the rich and the poor; and to signify that the people shall be all righteous in the kingdom of Christ—that from the least even to the greatest, all shall know the Lord. That no doubt of the certainty and universality of this fact may exist, it is stated in this definite and double form, that all the great and fat ones of the earth, and all the ignoble poor who now die, and are as unnoticed and valueless, in worldly estimation as the dust, shall then bow the knee, the head, the heart, in living, dutiful submission to Jesus of Nazareth, when he stands forth crowned King of kings, and Lord of lords.

It is not asserted that all of each of these two classes who ever lived on earth, shall then be raised out of their graves, and become the true servants of the Savior. No, some shall have no part in the first resurrection (Rev. 20:6). They shall lie in their graves, until the trumpet of the last judgment summons them to render an account of the deeds done in the body. There is no repentance in the grave. No purging of souls in the other world. As the tree falls, so it must lie. As life left them, so judgment shall find them. They who are unholy, shall then be unholy still.

There is indeed, however, a solemn period in the history of these individuals, in which they shall bow the knee before their once despised Lord. In the morning of the resurrection, when all that are in their graves shall hear his voice, and arise to receive his judgment, the unbelieving shall fall upon their knees in fear and consternation. The rich and the poor, in one undistinguished company, brought back from the chambers of death, shall behold Him who was crucified on the cross, crowned, and sitting on the throne of universal empire. "Every eye shall see him;" not a single human being that has lived on the earth shall be absent. Jew and Gentile, Barbarian, Scythian, bond and free, Christian and heathen, all shall be summoned to appear before the judgment-seat of Christ. "And they also, who pierced him," the judges and officers, the soldiers and people, Jews and Romans, who were the active instruments of his death, shall behold him. Annas and Caiaphas, Herod and Pontius Pilate, with the Scribes and Pharisees, and all that crowd of citizens and strangers, who took delight in his condemnation, and were spectators of his crucifixion on the mount of Calvary, shall behold the Savior in his glory. Of the certainty of this, he himself assured his judges: "hereafter you will see the Son of Man sitting at the right hand of the Power, and coming on the clouds of heaven" (Matt. 26:64). All those professing

Christians also, who have pierced the Redeemer by their sins, and unrepented backslidings, "wounding him in the house of his friends" (Zech. 13:6); and all those to whom the gospel of the pierced Surety came, but who denied the Lord that bought them (2 Pet. 2:1), shall be summoned there. "And all the tribes of the earth," who are then alive, and not prepared for his appearing, shall see him robed in majesty, and "will mourn because of him. Even so, Amen" (Rev. 1:7). "At the name of Jesus every knee should bow, of those in heaven, and of those on earth, and of those under the earth, and every tongue should confess that Jesus Christ is Lord, to the glory of God the Father" (Phil. 2:10, 11).

But this passage in the psalm before us speaks of the homage of love, and not the prostration of terror. The "prosperous," the rich and great men, shall, at that period, become one with the meek (ver. 26). They shall eat of the banquet of good things, which God has prepared for them that love him, and they shall worship the King, the Lord of hosts (Zech. 14:16). And "all those who go down to the dust," shall gratefully bow before him. This verse, then, must be understood to allude to those only, who shall be living on the earth when the Messiah reigns. At present, men are divided into two classes, the rich and the poor. Scripture does not assert that all the former reject the Savior, or all the latter receive his gospel. This is far from being the case. Many of both classes are now walking in holy obedience to his will, and many in disobedience. Such is the case with individuals, but in reference to the classes it is different. Those who are satisfied with their worldly portion, have always been distinguished as a body, by their opposition to the humiliating doctrines of the cross: "For you see your calling, brethren, that not many wise according to the flesh, not many mighty, not many noble, are called" (1 Cor. 1:26). While in every age of the church, the poor, as a class, have been, and are, distinguished by their attachment and devotedness to the Savior's cause. In the kingdom of the Messiah, however, both classes shall be eager to confess his name, and serve his cause. The rich and the poor shall meet together in love to one common Lord, in fidelity to one acknowledged Sovereign. "The people shall be all righteous" (Isa. 60:21). "Many people shall come and say, "Come, and let us go up to the mountain of the LORD, to the house of the God of Jacob; He will teach us His ways, and we shall walk in His paths... Nation shall not lift up sword against nation, neither shall they learn war anymore" (Isa. 2:3-4). The wild beasts of the forest shall be changed from the ferocity of their natures; "They shall not hurt nor destroy in all My holy mountain, for the earth shall be full of the knowledge of the LORD, as the waters cover the sea" (Isa. 11:9; Hab. 2:14). "No more shall every man teach his neighbor, and every man his brother, saying, 'Know the LORD,' for they all shall know Me, from the least of them to the greatest of them" (Jer. 31:34; Heb. 8:11). "All nations shall call Him blessed. Blessed be the LORD God, the God of Israel, who only does wondrous things! And blessed be His glorious name forever! And let the whole earth be filled with His glory. Amen and Amen." (Psa. 72:17-19).

THE AUTHOR OF THE FAITH

VERSE 29—*Even he who cannot keep himself alive...*
or, "And no man has quickened his own soul."[20]

WHEN our blessed Lord surveyed the picture of future glory which was placed before him in vision upon the cross, and, as it were, beheld the earth peopled with its righteous inhabitants, he instantly remarks, that notwithstanding the holiness of their perfect and blessed condition, they shall be as much dependent on the Author of life, as they were in their fallen state. None of them, even in that most favorable position, can quicken his soul, or maintain its pious frames, and feelings, one instant apart from Christ. Clusters of ripe grapes may hang abundantly on these righteous branches, but still they are only branches. The true Vine must have all the glory!

Such seems to be the significance which may, we trust not incorrectly, be attached to this passage. It is good at all times to be reminded of the grand and important truth that Christ is our life (Col. 3:4; John 15:6); and that in him alone are given to us the things that pertain unto life and godliness (2 Pet. 1:3). And it is especially suitable and right, when tracing before our ravished eyes

---

[20] Prayer-book version. The brevity of the original, (only three words,) in this place, occasions ambiguity of meaning, and difference of explanation. Some understand them to be simply expletive of the preceding truth, that men go down to the dust, and that none of them can prevent the stroke of the last enemy. On the various opinions of the learned, it is not suitable to our present purpose to enlarge. There seems to be no adequate reason, why our own excellent translation, or that of Cranmer's Bible, retained in the Book of Common Prayer, should not be adhered to. We humbly conceive that this passage contains a statement of vitally important truth, in an important connection.

this bright picture of the earth changed into a paradise, that there should be written underneath, as a motto for our instruction, when contemplating these happy children of the second, the living, Adam, and as an appropriate lesson and warning to themselves, as descendants of the first, the fallen, Adam, "No man has quickened, or can keep alive, his own soul."

Christ, by his Spirit, is the alone author of the faith, the only preserver of the soul's piety and peace. The purest, and highest, act of our earthly communion, is, in itself, and as far as our power extends, a transitory emotion, an evanescent feeling. We lie down at night in a calm and heavenly frame, and we awake in the morning heavy in spirit, and earthly in our desires. We retire to rest, mourning that we are not more holy, and we rise up blessing and praising God for that precious blood-shedding, which cleansed from all sin. So changeable is even the best Christian in himself. Our first father was so. Even in paradise, "very good," as he was pronounced to be, by his Creator, he could not keep alive his own soul. Like him, we are ever changing, not willfully, but unavoidably. When the new heavens and earth, however, are established, the inhabitants shall no longer be annoyed by the intrusions of self, with its sins, its weaknesses, and pride. The blessed truth that Christ alone is their life, shall not only be their strength and safety, but also their highest happiness and glory. The grace of Christ which did all for them in time, shall still do all for them in eternity. Salvation from first to last is all of grace. When the Capstone shall be brought forth, there shall be shouts of Grace, grace to it (Zech. 4:7).

In the "new creation," into which all those who have been introduced spiritually by Christ's reigning in the soul, shall be admitted actually and bodily by his reigning in the earth, all the redeemed, shining like stars in the firmament of heaven, shall revolve round the Sun of Righteousness, and reflect his pure, life-giving, and eternal, light. He is the center of life, and light, and gladness. As the material sun is to our world, so is Christ to the redeemed creation. He raised us from the ruins of the fall. He made us alive by his Spirit, from the death of sin, to the life of righteousness. He inspired the first desire after salvation. He inclined our hearts to pray. He taught us to abhor sin. He opened our understandings to understand the Scriptures. He blessed to us the various means of grace. He put love for the brethren into our hearts. He enabled us to take sweet counsel together. He strengthened us to resist the temptations of the world, the flesh, and the devil. He delivered us from dangerous trials. He encouraged us to persevere. He armed us for the fight. He made us more than conquerors. He animated our hopes. He dispelled our fears. He cheered our drooping faith. He restored our wavering souls. He enabled us to endure scorn and opposition. He supported us along the journey of life. He solaced and enlivened the bed of death. From the cradle to the grave every mercy is his gift, every good thought his suggestion, every charitable deed his operation. To him be all the glory! The Holy Ghost, who is the mighty worker in all these, is his Spirit. He acts by his direction, according to his will, and with his purchased blessings. The Spirit gives nothing, but what belongs to Christ. The Spirit promises nothing, but what Christ has spoken. The Spirit accomplishes nothing, but what is to carry on the work of Christ in our souls.

It was God, in Christ, that came near to man in time, and so it is man, in Christ, that is brought near to God throughout eternity. "In him dwells all the fullness of the Godhead bodily" (Col. 2:9). "It pleased the Father that in him all the fullness should dwell" (Col. 1:19). In him "are hidden all the treasures of wisdom and knowledge."—"And you are complete in him, who is the head of all principality and power" (Col. 2:3, 10). When sin shut up the fountains of heaven from man, Christ opened them again to him, in himself. When the sinner was banished from paradise, Christ obtained admission for him by his blood. The outraged law he magnified, and made honorable. The justice of God he satisfied, to the very uttermost. Man's name he took; man's debts he paid; man's death he died; man's deliverance he effected. All glory to the Surety! From him our hopes begin; in him our all is centered; on him our eternity of bliss depends!

Beware, then, O Christian, beware of self-confidence. Hold fast the head, even Christ, and let nothing beguile you from him (Col. 2:18, 19). The least thought of your own progress in virtue may open the fatal door of departure. Good-self is as dangerous to the Christian, to lead him away from Christ, as formerly bad-self was to keep him back from approaching him. Even at the very moment of your thanking God for those gracious changes, which he has wrought in you, and are concluding that now you shall not quickly fall, Satan may be secretly gaining an advantage over you. To defeat and counteract this, God may see it needful to send an afflicting providence. Learn this lesson from the experience of the psalmist. Hear how he declares in his spiritual prosperity, that he shall never be moved, and thanks God, saying, "Lord, by Your favor You have made my mountain stand strong." In this thanksgiving, not a word occurs, but what every Christian would desire to be enabled to use. But perhaps the great Searcher of hearts perceived that the psalmist trusted more in his own mountain that stood, than in that favor which made it strong. Therefore it became necessary to the welfare of David's soul, that this weed of sin should not be allowed to grow, and that a blast should nip its earliest bud. He informs us that this was the case; for he immediately adds, "You hid Your face, and I was troubled" (Psa. 30:6, 7). Do not tempt the Lord, then, O Christian, to deal thus with your soul. Keep your heart free for Christ; love him supremely; trust in him perpetually; draw all your supplies from his fullness. In life and death, in time and in eternity, lean on Christ, and say, "Not unto me, Lord, not unto me, but unto Your name be the glory" (Psa. 115:1).

Be humble, watchful, and prayerful. Remember that the Savior said, "Without Me you can do nothing" (John 15:5); and be assured that apart from him you are nothing. The supply of the

Spirit of Jesus, is absolutely necessary to the most advanced Christian, every moment of his existence. In heaven itself, his language shall still be, as before,

> "Hangs my helpless soul on thee."

Blessed helplessness, that makes us lie in the bosom of the Savior! This is *the heaven* of heaven; and, in proportion as we are enabled to realize it now by the Spirit, it is heaven on earth!

> "You, O Christ, are all I want,
> All my help from You I bring."

The angels do not stand, by their own inherent excellence. They depend on God for their support in holy adoration, as well as in activity of existence. And I would not, may the Christian say, I would not choose to have life, grace, strength, in myself; but all in Christ my Lord. I am content to be nothing, through all eternity, but what Jesus makes me. I can afford to lose all things, even the idol *self,* since God shall be my all in all. I rejoice to be humbled while on earth, by the recollection that can do nothing good of myself, and that God alone has done all my works in me (Isa. 26:12). I rejoice to know that even in the perfect state of glory, no man can make alive, or keep alive, his own soul; for these truths will ever constrain me to keep close to my head and Savior, to abide in him as my life (John 15:4); my temple (Rev. 21:22); the everlasting hiding-place of my soul, and eternal fountain of my bliss!

THE SEED

VERSE 30—*A seed[21] shall serve Him.*
It will be recounted of the Lord to the next generation.

THE unwillingness of man by nature, and his consequent inability to serve the Lord, arc truths plainly and unequivocally taught in holy Scripture (Rom. 3:9, 12; 8:7, 8; John 5:40). Unless then, the Lord should interpose, there could not be found in any human heart, a single good thought or desire towards God (Rom. 9:29). Satan would consequently enjoy a full triumph; the whole human race, without exception, would be his active and willing instruments against the God that made them. But the Lord Immanuel has declared that it shall not be so. Christ, as it were, looked down from heaven, and said, "I will enter the rebels' camp, and bring back many to their allegiance. The traitor shall not possess all for his own. On God's own earth a people shall serve him, and disown the usurper." Thus God's champion spoke. He laid aside his glory, assumed the human form, and came into the very midst of his enemies. They surrounded him on every side; he was seized, condemned, and executed. In his dying moments, they exulted over him as vanquished; but even then he triumphed in spirit over his foes, asserted that his object of turning many to God could not he baffled, and cheered his departing soul with this assurance: "A seed shall serve him."

This figurative expression signifies Christ and his people, who yield true obedience to God. They are called by this name in a spiritual and figurative, but most appropriate sense. The idea is

---

[21] NKJV reads "posterity." The King James has been retained for continuity of thought in the chapter.

taken from the operations of the farmer, who carefully reserves every year a portion of his grain for seed. Though it is small, compared with all the produce of his harvest, yet he prizes it very highly, and estimates it by the value of the whole crop it may yield in the succeeding autumn. Nor does he look only to the quantity, he pays particular regard to the quality of his seed. He reserves only the best: nay, he will put away his own, if spoiled, that he may procure better. The very smallest quantity of really good seed, is to him an object of great desire; and if, by grievous failure of crops, he should be able to procure only a single grain, yet he would accept it thankfully, preserve it carefully, and plant it in the most favorable soil. Such is the source from which this metaphor is taken. The good seed of human nature, which God planted, became corrupted in the earth; it failed to yield the return of righteousness. God looked over the successive generations of men, but found not even a single individual among them all, whom He could reserve as the new root, or seed, of another and a righteous succession. At last one man was found—only one man, perfect, and without spot; one single grain of human nature was obtained, and God took that, nourished it carefully, and planted it, in a fruitful soil. That one grain was Jesus Christ. He was exactly such as the Holy God had long been looking for. He was wholly a good seed. He spoke of himself, and said, "unless a grain of wheat falls into the ground and dies, it remains alone; but if it dies, it produces much grain" (John 12:24). Accordingly, as the one grain of pure wheat, He was laid in the earth; in due time he sprang forth, and became the fruitful source of a new and imperishable seed. He is therefore emphatically called "THE SEED." As such, he was promised to our disconsolate parents in the garden of Eden (Gen. 3:15). Under the same name, also, he was promised to Abraham, the Father of the faithful (Gal. 3:16). And in the fullness of time this promise was fulfilled. Woman, who was first in the transgression, was the first to obtain the promise (Luke 1:28). God sent forth his Son, made of a woman (Gal. 4:4; Isa. 7:14). And this seed of the woman became the stock and source of a new and holy race. These, after him, are called the seed. They receive their life from him, their new nature, and their new name. Yet in every age until now, they have been only as a seed, as a handful in the earth. But they are the seed whom the Lord has blessed. As the various generations come and depart, the Great Husbandman, through the seed of the woman, reserves a seed to himself from amongst them. They are spoken of in this verse: "a seed shall serve him."

The latter clause informs us that, "it will be recounted of the Lord to the next generation." It seems, from this expression, considered as referring to the Almighty Father, as if God were waiting to find an entire generation on the earth, living wholly to his service. Every earthly father desires, when surrounded by his family, to behold them all loving, all obeying him. God seeks this from his human family. What a happy scene would it present! What a subject for prayer does it furnish! Had all the people of Enoch's generation walked with God, as he did, they might all have been translated with him to the regions of joy! Blessed termination to this sin-sorrowing world!

But there is another, and a more appropriate sense in which we should understand these words, namely, in reference to God the Son. The term "generation" may be regarded as synonymous with "seed," and the whole verse taken as an instructive reply to the question of the prophet, when, having stated that Christ was cut off from the land of the living, he inquires, "Who will declare his generation?" (Isa. 53:8); that is, his seed. Answer, "A seed shall serve him, it shall be accounted to the Lord for a posterity."

To die childless, having no descendant to carry down their name to future periods, was considered as a great curse by the ancient Hebrews. A father was considered by them to live in his children, and to prolong his days in those of his descendants. But if he left none behind him, his existence appeared to them to be blotted out, and to become as if it had never been. The Jews, therefore, have always been remarkable for their genealogies and their posterities; the fathers looking forward to their descendants, and the children looking back to their progenitors. Our Lord himself is an instance of the latter. Two Evangelists have been careful to record the pedigree of the Savior. Those two chapters, the first of Matthew, and the third of Luke, are more important than is generally allowed. They prove, respectively, that Joseph and Mary were the lineal descendants of King David; and that therefore in the adopted son of the one, and true son of the other, the two royal lines, from Solomon and Nathan, centered and terminated. He who was born of Mary had a right by birth, according to the flesh, to sit upon the throne of Israel. Had the crown not departed from Judah, it must have rested by descent on the head of Jesus of Nazareth. He died, however, and left no seed. The lineal descent therefore became extinct in him. But He lives again, and will return to reign. No one, consequently, has any legal claim to sit upon the throne of David but himself. "Thus says the Lord GOD: Remove the turban, and take off the crown... UNTIL HE COMES WHOSE RIGHT IT IS, and I will give it to Him." (Ezek. 21:26-27). Shall Christ, then, possess no name in the earth? Shall he who died for us, be as though he had never been? By no means. His very death shall be the source from which a numerous seed shall spring. "If it dies, it produces much grain." "He shall see his seed, He shall prolong His days" (Isa. 53:10). "A seed shall serve him, it shall be accounted to him for a posterity." The children of the flesh are not counted for the seed, but the children of the promise (Rom. 9:8; Gal. 3:26-29). As a man he has no descendants to represent him in the earth; but as the second Adam, he has, among all nations and languages, a seed given him by God the Father, who shall transmit his name to the end of time. The seed of Christ are a spiritual posterity. They derive their birth from the travail of Christ's soul. The Father comforted him by the assurance that he should see the fruit of his labor, and be satisfied (Isa. 53:11). Christ the seed is also the word. And it is by the incorruptible seed of the word that we are born again (1 Pet. 1:22, 23). Those who believe the word, that is, have the seed of eternal truth sown in their hearts, are the sons of God (John 1:13). This enables us to understand how the Old Testament believers are one with Christians because Christ, in the form of the Word, was preached unto them, and thus proved a seed of life to their souls, as well as to ours (Heb. 4:2; Gal. 3:8; John 8:56; Luke 8:11). By believing the word, we become the children of God, under the form of adoption. Christ is the true Son, we are adopted sons through him. He who was born of the Virgin Mary, thereby became the adopted son of his earthly Father: and we who are born of the travail of Christ's soul, that is, born of his Spirit, thereby become the adopted children of our heavenly Father. As Christ's claim to Joseph's special care, kindness, and protection, lay through Mary; so our title to the special love, and blessing, and protection, of our heavenly Father, lies through Christ. We first belong to him; and then in and through him we belong to God. Therefore he says, "Go to my brethren and say to them, 'I am ascending to my Father and your Father, and to my God and your God.'" He does not say, to your Father and my Father, and to your God and my God, but "to my Father and your Father, and to my God and your God" (John 20:17). Therefore he elsewhere calls them his children. "Here am I and the children God has given me" (Heb. 2:13; Isa. 8:18). With full confidence, therefore, that they should all be given to him, the Savior resigned himself to death upon the cross. He left no name behind him in a posterity, but he knew that his name and his seed should endure forever (Psa. 72:17; 89:36). He beheld around him an infuriated multitude, whose hearts were set on his destruction, and who hated both him and his Father; but he consoled his dying spirit with this comforting consideration, "a seed shall serve him;" my children shall yield due homage to my Father; they shall take delight in the performance of his commandments; "for from the rising of the sun, even to its going, My name shall be great among the Gentiles; in every place incense shall be offered to My name, and a pure offering; for My name shall be great among the nations" (Mal. 1:11).

"Service," willing, active, unremitting "service" is the characteristic of Christ's seed. Mere professors are content to express their gratitude and love by words, the true seed seek to prove it by their lives. To promote God's glory, to extend the knowledge of the gospel, and to testify their love to the souls, by doing good to the bodies, of their fellow-men, are the great objects for which they live. Their food and drink is to DO the will of God. The conclusion of our General Thanksgiving expresses the full desire of their hearts, "Give us, we beseech You, such a due sense of all Your mercies, that our hearts may be sincerely thankful, and that we may show forth Your praise not only with our lips, but in our lives, by giving up ourselves to Your service, and by walking before You in holiness and righteousness all our days: through Jesus Christ our Lord."

Reader, is this prayer the true utterance of your inmost soul? Do you not only offer, do you endeavor to perform it? Are you accustomed to serious self-examination on the momentous question of your daily service? Every wish is a prayer, every action is an offering, at some shrine or other; every day of your life pays its tribute of homage to self, and the world, to Satan, or to God. Watch then, over yourself. Be as a faithful soldier in an enemy's country; examine all that pass. Demand of every outgoing of thought, and word and deed, Where do you come from? Where do you go? What is your object? Let nothing doubtful escape you. Inquire into every secret motive that actuates your heart, and what master is about to obtain your services. The seed of Christ do not serve sin; they strive even against themselves, and deny their besetting propensities. Do not, then, speak or pray in the name of God, and yet live and act for self, or Satan, or the world. Your words, indeed, tell what you profess; but your deeds tell what you are. Remember, we are only so far Christians as we live and act on Christian principles. Were we to ask, 'Are you one of Christ's seed?' It might, perhaps, be difficult to reply. But when we ask the same question in this other form, 'In what kind of service are you engaged?' The answer is at hand, supplied by every hour of every day, and by every look, and word, and deed, of that hour. Do you serve God? Have you a desire to do so? Do you put that desire into practice? Do you propose to yourself to live in such a manner as to bring honor to God? Is this your consideration in the expenditure of money, of time, and of opportunities? What is my object? Do you take yourself to task? Do you enter at times into the chamber of your conscience, and honestly ask, 'Am I now acting with an express intention to please God, as I would wish my servant to do to please me?' When you rise in the morning, do you say to yourself, 'What can I do this day to show my gratitude to God? What example can I set for others? What benefits can I bestow upon them?' Or do such thoughts never enter into your mind? When you lie down at night, do you call yourself to account? Do you inquire, 'Have I really served God this day? When I did speak, or write, or read, or transact business, did I do so for myself, or with a desire and intention to glorify my Savior?' (Zech. 7:6). If I did any good to the poor, was it done with a right motive? What *more* could I have done? In what should I have been more humble, more holy, more diligent, this day? Are these, reader, some of the questions on which you and your own heart converse together? Or are you a stranger to your own conscience? Most earnestly we beseech you to be so no longer. Let the love of a crucified Redeemer take full possession of your soul. Invite him to enter the temple of your heart, even though you know it to be polluted. His scourge of small cords will effectually cleanse it (John 2:15); do not be afraid, they are cords of love (Hos. 11:4). Rejoice to be purged. Thank him for so blessed a work, which you could never accomplish. Then ask him to enlarge your heart as he cleanses it, so that you may run in the way of his commandments (Psa. 119:32). Pray for the Spirit to enliven and strengthen you and to make your heart *"sound"* in the statutes of the Lord (vs. 80). In this way you will be enabled to "serve" the

Redeemer of your soul. Holy service, or earnest desire and persevering attempt thereafter, is the only sure proof that you belong to the number of Christ's seed. If, then, O reader, you are not only a professing, but a serving Christian, you are one of Christ's seed. To you he looked forward when expiring on the cross. Of you he spoke when he declared that a seed should "serve the Lord." In you he beheld prospectively, he now sees actually, and shall hereafter see perfectly, the travail of his soul; and was, and is, and shall be satisfied!

THE GATHERING

VERSE 31—*They will come.*

THESE words set before us the certainty of what had been declared in the preceding verse, and unfold also the gradual gathering, and final meeting of the righteous seed. "THEY," that is, the seed; those who belong to Christ, who are accounted or reckoned to him for a posterity: those in whose hearts the seed of the word has been sown; who, having been born again by the Spirit of God, are reserved by the Great Husbandman to be the seed of the new heavens and the new earth: these "SHALL," in spite of all the efforts of the adversary; notwithstanding the temptations of the world, and their own many sins and daily short-comings; contrary to their own fears, and notwithstanding their manifest unworthiness; they shall, beyond all doubt, without a single loss, and with unfailing certainty, "COME;" that is, born of the flesh, they all arise, one after another, each in his proper season, during the progress of time; *born again* of the Spirit (John 1:13; 3:7), they shall come, each in his appointed hour of the day of grace; and united together in one body, they shall ALL come in the consummation of glory.

They shall come one after another in time. However few may be the inhabitants of the earth, there shall be one of the seed of Christ among them: one on whom the eye of the great God may rest with delight (Zeph. 3:17). However degenerate and corrupt this crowded world may become, there shall be found more or less of the good seed, bearing the fruits of righteousness, here and there amongst them. This is no doubtful matter. There was not more certainly a wicked Cain in the first family of only two brothers, than there was a righteous Abel. When the desponding prophet exclaimed amidst the multitudes of the ungodly, "I alone am left;" He, that knew his own, could reply, "I have reserved for Myself seven thousand men who have not bowed the knee to Baal," (Rom. 11:3, 4). It is even so today. The seed shall come. Christ, from whom they spring, came in promise and in person; so likewise do his seed. They were given to him in promise by God the Father, before the foundation of the world (Matt. 25:34; Eph. 1:4). Having come in the promise, they come also at the appointed time in the flesh.

Abel came, the first of mortal born that lived a righteous life, and died a righteous death. Abel once lived in the flesh, but he lived to God; his spirit drew near to the Most High by the appointed sacrifice; he came and was accepted; he sung the praises of the God he loved; he served him with a willing and steadfast obedience; and by faith looked forward to the promised Seed, which, doubtless, Eve had told him was his parents' confidence (Heb. 11:4). In this way Abel came in grace, as well as in time, and he shall also come in glory. No sooner did his mangled body fall in death, than his soul was received into life. He entered the world of spirits the first of all the redeemed. There his spirit would raise a song of thanksgiving which angels never heard before. Listening with admiration, they would pause for an instant that all heaven might learn the strain. Astonished beyond measure, they hear, for the first time, it may be, a song in which they cannot join. It is one which he alone can sing, of all the millions that surround the throne. And Abel is singing that song. His soul has long enjoyed the abodes of the blessed, but so long also has it looked forward to the adoption, specifically, the redemption of his body (Rom. 8:23). It shall not hope in vain. When the Savior comes in glory, the soul of Abel shall come in glory with him, to be reunited to its raised and incorruptible, its glorious and spiritual body (1 Cor. 15). Then Abel, in the new heavens and the new earth, shall again sing the praises of that God whom he had loved and served in the earliest period of the departed world.

The first parents of our race shall also come. With penitential tears, we may suppose, did Adam and Eve seek admission again to the fair bloom of Eden. Confessing themselves to be sinners, and their condemnation to be just, they pleaded for its forgiveness in the name of the promised Seed. Painfully conscious from where they had fallen, and fatally taught that no created being can stand in his own righteousness, "can make alive or keep alive his own soul." They knelt as suppliants for mercy, through the imputed righteousness of the second Adam; and the sinful parents, while they lived, came, doubtless, in the name of their holy child Jesus, into the kingdom of God's grace, and at their death entered into the kingdom of God's glory, and joined the song of their beloved Abel. There they are now; and when the Savior's glory is to be revealed, when the Almighty Father brings Him forth, crowned King of kings and Lord of lords, their souls shall come as attendant trophies of his triumph, gracing the Conqueror's entry on his new possessions.

The patriarchs who lived before the flood shall come. Amongst them Enoch, who was not found, shall again be found. He walks now, among the redeemed souls in paradise, with a glorified and spiritual body, as before he walked among the sons of men with God and with a heavenly mind. His body does not sleep in the dust. He does not need the power of the resurrection morning. Mortality in him was swallowed up in life (2 Cor. 5:4).

The preacher of righteousness, the father of the second world, shall come. When the wickedness of men became great, so that the Lord was sorry that he had made them (Gen. 6:6), Noah came. He came to men for God, and reasoned with them of righteousness, self-control, and judgment to come. He came to God for man, and pled for mercy upon those who never asked for mercy upon themselves. He is one of the seed whom the Lord promised. He was the salt of his time; "You only have I seen righteous in this generation" (Gen. 7:1). The ungodly are to be destroyed, yet the seed must be reserved. An ark is ordered for him; and the long-suffering of God waited one hundred and twenty years, while the ark was being prepared (1 Pet. 3:20). Noah came into the ark, and the flood came upon the world. The seed shall be safe; they shall be brought without loss even through the destruction of worlds, and shall eventually appear in peace in the kingdom of the saints (Dan. 7:18, 22).

Abraham shall come. Though born in the country of the Chaldeans, he shall be made willing to seek a better country, that is, a heavenly country (Heb. 11:16). The "father of the faithful" shall arise in the earth to preserve the name of the living God from being altogether blotted out. "He will command his children and his household after him to walk in the ways of the Lord." His faith shall be more severely tried than any man's, but he shall be brought out of the furnace, a vessel fit for the Master's everlasting use.

Isaac shall come. That double type of the Messiah shall be found, amongst the children of men. His long promised birth shall be accomplished at last. And as a sacrifice upon his father's altar, he shall prove an accepted offering, and become a picture of the resurrection (Heb. 11:19).

Jacob shall come. Not more surely shall his brother Esau, after his own nature, love earthly things, and sell his birthright, than the other shall, by the implanted seed of the word, bear fruit of better desires, and be called a man of prayer. No longer Jacob, but Israel, a prince that prevails with God (Gen. 32:28).

Joseph, too, shall come, and his brethren also, the fathers of the tribes of Israel. Out of the pit and out of the prison-house he shall be brought, the type of Christ, the preserver of his brethren who sold him, and the ruler over all the land.

Moses shall come. Out of the waters he shall be drawn, and not more surely shall he be called the son of Pharaoh's daughter, than he shall be named the servant of the most High God. The dazzling honors of Egypt's kingdom shall be presented to his ambition, but he will esteem the reproach of Christ greater riches than all its treasures (Heb. 11:26). The seed of a new and heavenly life shall bear within his heart its holy fruit; being brought out of bondage to sin, he shall lead out the people of Israel from the slavery of Egypt. He will conduct them through the Red Sea as upon dry land and, after the wanderings of many years, shall bring them safe to the borders of Canaan. Moses, the picture of the law, cannot bring us into the heavenly Canaan. The law leads us to Christ (Gal. 3:24) and there its office ceases, as did that of Moses on the borders of the land of promise. Therefore...

Joshua shall come, the type of the true Joshua, or Jesus, (Heb. 4:8) to lead the seed into the chosen possession. There the preserved seed shall dwell in the reserved country; and in their various generations, the faithful and spiritual seed shall be found, not united, but intermingled with their worldly and carnal brethren.

Time would fail to tell of all who came, and by the seed of a living faith, brought forth the fruits of righteousness and glorified God amid the trials of a world that was not worthy of them (Heb. 11:32-38).

When, too, the fullness of time had come, God sent forth his Son. The Seed of the woman appeared (Gal. 4:4). The long promised heir did come. The life of the new creation by His double birth brought life and immortality to light. The seed, the one grain of pure wheat, fell into the ground and died. It revived again, and brought forth much fruit (John 12:24). It shall bring forth much. As certainly as they came in the generations that are passed, so surely shall they come in the generations that will succeed. Together with his flesh, the Savior laid aside the Jewish church, his representative body. And with his spiritual body, he took also to himself a new and spiritual representative, the Christian church.

From the height of Calvary's cross, he could look down the vista of futurity, and console his dying spirit with the vision of a Christian posterity, and exclaim, "They shall come!" "Your dead shall live; together with my dead body they shall arise" (Isa. 26:19). The apostles, martyrs, and confessors came. The newly implanted seed was watered with their blood, and it grew and became a fruitful tree. As time rolled on, its branches spread; and in every succeeding season of a generation it yielded abundantly. Not one year has it failed. Even on its outmost branch, the fruit, whose seed is in itself, was found. Two thousand years have passed away, but still it has not ceased to bear. In this remote island of the sea, its boughs are strong, and its fruit cannot be numbered. Widely extended to the four corners of the earth are its branches, and none are wholly barren among them. We now behold in our world, what Christ predicted, what his dying eye beheld, with delight, in the vision of joy that was set before him on the cross. Then and there he was able to say, "They shall come." From the circumcised Jews, and the uncircumcised Gentiles, they shall be gathered into My church. From Ephesus, and Corinth, and Galatia, they shall come, with hearts purified from their unholy and debasing superstitions. The haughty Romans, too, shall bow to the doctrine of the cross. The sons of Africa and the East shall come to the obedience of the faith. The wide-extended lands shall acknowledge My name. Kings of the earth shall become the nursing fathers of my Church, and their queens her nursing mothers (Isa. 49:23). They shall come from the distant south, and the north shall not keep them back. The British isles shall be converted to Me, and shall become My willing messengers to the most remote nations. To every one of them for a witness shall the gospel be proclaimed, and then shall the end of My gospel kingdom come, and the commencement of My kingdom of glory.

Then, too, shall they come in the royal retinue of King Messiah. He will bring them all with him. He will show that He has gathered them safely, one after another, and at that glorious moment He shall collect them into one perfect, spotless company. "Our God shall come, and shall not keep silent... He shall call to the heavens from above, and to the earth... Gather My saints together to Me, those who have made a covenant with Me by sacrifice" (Psa. 50:3-5). Then the graves shall give up their pious dead; then the living saints shall be changed; and both together shall be caught up in the clouds, to meet the Lord in the air (1 Thess. 4:17). Then two in the field shall be separated. Two in one bed shall be suddenly parted. Of two at the mill, there shall be left but one. And why? Because the time shall have arrived for the separation of the righteous from the wicked. Intermingled as now they are, there shall then be an instantaneous and everlasting separation, as these three illustrative cases represent. Then also shall be fulfilled the prophecy of the Savior, "They will come from the east and the west, from the north and the south, and sit down with Abraham, and Isaac, and Jacob, and all the prophets, in the kingdom of God," (Luke 13:28, 29; Matt. 8:11).

All the seed shall come. As certainly as each came in his proper season during the progress of time, and the continuance of grace; so certainly shall they all come together in the consummation of glory. Nor will it be these alone. From amongst the nominal professors of the Christian faith who shall be left it may be on the earth, a seed, we trust, shall come. While the gathered spiritual Church is blessed with Christ on high, the nominal Church shall in all probability pass through fires of tribulation below. Doubtless the great Refiner will watch by the furnace and bring out vessels fitted for his holy use. Even at that period, judging from analogy, God shall not lack a witness for His truth, here and there throughout the earth. The Jews also shall be grafted into the tree of life. The Lord has spoken it. "Therefore they shall come... streaming to the goodness of the Lord and their souls shall be like a well-watered garden," (Jer. 31:12). The sweet fruits which it bears will gladden the whole world. "For if their being cast away," because unfaithful branches, "is the reconciling of the Gentiles, what will their acceptance be, but life from the dead?" (Rom. 11:11-15). "Then shall the earth be full of the knowledge of the Lord as the waters cover the sea" (Isa. 11:9). "All shall know him, from the least of them to the greatest of them" (Jer. 31:34). Instead of a few here and there, as at former periods, that age shall produce the ripened harvest of righteousness, the holy seed shall be the substance of it (Isa. 6:12). Blessed shall be that time, and blessed shall be that people, for the meek shall inherit the earth (Matt. 5:5).

When the period of that earthly blessedness is completed, when every foe shall be subdued and the last enemy, death itself, destroyed, then shall THEY ALL COME into the new heavens and the new earth. "And there shall by no means enter it any thing that defiles" (Rev. 21:27). But there shall be gathered together all who have loved and served the Glorious God from the beginning to the end of time. In the glorious city they shall dwell. In the everlasting Presence they shall rejoice. No temple shall be able to contain the ransomed millions, and the Lord God Almighty and the Lamb shall be the temple of that new Jerusalem. God himself shall be with them, and be their God. They shall see his face. The Lamb shall feed them with his love, and lead them by the living and everlasting fountains (Rev. 7:15-17; Rev. 21-22). The once afflicted and crucified Jesus shall then see the travail of his soul, and shall be satisfied with an unutterable satisfaction, full and perfect in its nature, and eternal in its duration. It shall be the satisfaction of his sufferings, of is righteousness, of is providence, of his earnest desires, and of his inmost affections. It shall be a satisfaction of a new, uninterrupted, and increasing nature. When Christ presents himself, and all his seed, before the throne, and says, "Here am I, and the children You have given me," there shall exist in his heart the full, lively, and unmeasured satisfaction of a paternal heart. Therefore he is called the everlasting Father, or Father of the ever lasting age (Isa. 9:6). The head of a large family, he shall behold his own holy image in every one of them. Dwelling with them in the many prepared mansions of his Father's house, he will listen to their praises of that Father's name, and hear them ascribe all glory, and honor, and blessing, to the Triune Jehovah. "I looked, and behold, a great multitude which no one could number, of all nations, tribes, peoples, and tongues, standing before the throne and before the Lamb, clothed with white robes, with palm branches in their hands, and crying out with a loud voice, saying, "Salvation belongs to our God who sits on the throne, and to the Lamb! (Rev. 7:9, 10).

THE EVERLASTING THEME
AND OCCUPATION

VERSE 31—*And will declare His righteousness
to a people who will be born.*

THE first clause of this verse we have seen refers to the seed, the spiritual children of the Lord Jesus. It asserts the certainty of their existence, and exhibits them as arriving on the stage of time, each in his proper season—introduced into the kingdom of grace, one after another, each at the appointed hour of his spiritual birth—and, all together, gathered into the kingdom of glory, not one lost or lacking among them.

This second clause discloses the high and blessed object for which they were brought into existence at first and for which they are all united into one company forever. It informs us that as the glory of God was the principal object of their life on earth, so it shall form the sole business of their eternal existence. Here at once, and in few words, is set before us their occupation, their theme, and the objects of their instruction both in time and in eternity. The unity of God's purpose is in this way exhibited; a true view of our present state and duty presented; and a glimpse of the heavenly life unfolded.

The occupation of the seed is "to declare" —to testify from their own experience, from their own knowledge and conviction, that grand subject, theme, or lesson which they have learned. This theme is his "righteousness." The righteousness of God the Father, in his law and in his providence, they will declare. To maintain the integrity and strictness of the one, and justify the diverse nature of the other is what they will regard as their bounden duty. To silence all fretful murmurs in their own hearts and in the hearts of others against the sovereign dealings of a wise and holy God, they will continually apply themselves (Psa. 73 and 37). They will avouch his righteousness in accepting the willing but innocent substitute in the place of the guilty; in justifying through him the ungodly who believe (Rom. 3:26; 4:5); and in condemning all classes of men who commit sin (Rev. 21:8; Psa. 19:9; 145:17). They will declare the righteousness of God the Holy Ghost in his convictions of sin, reproofs of conscience, forsaking of the impenitent, and abiding with the believer. And in a special manner they will declare the righteousness of God the Son, in his human life and sufferings and death as man's surety, by which he magnified the law and made it honorable (Isa. 42:21), and by which they are able to call him by this name, "The Lord our righteousness" (Jer. 23:6). And lastly, the objects of their instruction, those to whom this declaration of the righteousness of the Triune Jehovah is made by the seed, are pointed out, "A people that shall be born." The men of their generation, and especially the young, shall be the immediate objects to whom the seed will declare this righteousness during their numerous pilgrimages on earth. When gathered together in one, they will declare this righteousness to the principalities and powers in the heavenly places (Eph. 3:10), as even now they are called to do. Then, perhaps, to all the worlds of intelligent beings that shall successively be created throughout eternity, it may be their glorious privilege to furnish an instructive lesson of the righteousness of God in Christ.

Such seems to be the meaning of this passage. It represents the Savior as looking with minute and intense interest into the joy that was set before him. From the cross on Calvary he could behold the remotest future, and present before his mind a picture of the completion of all things. His own Spirit had inspired this psalm, perhaps for him to use on this solemn occasion. In these concluding verses, it consoles his mind with gracious assurances and glorious prospects. It sets before him his own faithful seed, bearing witness to his love and righteousness through changing time and ceaseless eternity.

We understand the last two verses of this psalm to contain this double, rather this unlimited reference. It seemed necessary to explain the previous clause and verse, with regard to the seed, both individually and collectively, and we are bound to adhere to the same interpretation now. It might even be argued that, in strict propriety, the words cannot bear a limited significance. For being spoken of the seed generally, as something accomplished by every one of them, we must necessarily send forward our thoughts to that period when all the seed shall exist and be gathered into one, and when consequently they shall all be able to declare the righteousness of our Emmanuel. Thus, this clause, with the entire passage in which it occurs, obtains full, adequate, and most satisfactory explanation, by referring its significance to the church militant, and to the church triumphant.

We ought ever to bear in remembrance that the true Church is a spiritual body, and that the universal Church of all ages is *one*. The great object to be effected by her is also *one*, namely, "to show forth the praises of Him who has called her out of darkness into His marvelous light" (1 Pet. 2:9). Alas! How inadequately has this duty been discharged! What a sad sight must the Church present to the high intelligences, till she shall be freed from her divisions, gathered to her Lord, and made perfect in the unity of holiness!

The employment of the Church of God from the beginning has been the same as should occupy her now, and onward forever. True believers, in all countries and periods, have been diligent to declare the righteousness of their God and Savior. This was considered by them all to be their most incumbent duty, the one great object for which life was valuable, and the highest privilege and honor to which they could be here advanced. They testified for God to all who were around them, and more specifically to the young. Over their own children they watched with unwearied care, and early instructed them in the way of righteousness. To deliver the "people that are born" from the error and ignorance, and from the sinful customs and practices of the world around them, has always been a distinguishing characteristic of the Church of God. With maternal attention and concern she seeks the welfare of the souls of children, and thus tenderly instructs each of them, "Remember now your Creator in the days of your youth" (Eccl. 12:1). The great Father of all has made this a special subject of his commands, "And these words which I command you today shall be in your heart. You shall teach them diligently to your children, and shall talk of them when you sit in your house, when you walk by the way, when you lie down, and when you rise up" (Deut. 6:6, 7). Is this not the reason which God assigns for his communing with Abraham, and revealing to him His purpose? "For I have known him, in order that he may command his children and his household after him, that they keep the way of the LORD, to do righteousness and justice, that the LORD may bring to Abraham what He has spoken to him" (Gen. 18:19). Was not Noah called a preacher of righteousness? He fulfilled this duty to the people of that wicked generation; but none, save his own family, were brought with him out of the destruction of the flood into the safety of the ark.

It was the invariable practice of the spiritual seed, during the continuance of the Jewish Church, to declare the righteousness of God. Even in the time of their greatest corruption, Malachi testifies that "then those who feared the Lord spoke to one another" (Mal.3:16). Doubtless also they spoke words of warning to the ungodly around them, and watched over the young, seeking to impress their hearts before the allurements of the world had fatally ensnared them. How fully and faithfully does the Christian Church follow in the same path! See how our gracious Head set her the example. To all with whom he met or conversed, the Savior declared the righteousness of God, as well as testified of the world that its works were evil (John 7:7). How often do we find him with children around him and with children following him? Do we not rejoice to hear him say, "Let the little children come to Me, and do not forbid them?" (Matt. 19:14). And when this great and good Shepherd was about to leave his earthly flock, the first of his threefold injunctions to all ministers, through Peter, is this, "Feed My lambs" (John 21:15). The early Christians were particularly attentive to this duty, and greatly did the Lord bless them in it. Timothy is reminded by St. Paul that from a child he had known the Holy Scriptures, and is admonished not to forget from whom he had learned them. Doubtless the apostle referred to his mother Eunice and his grandmother Lois, in whom dwelt an unfeigned faith (2 Tim. 1:5; 3:15).

The history of the true and spiritual Church of Christ is one continued narrative of God-honoring and sin-condemning Christians. The Church is an embodied testimony. Every member of it ought to be a witness and a testifier for God. The two things in which they especially differ from the world around them are these — they seek to bring men to the Savior by declaring His righteousness as the only ground of their salvation; and they desire to exclude and banish sin by testifying against it in every form (2 Tim. 2:19). This is the duty in which every real Christian is engaged at the present day. As ministers or people, as parents or children, as masters or servants, and in whatever station of life they may be, they make it their aim to declare the righteousness of the Lord Jesus as the only ground of a sinner's acceptance and the only source of his sanctification. The Holy Scriptures they make the basis of all learning, and exhibit Jesus and his righteousness as the first and last object of knowledge. What we are now privileged to witness of the increase of vital godliness and faithful declaration of the truth as it is in Jesus, was contemplated with satisfaction by our dying Lord. He could fix his eye on every self-denying effort which the most humble Christian is now making on behalf of the cause of truth and righteousness. It imparted joy to the last moments of our dying Master to know, that though a multitude was then despising him, multitudes would now and in every age render him a willing and most cordial service. He could not only contemplate the present generation, he could look also to all that shall succeed. His all-knowing eye could survey them all to the end of time, and with full certainty of the fact, and blessed gratification at the event, he could exclaim, "They shall come, and will declare My righteousness to a people who will be born."

Reader, it is a solemn question, but for our soul's own good we should not fail to ask ourselves, 'Did my Lord and Master, looking forward from the cross, behold me among the number of those who declare his righteousness? Do not evade this question by saying that you art not called to any office in the Church. Ministers have, indeed, the solemn responsibility of *publicly* declaring the righteousness of the Redeemer. Woe to us if we cannot answer this question affirmatively, as in the sight of God. But, as a professing Christian, the duty is binding on you to declare by your *private* life and conversations, that the righteousness of Jesus the Surety, is that alone by which your own soul and those of your fellow men can be saved. Alas! How few consider the weighty obligations under which they lie! For all that we know of right and truth by the Scriptures, and for the use we make of it for our own souls, and the souls of those with whom we meet in the activities of life- *we must give an account to God.* Do we allow our wives and children, our friends and neighbors, our co-workers, employees and employers to continue in ignorance of the things that belong to their peace? Do we allow them to remain in error on the most important of all questions, the salvation of their souls? Alas! How many bosses have kept an employee for years, and never told him that an immortal soul was lodged within him! Let it not be so. Do not let your wife be constrained to declare that she never heard you say there was a heaven to seek, or a hell to shun. Do not let the children God has given you rise up in the judgment and testify that they were not taught to pray, or to know and love that Savior who had finished a work of righteousness. Do not let your friends and servants go unwarned from day to day, but faithfully declare to them the way of righteousness and plead with them to walk in it so that they may find peace and salvation to their souls.

Blessed is that resolution of the Psalmist, "I will meditate on the glorious splendor of Your majesty, and on Your wondrous works.

Men shall speak of the might of Your awesome acts, and I will declare Your greatness. They shall utter the memory of Your great goodness, and shall sing of Your righteousness" (Psa. 145:5-7). "We will not hide them from [our] children, telling to the generation to come the praises of the LORD, and His strength and His wonderful works that He has done." For, "He commanded our fathers, that they should make them known to their children; that the generation to come might know them, the children who would be born, that they may arise and declare them to their children, that they may set their hope in God, and not forget the works of God, but keep His commandments" (Psa. 78:4-7). This is the duty and privilege of the church. Since Christ ascended one generation of the seed has been telling another, and they to those that came after them of the Lord Jesus, his holy life, sufferings, and death. One word comprehends it all; they declare his *"righteousness."* That perfect and spotless life of obedience to all the will and law of God, which Christ exhibited on earth, and which enabled him to offer a pure offering of holy blood, and to give an unstained soul in ransom for a world's redemption, is their grand theme. This is the work of the church through her various members. In her collective capacity, it is intended that she should afford an everlasting lesson to all the inhabitants of the universe who are, or shall be created. "You are the light of the world" (Matt. 5:14). They shall look upon the Bride, the Lamb's wife, and they shall glorify God in her. She shall be at once the Teacher and the Lesson. And it is not improbable that there shall be called into existence, throughout eternity, various races of intelligent beings, who shall learn by the glorified church the manifold wisdom of God. How fully and perfectly shall the redeemed be able then to declare the righteousness of the Father, of the Son, and of the Holy Spirit! They shall know as they are known. No longer beholding through a glass, dimly, they shall understand what is now mysterious, and approve what is now hard to bear. Their eye shall shed no tear; for their heart shall feel no sorrow. The past shall all be explained; and, in the light of eternity, they shall be able to bring forth glory to the Lord from every part of it. Jesus, by his Spirit, shall be their Eternal Instructor. "He will dwell with them." They shall see his face. As the Lord their God, he will give them light. With them he will look back to the manger of Bethlehem, the garden of Gethsemane, and the cross of Calvary: and with them he will be fully satisfied with the abasement of the one, the anguish of the second, and the desertion and death of the last. With them also he will look back to their own places of nativity, their periods of birth, their country, and their kindred. The trials that were sanctified, the seen and unseen dangers to which they were exposed, and the amount of undeserved blessings that were graciously granted, shall be rehearsed. The means of their conversion, the preservation of their faith, and the time and circumstances of their death, shall be fully remembered. In the abundance of their satisfaction, the redeemed shall exclaim, "He has done all things well. The covenant was ordered in all things and sure. Not one pain too many. Not a sorrow too great. Not a trial too severe. From the cradle to the grave, all was right, and wise, and good!" The minister and the missionary shall say, "We have not labored in vain, nor spent our strength for nothing!" The parent shall exclaim, "My prayers have not been lost upon my child." The tried and afflicted Christian shall acknowledge that his trials were his greatest blessings. All classes among the saved shall be PERFECTLY AND ETERNALLY SATISFIED. In the gladness and gratitude of their hearts, they shall come to the throne of glory. Arrayed in white robes, faultless and spotless in body and soul, bright and attractive with the beauty of the imputed righteousness of their Head and Savior, they shall there present themselves, cast their crowns before him, and strike their golden harps, saying, "Blessing and honor and glory and power, be to Him that sits on the throne, and to the Lamb, forever and ever" (Rev. 5:13).

THE FINISHER OF THE FAITH

VERSE *31—That he has done this,* or, *for he has fulfilled it.*[22]

THESE words express the concluding argument—the triumphant termination, of this psalm. Here is assigned the reason why the seed shall be able to declare, with truth, the righteousness of their Lord and Savior. During the period of time while they individually sojourn in this world, and throughout their everlasting existence in the new heavens and the new earth, this shall be their theme—the finished righteousness of Emmanuel. This shall be their occupation—to declare and celebrate the perfected work of the eternal redemption. This shall be their all-convincing and conclusive argument, "for he has fulfilled it."

The statement in this passage will powerfully recall to the Christian's recollection, the dying exclamation of his Savior, "It is finished" (John 19:30). We have already seen, that our Lord quoted the commencement of this Psalm, with the first "loud voice," which He uttered on the cross. We have observed that throughout the entire Psalm, all the sentiments bear a direct and close reference to what He then experienced, and that many of the expressions of sorrow and joy which it contains, are expressly applied to him in the New Testament. Therefore, in harmony with the view which

---

[22] The Hebrew verb, in this passage, is synonymous with our English verb, *to do,* the various significance of the word being, perform, execute, transact, finish, and conclude are too well known to be enumerated. In different passages of the King James translation, the word is rendered; *make,* Dan. 9:24; *make ready, dress, prepare,* as a sacrifice, Ezek. 45:17; 1 Kings 18:23; Num. 15:5, 6, 8, 12; *offer,* that which has been so prepared, Lev. 9:7 ; *effect,* Jer. 48:30; *execute,* Exod. 12:12; *perform,* Jer. 44:25; and, as it is here translated, *fulfill,* Psa. 145:19; 148:8; 1 Chron. 22:13; 2 Sam. 14:22. The authors of the Hebrew New Testament have also given it this sense in Acts 13:22; Eph. 2:3; and Rev. 17:7.

we have taken of this Psalm, that our Lord inwardly repeated its various verses, we now conclude that in his second "loud voice," when He exclaimed, "It is finished," the Redeemer had reference to the termination of this Psalm, in which his church is represented as declaring his righteousness, and proving its finished and perfect excellency by his triumphant argument "for he has fulfilled it."

This is the standing position of the church of Christ, in time and in eternity: Her Lord, in her name, and in her nature, fulfilled all righteousness. The powers of evil can no longer boast. Their exultations over fallen man are put to silence. One of our race has kept the law; yes, he has magnified it, he has made it honorable (Isa. 42:21). A man has been found who, from his cradle to his grave, never thought an evil thought, or spoke an idle word, or omitted a single duty, or transgressed the will of God in the slightest particular. A man has been found, "bone of our bone and flesh of our flesh," who "was tempted and tried in all points, like we are," and yet remained "without sin" (Heb. 4:15). Yes, against whom all the wickedness of man and all the power and malice of the hosts of darkness were let loose: on whose single person, in body and soul, were concentrated every conceivable, and inconceivable, pain, and sorrow, and anguish; and who, in the last and most trying hour of his death, was forsaken by the comforting presence of his Father and his God. Yet under all these, he never uttered a murmur or impatient exclamation; and in opposition to them all, persevered in the narrow path of duty, still loving, still obeying his absent Father; praying for man, his murderer; repudiating Satan, his tempter; and, in the midst of excruciating torments, attending to the minutest detail of Scripture, and saying, "I thirst," in order that it might be fulfilled. Then, with a "loud voice," that heaven and earth might hear, and challenge, if they could, his perfected righteousness, exclaiming, before he bowed his head, "It is finished."

If the view here given is correct, this concluding passage of the Psalm serves to explain that concluding sentiment of our Savior's mortal life. This verse informs us, that when he said, "It is finished," he meant by this that his "righteousness was fulfilled."

The term "righteousness," strictly denotes conformity to law. When we wish to express what Christ was in himself, we not only state that he was righteous, but something more; we affirm that he was holy — "the Holy One of God." His righteousness proceeded from his holiness. It was his holy nature exhibiting itself in acts cognizable and commendable by law that constituted his righteousness. Our Lord, as the Surety of sinners, was under two laws, the law of the curse, and the law of the commandments. To each of these his obedience was full and perfect; his righteousness is, therefore, twofold, passive and active. Under the law of the curse, he passed more than thirty years with perpetual and perfect endurance. For CONSIDER HIM who ENDURED such hostilities against himself—pains and trials, labor and sweat, poverty and hunger; sorrows, griefs and disappointments; weariness, fatigue and exhaustion; shame, spite and spitting; reproach, distress and persecution; the forsaking of friends, the mocking of fools, and the persecutions of enemies; accused of the worst of crimes, and of associating with the worst of company; charged before the highest tribunals in the land; solemnly condemned in the spiritual court for the greatest sins against the law of God of which man can be guilty—the dreadful crimes of descending, as it were, to the lowest hell, by calling up the dead in union with Beelzebub, and of aspiring to the highest heaven by blasphemously making himself equal with God; sentenced in the criminal court for the highest offence which could be committed against the law of the land, namely, sedition and treason; subjected after each sentence to the most insulting and abusive treatment; mocked and struck; blindfolded and buffeted; scourged on the back, crowned with thorns on the head, and arrayed with a fool's insignia of royalty. CONSIDER HIM in all this, and how HE ENDURED to be led away to a painful, lingering, and shameful, death; to be hung upon a cross like a common criminal; and, worse than these, while under the curse of man and the law, to be afflicted by the most trying of all sorrows—the hiding of his

Father's countenance. Yes, consider how he endured and you shall behold the passive righteousness of the Son of God, shining forth, calm and undisturbed, like the silent moon amid the storms of night. Clouds encompass, winds roar, and tempests rage, but every glimpse we obtain of her silver light serves only to exhibit the queen of heaven more lovely, clear, and unruffled, in the composure of majesty. Such was the passive righteousness of Jesus Christ. He never fretted at the prosperity of the wicked, or felt disconcerted at their frown. He murmured not at trials, nor grew angry at disappointments. A man of sorrows, and acquainted with grief, yet he knew neither impatience, or discontent. There was no sullenness and no selfishness in his nature. Though ready to forgive, he was not quick to resent. And amidst the strife of tongues that vied in reviling him, he did not revile back. "As a sheep before its shearers is silent, so He opened not His mouth." Like a lamb led to the slaughter, in simplicity and silence, he used no craftiness for his escape. And when death was transfixing him with its sharpest stings, He endured the most piercing of them all without a single murmur. Thus every sorrow, trial, and suffering, which the law of the curse had denounced, and which the Scriptures of truth had foretold, were endured by Christ in the most holy and innocent manner. His passive obedience, or righteousness, was proved to be immaculate and perfect. He had neither sinned, nor come short in the smallest particular which the law of the curse prescribed, but had fulfilled it to the very uttermost.

The active righteousness of Christ consists in his having fully discharged all his obligations as a Surety, all the requirements of the law as a man, and all the commands of God as an obedient servant and a willing sacrifice. To state it in a few words, we may say that his heart and life overflowed with love to God and man; that he perfectly fulfilled those two commandments on which hang all the law and the prophets. He loved the Lord his God with all his heart, and with all his soul, and with all his strength, and with all his mind, and he loved his neighbor as he loved himself. The duty of every relationship, by which he stood connected with his fellow men, he discharged to the utmost. When a youth, he was subject to his parents and obedient to them (Luke 2:51). When a man, he did not evade his duty to the state, but wrought a miracle so that he might pay the tax that was levied upon him. In his conversations with men, the law of kindness was on his lips and gifts and blessings dropped from his hand. From the first dawn of reason, to the commendation of his departing spirit, he was always mindful with a lively readiness that he must be about his Father's business. Wherever he went and into whatever company he came, this was his first and only question, 'What can I now do for God? How shall I benefit these immortal souls?' Christ was always at his post; he never lost a single opportunity of warning a sinner, instructing an inquirer, or relieving the distressed. The active obedience of the Savior towards man is summed up in Scripture, "He went about doing good" (Acts 10:38). In regard to God, his religion, his life, his righteousness, were of the most perfect, energetic, and fervent kind. He did not rest in the outward form nor neglected or despised the holy rites of religion. As his custom was, he went into the synagogue every Sabbath (Luke 4:16) and worshipped the God of the Hebrews in their sacred language and services. On the solemn festivals he presented himself in the temple at Jerusalem, as the law commanded, and never failed to yield the most complete and cordial obedience to the divinely appointed ordinances. His was a spiritual worship. His soul did not slumber in the outward ceremonies, but ascended through them into the highest communion with God. The private duties of his religion, were discharged with an active vigor, and fullness of heart. There was no delay, no procrastination of prayer, no wandering of thought, no dullness of mind, no coldness of affection. In the morning, he rose up a great while before day so that he might be alone in prayer with God (Mark 1:35). At times he continued all night, pouring out his soul in fervent supplications (Luke 6:14). Never omitting the duties of prayer and fasting, he was always ready and prepared for the mightiest miracle of mercy that might be required of him (Matt. 17:21). Living and breathing for the glory of God, he moved amongst men and devils untouched by sin, and was acknowledged by both to be the Holy One of God (Mark 1:24; Luke 4:34; Acts 3:14). Every moment of his life, he possessed the most unhesitating readiness to accomplish all that his Father commanded: "I delight to do Your will, O my God, and Your law is within my heart" (Psa. 40:8). He came to Jordan to be baptized by John and his reasoning with this humble and declining minister prevailed, "Permit it to be so now, for thus it is fitting for us to fulfill all righteousness." And upon him who had performed this work of righteousness, in such a self-denying and God-honoring spirit, the Holy Ghost descended like a dove; "And suddenly a voice came from heaven, saying, "This is My beloved Son, in whom I am well pleased" (Matt. 3:15, 17). When he ascended Mount Tabor, and was transfigured in glory the same voice uttered the same declaration, proving that his righteousness in the sight of God was perfect and complete. Thus, by a testimony from heaven on two occasions; by the admission of his watchful enemies that they were at a loss how to lay hold of him; by the contradictions of the witnesses whom they induced to accuse Him; by the solemn, emphatic assertion of the judge who condemned him, "I am innocent of the blood of this just Person" (Matt. 27:24) and by the affirmation of one of the dying criminals, "this Man has done nothing wrong" (Luke 23:41). We conclude with the most triumphant assurance that in the sight of God and man, the active righteousness of Jesus Christ is pure, spotless, and perfect; bright with the luster of its excellency; clear as the sun, resplendent and beautiful before the throne of God with the brightness and purity of its effulgence; the admiration of heaven; the glorious light of the eternal day; and therefore, with all the emphasis of truth is HE to whom it belongs rightly called, "THE SUN OF RIGHTEOUSNESS," who rises on a dark and benighted world, and imparts a healing warmth and light and life with his unsullied ray (Mal. 4:2).

Having now considered the finished righteousness of the Lord Jesus, as it is in itself, let us direct our attention to it in relation to ourselves. We have remarked that it was of a passive nature, enduring the law of the curse; and of an active nature, fulfilling the law of the commandments. We now further add that it was a Surety-righteousness. That is to say, the Lord Jesus Christ fulfilled all righteousness, not in his own name, or for his own benefit, but in our name, and on our behalf. Let us remember that Christ's life in the flesh was entirely gratuitous. He did not need to become man, but he did so out of love to us. After he took our nature, he did not need to act righteous acts in order to become righteous for he already possessed that essential and perfect holiness which is the fountain of all righteousness, either of law commanding, or of goodness obeying. Yet, from love to us, he did perform all manner of righteous works. His intention in this was to produce and provide a perfect righteousness in the name of man and to give it forth as a second Adam, in place of that unrighteousness which had been transmitted by the first Adam. Therefore without consulting any man, he took our name. Without waiting for us to ask, he voluntarily undertook our bankrupt cause; and having conducted it to a successful resolution, he now invites us to become partakers of the benefits and privileges he has acquired. Our cause of bankruptcy was sin. To meet the penalty we had incurred, our Surety gave his life as a sacrifice; and for the debt we owed, he paid his righteousness as a price. Having undergone our death, he came forth from the prison of the grave, ascended to the hill of the Lord, and presented himself in the holy place before the Most High. There, in the court of heaven, he claimed, in his own right, that the name of man should be again restored to the book of life. He stood there as a man and he could challenge the whole universe to disprove his claim. Of all the human race, his hands alone were clean, his heart pure; no thought of his soul had ever turned on vanity; and without deceit or guile, he had faithfully fulfilled to the very utmost all that will of God which he had sworn to accomplish. Therefore, in justice, he received that blessing which he sought from the Lord and obtained the blessing of righteousness from the God of his salvation (Psa.

24). The name of man was again registered in heaven and the good news of our redemption, through the righteousness of this Surety, was commanded to be proclaimed to all nations for the obedience of faith (Rom. 1:5). He who refuses to believe what this Surety has accomplished for him, will naturally attempt, if he at all desires to be saved, to perform it for himself. But until he has fulfilled all righteousness and can prove before God and man that from his cradle to his grave, his hands were clean, and his heart pure, this attempt will only aggravate his ruin. He, on the other hand, who believes in this gracious Surety, who acknowledges his own utter failure, and accepts the "gift of righteousness" (Rom. 5:17) which Jesus bestows does not attempt to do anything towards the attainment of that which has already been so perfectly accomplished, but he rests on it, as all his salvation and all his desire. Filled with gratitude, he now works to show his love to Christ, not selfishly to merit his gifts. His religion becomes a service of love—a holy and a happy life. The name by which he now addresses the blessed Redeemer is, The Lord my righteousness (Jer. 23:6). The rights of the head become the rights of the members. The name of the husband is conferred upon the wife (Jer. 23:16). The satisfaction and gladness of the Christian's heart at this discovery of a finished salvation by a Surety-righteousness, and of everlasting union and betrothal with Christ therein, are so delightful that he exclaims, "I will greatly rejoice in the LORD, my soul shall be joyful in my God; for He has clothed me with the garments of salvation, He has covered me with the robe of righteousness, as a bridegroom decks himself with ornaments, and as a bride adorns herself with her jewels" (Isa. 61:10).

The doctrine of substitution, or imputation, is the life of the Christian. My sins were laid on the head of Jesus; that is, they were imputed to him by God the Father (Isa. 53:6). Jesus willingly became my substitute, suffered in my place, and died in my stead. In the eye of the law, I am regarded as one who has paid its penalty, suffered its curse, and died under its sentence. I have therefore become dead to the law, by the body of Christ (Rom. 7:4). It cannot lay hands upon me, and execute me twice. I was crucified with, and in Christ, under the curse of the law. What more then can it demand? The law of our land cannot justly apprehend an individual a second time for the same offence, after he has either suffered its recorded sentence, or been acquitted as innocent at its bar. Nor will the law of God lay hold on Christ again, nor can it seize on me; for it was only and expressly as my Surety that he died; it was with the full permission of the Judge and Lawgiver, and with the covenanted consent of the Great Creditor that he acted in my name and laid down his life for mine. In the eye of the law, therefore, I am discharged in Christ my Surety, because it has executed all its wrath and sentence upon him. It laid him dead; but he took to himself a new life, and I, therefore, ought to reckon myself to be dead indeed unto sin, but alive unto God, through Jesus Christ my Lord (Rom. 6:11). With full truth also I may say with the apostle, "I have been crucified with Christ; it is no longer I who live, but Christ lives in me; and the life which I now live in the flesh I live by faith in the Son of God, who loved me and gave Himself for me" (Gal. 2:20).

The full statement of the gospel is comprehended in one word, ATONEMENT. A Surety has appeared. He has offered himself as a sacrifice, and placed himself as a mediator between God and man, (1 Tim. 2:5). He has atoned for the misdeeds of the one, and satisfied the justice of the other. God and man ought therefore to be again at one; for the atonement, or the at-one-ment, has been fully accomplished. God, on his part, has cordially accepted that atonement. It was his kindness that suggested it, his goodness that allowed the substitution to stand good in law. "God so loved the world, that he gave his only begotten Son" (John 3:16). Nothing more, therefore, is required to be done, in order to incline God's heart towards a reconciliation. He has accepted the atonement, and retains no feeling but that of good-will towards men. The Scriptures, accordingly, never affirm that God must be reconciled to man, but, on the contrary, represent God as entreating man to be reconciled to him. The enmity lies on man's side, not on that of the Most High. The change to be effected must be in the heart of the offender, not in that of the offended. The ministry of reconciliation, therefore, is distinctly, even in legal phraseology, defined in this way: "that God was in Christ reconciling the world to Himself, not imputing their trespasses to them, and has committed to us the word of reconciliation. Now then, we are ambassadors for Christ, as though God were pleading through us: we implore you on Christ's behalf, be reconciled to God. For He made Him who knew no sin to be sin for us, that we might become the righteousness of God in Him" (2 Cor. 5:19-21). It is man, then, that is called upon in this passage to be reconciled to God, to be again at one with him. It is we who are invited to accept the atonement, and to feel, and to act, as those who are satisfied that it has made up the breach between ourselves and God. Too many conceive that Christ was accomplishing a work in order to make the Father favorable to man, as though Christ were more merciful than he. But this Scripture positively declares of God the Father, that he was in Christ, reconciling this world of ours unto himself, not imputing to us our trespasses. The Father laid them upon the head of his Son. Jesus cordially took our guilt, and suffered as our substitute. We are called upon to "accept [our] guilt" (Lev. 26:41). We are besought to lay our hands on the head of this substituted victim, and to confess over him all our iniquities, and all our transgressions, in all our sins (Lev. 16:21). We thus make a covenant with God by means of the sacrifice (Psa. 1:5). This covenant is, that since he has so graciously accomplished all this redemption-work for us, which we cordially and gratefully accept at his hands, we will unreservedly present our bodies and souls, our time and talents, to him as our reasonable service. This is the only return we can make for such glorious and gratuitous kindness, and the only proof we can give of our confidence in his word, our acceptance of his sacrifice, and our gratitude for his benefits. (See Rom. 12:1; 1 Cor. 6:20; Rom. 6:11, 12, etc.).

This is the salvation of the soul. This is the reconciliation, the at-one-ment, attaining its full effect. A principle is thus introduced into the human heart, which produces hatred against all sin. The end of Christ's death, as our Surety, is accomplished: "We are made the righteousness of God in him." Being delivered out of the hand of our enemies, we begin to learn to serve God without fear, in holiness and righteousness all the days of our life (Luke 1:74, 75). We recognize how appropriately our Surety is named, "Jesus," because he saves his people from their sins (Matt. 1:21). We no longer regard the work of Christ as something done to obtain for us merely a place of safety, but to introduce us to a state of holiness. Instead of hoping that Christ may save us from hell at our death, we are chiefly anxious to be delivered from the love of and the commission of sin while we live. And with greater earnestness of desire, we long and pray for the restoration of God's image to our souls, than for bare admission to the happiness of heaven. Man is in this way brought to be of one mind with God. Formerly, he meant only safety and happiness by the term "salvation." Now, he understands its full signification to be restoration to purity and holiness. While natural men set themselves to "work out their own salvation," that is, their safety, with slavish "fear and trembling," lest after all they should be lost; he instead comes to the Savior as one who is lost already, and, from love and gratitude to that Savior, applies himself with perseverance and alacrity to work out his salvation—that is, his deliverance from pollution and his restoration to holiness. He does so "with fear and trembling," because he feels the power and multiplicity of sin within him; because he knows that he cannot, of himself, either be willing or able to eradicate it; and because he has learned that it is God alone who can work in him, first to will, and then to do, of his good pleasure (Phil. 2:12). Therefore he is ever fearful lest he grieve the blessed Spirit, and quench his light and convictions. He wrestles in agony of contention against every species of sin. He trembles to think what little progress he is making in holiness, and what a deceitful and powerful enemy is lodged within him. Thus "fearful and trembling" in regard to his own workings, the Christian's peace and confidence flow entirely from the knowledge of his Surety's finished righteousness. A righteousness which assures him that the Lord does not work an imperfect work, but that good thing he has begun in him, he will perform until the day of Jesus Christ (Phil. 1:6; Psa. 138:8). Therefore, as with the apostle, his life, his religion, consists mainly of three things: he worships God in the spirit, he rejoices in Christ Jesus, and has no confidence in the flesh (Phil. 3:3). And as with another apostle, he casts himself for support entirely on his Lord and Master, saying, "Now to Him who is able to keep you from stumbling, and to present you faultless before the presence of His glory with exceeding joy, To God our Savior, who alone is wise, be glory and majesty, dominion and power, both now and forever. Amen." (Jude 24, 25).

Such, Christian reader, is the result of the finished work of our Emmanuel. "The work of righteousness is peace, and the effect of righteousness is quietness and assurance for ever" (Isa. 32:17). Has it produced this "effect" upon your soul? Or, are you laboring after peace and not believing Him who says, "My peace I give to you?" (John 14:27). Are you "going about," in all your religious duties, to establish a righteousness of your own, or have you submitted yourself to the righteousness of God? "Christ is the end of the law for righteousness to every one that believes" (Rom. 10:3, 4). You doubtless wish for admission to the realms of glory. Those who receive, who accept, the gift of righteousness, shall reign in life by the one, Jesus Christ (Rom. 5:17). Do you engage in works of charity, in order that God may count you a righteous person, and worthy of reward?" "But to him who does not work but believes on Him who justifies the ungodly, (through the provided Surety,) his faith is accounted for righteousness..." (Rom. 4:5).

Come then, to the Lord Jesus, who is both the author and the finisher of our faith (Heb. 12:2). Accept him as given. He is made of God unto you righteousness (1 Cor. 1:30). Receive him into your heart, and call him ever after, "The Lord your righteousness" (Jer. 23:6). "He shall say, 'Surely in the LORD I have righteousness and strength." (Isa. 45:24). Count then, with the apostle, all things to be loss for the excellency of the knowledge of such a Savior. Yes, count every thing as dross so that you may win Christ and be found in him, not having your own righteousness which is from the law, but that which is through faith in Christ, the righteousness which is from God by faith (Phil. 3:8, 9). So in Christ shall you be made a new man, created in righteousness and true holiness (Eph. 4:24). Through him your soul shall be united to God; "he will betroth you to himself in righteousness" (Hos. 2:19). You shall be counted a member of the Bride, the Lamb's wife. Arrayed in the fine linen which is the righteousness of the saints (Rev. 19:8). You shall be a welcome guest at the marriage-supper of the Lamb. As an inhabitant of the new Jerusalem, the brightness of your unstained purity shall be an object of everlasting admiration to all angelic beholders. Yes, rather, the Lord of the glorious church shall be admired in the perfect appearance of all her members (2 Thess. 1:10; Ezek. 16:14; Eph. 5:27). Many shall inquire, "Who are these?" And the reply shall be, "These are the ones who come out of the great tribulation, and washed their robes and made them white in the blood of the Lamb. Therefore they are before the throne of God…" (Rev. 7:14, 15).

SUMMARY

THIS Psalm, Christian reader, which we have now considered has fixed our thoughts on the Savior of the world and unfolded to us, as it were, his secret feelings and inmost thoughts during the latter part of that awful period in which he hung upon the cross. After almost three hours of silence, in which he endured the conflict of the powers of darkness, suffered inconceivably acute mental anguish under the hidings of his Father's face, the Savior uttered, and this Psalm has recorded, his astounding cry, "My God, my God, why have You forsaken me?" Here we considered the Lord Jesus as our Surety, standing at his Fathers judgment seat, and conscious of innocence, inquiring what new charge was laid against him, to cause this new and severest of all afflictions, the hiding of his Father's face. We concluded that one reason why our Lord so earnestly cried to his Father was, that he might ascribe the glory of his deliverance to him, being unwilling to appropriate it to himself by an exertion of his own power; and we found that the whole verse comprised three inquiries, to which we conceived these to be appropriate answers: 1. Why have you forsaken me? Because you are bearing the sins of the world. 2. Why are you so far from helping me? So that the victory may be altogether your own. And, 3. Why are you so far from the words of my groaning? So that you may learn all the obedience by the things which you are suffering. We perceived that our Lord in continuing his supplications, complained *to* his Father, but would not complain *against* him; and yet instantly acquitted him of unkindness or injustice, and sub-joined this filial and beautiful acknowledgment, "But you remain holy." In the fullness of his sorrow, our Lord next contrasted his own experience with that of the fathers, whose prayers were heard, whose expectations were not confounded. He called himself a worm, allied by his human nature to the basest part of creation; a scarlet-colored worm, covered with the imputed guilt of men. He regarded himself as "no man;" not what man now is by sin, nor what man was intended to be by his Creator. Our Lord's life in the flesh, we saw, might be illustrated by the heathen doctrine of metempsychosis. For he brought the recollections of the world of glory into this state of being and therefore human life must have appeared, in his eyes, infinitely more base, wretched, and loathsome, than we can possibly conceive. We were next led to contemplate the numerous mental sufferings of our much-tried Lord: the reproaches with which he was assailed, the mockery by which he was insulted, and the taunts which wounded his spirit to the quick. In the ninth and tenth verses, we considered that pathetic and touching appeal which our dying Redeemer made to the heart of his Father, arguing from the helplessness of his infancy to the helplessness of his manhood, and casting the latter upon that Paternal care, which had provided for the former. We perceived how earnestly our Lord followed up this appeal with renewed entreaty for his Father's presence, expressing this great and only desire of his heart in these words, "Do not be far from me." The bodily sufferings of the Man of Sorrows, were next brought to our notice. The assault and encompassing of his enemies on every side, was the first particularized; where also we considered the assault of Satanic hosts upon the spirit of our Lord. Consequent on this assault succeeded universal faintness over his body, complete languor and extreme exhaustion, with an intense and burning thirst. The piercing of our Lord's sacred body in his hands and feet was then considered, and the lingering death by crucifixion described. Extended on the cross, the emaciated state of the Savior's worn-out frame was exposed to view, and all his bones could be counted. In this condition he was subjected to the insulting gaze of the multitude. The soldiers also seized every article of his clothing, divided his garments among them, and cast lots for his garments. Urged by these various and painful afflictions, and desiring with intense anxiety to enjoy again before he died, the light and peace of his Father's presence, our blessed Savior then, with the most vehement importunity, prayed for a speedy and immediate answer. And, while he was still praying, his Father granted his petition. Light dawned upon his soul; darkness was dispelled from the face of nature, and from the heart of the Redeemer. Then as though coming forth from a kind of spiritual death, and enjoying a spiritual resurrection, our Divine Surety exclaimed, "You have heard me." Importunity prevailed with God. The whole tone of feeling and sentiment in the Psalm became changed from this verse. Gratitude and thanksgiving, we observed, occupied its remaining portion. The Savior, as it were, invited from the cross the members of his Church to join his blessed song. He called them his "brethren" to whom he would declare his Father's name and testified that God is worthy to be praised, because he had not hid his face from him, but had heard his prayer and answered his cry. Therefore he himself again expressed his determination to praise the Lord, and to fulfill all his vows in the presence of the redeemed. Our blessed Savior was next presented to our view as contemplating the vision of joy that was set before him— casting a long look through successive time into the eternal age, and beholding with delight all things gathered together in himself (Eph. 1:10). He contemplated the satisfaction of his meek and lowly disciples—the seekers of the Lord, all praising him; and the eternal spiritual life which they should enjoy. Then the conversion of the world, the establishment of his own glorious kingdom, the universal worship which should be rendered to him by all classes of human beings, and their entire dependence on himself, even in their most holy and exalted condition, as the sole Author of the faith. And lastly, the Psalm represented the Savior as giving solace to his dying spirit in the midst of his enemies, with the assurance of a holy and numerous seed, who should be accounted to him for a posterity. These his children, the fruit of the travail of his soul, he beheld, with satisfaction, faithfully serving God in every age of the world and, without fail, coming each in his proper and appointed hour into his kingdom of grace, and all at last, gathered together into his kingdom of glory. Their theme in time and in eternity is one; their occupation also is one, to "declare" to all that surround them, or that rise up under them in time; and to all the principalities and powers that behold them, or worlds of intelligent beings that shall be created after them throughout eternity, the unsullied and accepted Surety-righteousness of Jehovah Jesus, which completely secures their everlasting salvation, for he has fulfilled it all!

"To God our Savior, who alone is wise, be glory and majesty, dominion and power, both now and forever. Amen."
Jude 25.

PUBLISHERS' POSTSCRIPT

As a young Christian I picked up a little paperback from the church bookstore that was a character study on the life of Paul. It was an exercise in sheer perseverance to finish the book. When I finished, I looked at the cover and reminded myself never to read a book by that writer again as he was such a horrible writer. Many years after that experience I was in a bookstore in England. I picked up a little work that grabbed my eye. After perusing its table of contents, I decided the book was worth the few dollars being asked for it. I sat down that day to begin reading the little book and I did not rise until I had finished it. I was riveted. I had never read such a clear, simple, and yet profound understanding of Christ, outside of Scripture. I closed that book and thought to myself, "who is this warrior-poet?"

When I returned home from overseas I placed this literary treasure I had found in its rightful (alphabetical) place on the bookshelf. As I did so, I noticed a paperback right next to it bearing the same last name. I had no idea I had other books by this wonderful author- surely I would remember that! As I looked at the paperback, sure enough, it was the same author. It was also the same author I swore I would never read again years earlier (blessed forgetfulness in this case!). As I wondered at the difference in writing between these two books, my puzzle was soon solved by a statement on the front cover of the paperback. It said this: "edited for today's reader."

Being in the business of selling old, out of print books for over ten years now, I have come to learn that when a book is "edited for today's reader," editing is not at all what is being done. A more fitting expression would be, "butchered," "slaughtered," or "hacked apart." In their efforts to modernize the books of great men, editors often destroy and lose the meaning that made the books so great in the first place. Meaning is sacrificed for modernization.

I also recognize that the King James language in which these books were written is obsolete. We are at a point in time that we are so far removed from it, that books written in the good old Saxon of King James are not being read because the language is not understood. As a result, many people are missing out on the richest Christian writing the world has ever seen.

The aim of our ministry has always been two-fold. To spread the gospel of Jesus Christ among the unreached area's of this world; and to further sound doctrine among the English speaking world. The first part is accomplished through the sale of good books. So is the second.

The longer we sell the original's, the more we are realizing there is a limited supply. Someday that supply will run out. Our goal is to reproduce these works, without losing their meaning, and make them available to the English speaking world.

There is a depth of the knowledge of Christ in these authors that is missing today. Today's writers write to teach the Christian what to "do." Seven steps to—, five keys to a successful—, etc. Scanning titles in the devotional section of a Christian bookstore, one would think the devotionals are written for people who are too busy for God, but would love to fit Him in somewhere if they could. They are anemic writers often writing for anemic Christians. The old writers whom we have come to love were not pragmatists, they *beheld* the Lord. It comes out in their writing. They *know Him* who said the greatest thing to boast of in life *is knowing Him* (Jer. 9:23-24), who said that knowing Him *is eternal life* (John 17:3).

We have found ourselves so blessed by the spiritual depth of these works that we desire others to have the opportunity to read them. Recognizing therefore the richness of the work and the difficulty of the outdated language we have created an editorial approach that does not lose the meaning, but does modernize the language *where necessary.*

The spelling of many old English words are different. Many words used two hundred years ago are obsolete today. Many words also have very different meanings today. The Old King James with its, "hither," "thither," "runneth," and "spunneth" is not used today. While some preachers will open their sermons with a prayer addressing God using "thee's," "thy's," and "thou's," they quickly move into their native tongue when addressing the people. They have to, or their audience would not know what they are saying. Not only that, but Scripture references were given using Roman numerals. Hence, most people reading the book today would not even be able to find the Scripture reference.

Truth always advances when it is in the language of the people. To keep truth hidden behind the pious robes of a language form a former era is to impede the growth of the church. To dilute the truth and dumb it down is to dumb down the church— and impede its growth.

We have updated all pronoun's (thee, thy, thou, etc.). Roman numerals have been replaced with the numbers that we all read on our phone's keypad. Word endings have been updated to their current spelling (i.e. "runneth" updated to "run"). We have replaced Old King James Scripture quotations using the New King James translation. Words that are obsolete, or unheard of today we have either footnoted, or used modern synonyms. The grammar and syntax we have left nearly entirely alone. These old writers were fond of long sentences, semi-colon's, and lot's of commas. As a result, you will find the sentences longer than what you may be used to, and filled with enough comma's to make your Post-modern English Professor have a heart attack.

In this way, we have preserved the entirety of the text. Our editing does not consist of removing what was written. We have also, using this method of what we call "minimal editing," preserved the meaning which is so rich.

We hope you have enjoyed the work and are drawn more to Christ and what He accomplished for you on the cross. As you see

Him in all of His greatness may it increase your faith in Him, love for Him, and service to Him.

Ryan Ellsworth
    Scattering Seed Press

Made in the USA
Middletown, DE
10 September 2024

60705310R00186